MACHINES, MONEY AND MEN

An Economic and Social History of
Great Britain from 1700 to the 1970's

D. P. Titley

Hart-Davis Educational

© 1969, 1977 D. P. Titley
First published in Great Britain 1969 by Blond Educational.
Reprinted 1970, 1972, 1973 (revised), 1974, 1975.
Second edition 1977, reprinted 1979, 1981, 1982,
published by Hart-Davis Educational Ltd
a division of Granada Publishing
Frogmore, St Albans, Hertfordshire

Granada ®
Granada Publishing ®

ISBN 0 247 12768 X

*Printed in Great Britain by offset lithography by
Fletcher & Son Ltd, Norwich*

Contents

Acknowledgments

The author and publishers wish to thank the following: Mrs L. Benzimra for Plate 1; the Mansell Collection for Plates 2, 32, 38, 41, 51, 52, 53, 56, 75, 77, 78, 89, 103; John Cornwell for Plates 6, 9, 11, 12, 13, 19, 20, 34, 35, 43, 80, 81, 82, 92, 109; the Fitzwilliam Museum, Cambridge, for Plates 4, 7, 14, 21; the Royal Mint for the George III penny; the National Coal Board for Plates 57, 81, 110; City of Stoke-on-Trent Museum and Art Gallery for Plate 18; the Science Museum for Plate 22; Lewis Textile Museum, Bolton, for Plates 25, 26; Museum of English Rural Life, Reading, for Plate 29 and Page 46; the Essex County Archivist and Essex County Council for Plate 31; J. R. Freeman Ltd. for Plates 45, 46, 47, 54, 55, 58, 76, 90; Samuel Whitbread Ltd. for Page 88; H.M. Postmaster General for Plates 37, 69, 93, 94, 95, 96; the TUC for Plate 48; the CWS for Plate 50; Radio Times Hulton Picture Library for Plates 59, 60, 68, 98, 99, 100; *The Bristol Evening Post* for Plate 61; *The Illustrated London News* for Plate 62; Cunard Steam-Ship Co. Ltd. for Plates 63, 64; Dr. J. R. Kellett for Plate 65; the Greater London Council for Plates 67, 73; the Shaftesbury Society for Plate 72; Manchester Libraries Committee for Plate 91; the London Museum for Page 207; Leyland Motors for Plate 102; British Railways Board and the Museum of British Transport for Plates 104, 105, 106; British Airways for Plates 107, 108; Frederick Muller Ltd. for the extract from *Scrapbook for the 1920's,* by L. Bailey; the Bodley Head for the extract from *Life's Enchanted Cup,* by Mrs. C. S. Peel; Chappel & Co. Ltd. for the words of *Brother Can You Spare A Dime?* by E. Y. Harburg (composer Jay Gorney. Copyright 1932 Harms Inc. Copyright renewed); the Estate of the late Sir P. Gibbs for the extract from *Pageant of the Years* (Heinemann) John Cornwell for the pictures on the cover of Brunel, a nineteenth-century miner, the Concorde, the airship R33, a Bessemer converter and a cholera poster.

The author also wishes to acknowledge his indebtedness to *Abstract of British Historical Statistics,* by B. R. Mitchell (C U P) and *English Trade Tokens,* by P. Mathias (Abelard Schuman) for helpful reference.

Maps and diagrams by David Watson.
Cover design by Ken Vail.

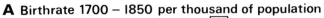

A Birthrate 1700 – 1850 per thousand of population

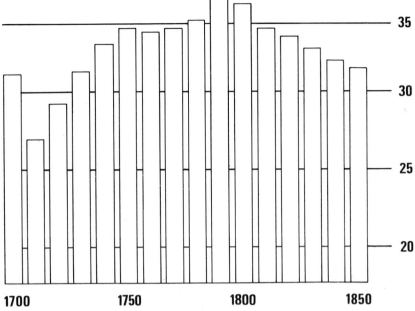

35
30
25
20

1700　　　　　1750　　　　　1800　　　　　1850

B Mortality rate 1700 – 1850 per thousand of population

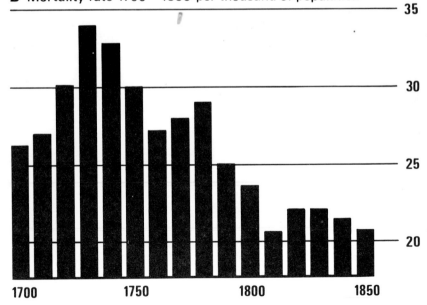

35
30
25
20

1700　　　　　1750　　　　　1800　　　　　1850

1 Population 1700-1850

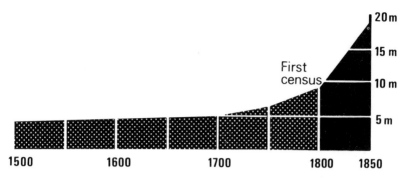

The above graph shows the growth of population in England and Wales from 1500 to 1850. From 1500 to 1700, when the estimated population was 5,750,000, the rise was only slight but by 1801, when the first census was taken, the figure had risen to 9,000,000. After 1801 the population increased rapidly and by 1851 it had reached 18,000,000; so in 150 years the population had more than trebled. In those years the face of Britain was changed beyond recognition.

Why did this great increase in population take place? Quite obviously any population increase must be due to more people being born, or to an increased number of immigrants, or to fewer people dying. We must consider each of these factors in turn.

The Birth Rate

There was a slight rise in the birth rate between 1750 and 1850 due to a number of causes.

1. Farm labourers were ceasing to live in the farmers' houses which meant that they could set up their own cottages and marry earlier.

2 It had once been common for many youths to serve an apprenticeship at low wages. This practice declined throughout the 18th century until it was abolished in 1813. Men began to earn full adult wages when they were still quite young, which again led to earlier marriages and larger families.

3. Young couples living in the towns knew that their children could obtain work in the factories and thus provide money.

1

Nevertheless the rise in the birth rate was not great as you can see in graph A facing page 1, and played only a minor part in the population increase.

Immigration

There was a steady trickle of Irish immigrants in the 18th century. However, after 1800 many settled in Liverpool and Glasgow. Against this must be set the number of people who emigrated from England. Although the emigration of skilled workers was banned from 1719 to 1825, thousands of Englishmen evaded the law and went to work in France and other continental countries. It is possible that the number of immigrants was not much greater than the number of emigrants. Therefore immigration did not play a particularly important part in the population increase. The really great influx of Irishmen into Britain came after the 1845 potato famine when millions starved in Ireland.

The Death Rate

It was the fall in the death rate that proved to be the real cause of the increased population. From 1740 until 1820 the death rate fell almost continuously (see graph B facing page 1). There were a number of reasons why people were living longer.

1. In the early 18th century gin drinking had been rife in London. Gin-shops were common and outside many of them was the sign, "Drunk for a penny, dead drunk for twopence". Drinking this crude spirit caused many deaths and it was not until spirits were heavily taxed in 1751 that the evil was checked.

2. As agricultural methods improved it became possible to keep more cattle alive during the winter which meant that additional fresh meat was available. More wheat was being grown instead of inferior cereals like rye, and greater quantities of green vegetables were being eaten. This meant that people's diets were improving and they had greater resistance to disease.

3. There were some improvements in medicine. William Smellie's work in training midwives saved the lives of thousands of mothers and babies. Then in 1798, Edward Jenner, a Gloucestershire doctor, discovered a vaccine against smallpox. At this time smallpox was one

2

1 *Hogarth's engraving "Gin Lane" vividly evokes the perils of gin drinking.*

of the most dreaded diseases. Each year almost 40,000 people were killed, blinded, crippled, or disfigured by the disease. Jenner noticed that milkmaids, through catching a mild complaint called cowpox, were immune from smallpox. For years Jenner studied the effects of cowpox and experimented with inoculations. When he was fully satisfied with the results of his research he inoculated an eight-year-old boy, James Phipps, with cowpox. A few weeks later he inoculated the boy again, but this time with smallpox germs. The boy was not even slightly ill, for, as Jenner had predicted, the vaccine had made him immune to smallpox. Jenner's success was widely publicised and within his own lifetime, smallpox, as a major disease, was eliminated from Britain.

Most provincial towns began to build hospitals and the standard of surgeons slowly improved. However, in an age when anaesthetics were unknown surgical progress was limited.

4. In some of the large towns attempts were made to pave and clean the streets and to provide proper water supplies and better drainage facilities. These measures did help to prevent diseases at the beginning of the 19th century. Unfortunately after about 1820, the already crude public health facilities could not keep up with the rapid growth of the towns. Between 1820 and 1870 there was

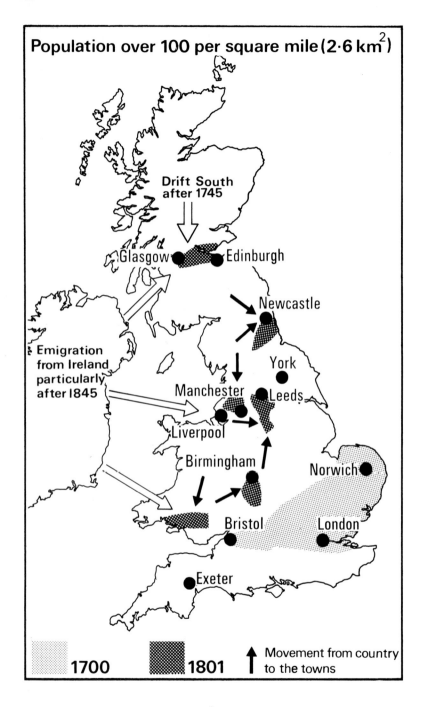

Population over 100 per square mile (2·6 km^2)

Drift South after 1745

Glasgow Edinburgh

Newcastle

Emigration from Ireland particularly after 1845

York

Manchester Leeds

Liverpool

Birmingham

Norwich

Bristol

London

Exeter

1700 1801 Movement from country to the towns

4

a rise once more in the death rate, particularly in the industrial towns.

All the factors mentioned enabled people to live longer, but their most important result was the fall in the death rate of children. In 1700 three-quarters of all children died before they were five. In 1800 the proportion was one-third. In London, between 1750 and 1830, the number of child deaths was halved. Clearly if the children survived they themselves would eventually become parents and the population would rise even more rapidly.

In conclusion it can be said that although the birth rate, immigration, and the death rate all played their part in the increased population, the greatest single cause was the fall in the death rate.

The Distribution of Population

Equally as important as the growth in the population was its geographical change. Look carefully at the map opposite. It shows the distribution of population in 1700 and in 1801. In 1700 London was by far the largest city with about 700,000 inhabitants. Bristol and Norwich were next with over 20,000, and then a number of towns like York, Exeter, and Newcastle had over 10,000. Towns such as Liverpool and Manchester were already growing rapidly.

Most of the population still lived in the country and, as you can see, the South was more heavily populated than the North. One reason for this was the woollen industry in Suffolk and the West Country. Even so only Surrey and Middlesex had more than 150 people to the square mile (2.6km^2).

By 1801 the distribution of population had changed considerably. Apart from the area around London, the most heavily populated counties were the Black Country districts of Staffordshire and Warwickshire with coal and iron industries, and South Lancashire and the West Riding of Yorkshire with cotton and wool. The towns in these regions had grown rapidly. Manchester's population had risen from 9,000 to 95,000. In 1760 Oldham was a village of 300 people; by 1801 it was a town of 12,000. In the Midlands the population of Birmingham had grown from 15,000 to over 70,000.

One very important point to note is that these towns drew their inhabitants from the countryside close to them. For example, some of the villagers in Cheshire moved to Lancashire towns for higher wages, while the country people of Warwickshire were attracted to

Birmingham. But there was never any large-scale movement of population from the South to the North. The only important long-distance movement was that of the poverty-stricken Irish to places like Glasgow and South Lancashire.

Follow up Work

1. *Learn the main reasons for the slight rise in the birth rate, the effect of immigration and emigration, and the rapid fall in the death rate. Then without referring to your book explain fully why the population rose from less than 6 millions in 1700 to 18 millions in 1851.*

2. *"One of the most outstanding features of the rise in population in the 19th century was the growth of towns, particularly in the north of England. In this period the population of the agricultural districts in the south did not decrease but it fell proportionately to the industrial areas of Lancashire, Yorkshire, and the Black Country."*

   a) *Why did the population of Lancashire, Yorkshire, and South Staffordshire rise at the beginning of the 19th century?*

   b) *Name three industrial towns in which the population grew rapidly.*

   c) *There was no large-scale movement of population from the South to the North. From where then did the towns obtain their extra inhabitants?*

   d) *From where did many of the newcomers to Glasgow come?*

2 Power and Industry

2 *The domestic system. How many different jobs are being done by the people in this picture?*

Industry in 1700

Today factories are commonplace, whether they are grim buildings blackened by years of smoke or modern pre-fabricated structures rising on the outskirts of our towns. We accept them as an essential part of our industrial society, but had we lived in 1700 we should have known a very different Britain.

Although most people worked on the land at the beginning of the 18th century, industry was important. Most of this industry was not carried on in factories but in the workers' own homes; for this reason we call it the *domestic* system.

This domestic system was common in the hosiery trade around Nottingham and Leicester, in hat making at Bedford, cutlery at Sheffield, nail manufacture in the area near to Birmingham, and cotton in South Lancashire. In most of these industries the work was "put out" by merchants. They distributed the raw materials and collected the finished product. Gradually they gained control over the workers and would often own the tools used.

The woollen cloth industry provides the best example of the domestic system. Although woollen cloth was manufactured in many areas there were three regions where it was of particular importance; the West Country, East Anglia, and the West Riding. In 1700 the cobbled streets of small towns like Stroud in the Cotswolds, Lavenham or Coggleshall in East Anglia, all echoed daily with the rattling hooves of laden packhorses carrying raw wool to the workers' cottages or taking the finished cloth to market. In all the villages around women sat in their homes spinning and men worked on their weaving looms. The cloth was taken to small mills where the fullers beat the material with water and fullers' earth to make it shrink, the shearmen cropped the nap with huge scissors to make the surface smooth, and the dyers immersed the grey cloth in great vats of coloured dyes. The whole production took place either in a worker's home or in a small mill usually employing only a few men.

Behind this manufacture was a complex organisation controlled by a man called a clothier. It was the clothier who bought the wool from the farmer, arranged for it to go through its various processes, and finally sold the finished product. Sometimes he employed just a few spinners and weavers, but there were clothiers who employed two or three thousand and grew so powerful that they even owned their workers' looms and spinning wheels. Such men were capitalists, but because the machinery used was simple and the only power needed was the water wheel to drive the fulling mills, there was no real need for factories.

In the West Riding the situation was different. There the clothier was usually just a farmer-weaver who employed a few other weavers in a workshop attached to his home. The wool was spun by the women in the village and the farmer took his unfinished cloth to the weekly markets held at Wakefield, Leeds, Bradford, or Halifax.

The domestic system appeared to have many advantages for the workers. There was no travelling to work and no factory discipline. If they wanted, and they often did, they could take days off to follow the hounds or just idle. Their needs were simple and they lived in a healthy countryside, not in the crowded towns which were later to grow up.

In practice the system was never as agreeable as this, and certainly not as cosy as Plate 2 might suggest. The workers' cottages were small

3 *Handloom weavers and spinners at work in a London textile merchant's "factory" in the 1740's.*

and they must have lived in an atmosphere of forged iron or dusty wool. They were never sure when they would be paid, and work could be infrequent. Employers sometimes tried to rob the workers by giving too little iron or wool, and in turn the workers produced inferior goods. It is impossible to say how well paid domestic workers were since wages varied over the country.

The domestic system prevailed in many industries but there were some to which it was unsuited. Coal, lead, and tin mining obviously could not be done at home, and there were many industries where workers were employed together under factory conditions. These included iron smelting, brewing, brick making, and cannon manufacturing.

This, then, was the picture of industrial England in 1700. With the exception of London most industry tended to be rural rather than urban. This was true both of the domestic system and the early factories and mining. Power was not yet important and where it was used, as in iron smelting, waterwheels sufficed. Most industrial production was on a small scale but there were some wealthy capitalists who invested large sums in their businesses.

Many industrial changes had taken place before 1700 and industry was already important. But it was in the second half of the 18th century that the remarkable transformation known as the Industrial Revolution really began.

Follow up Work

1. *What was the domestic system and in which industries was it common in the early 18th century?*
2. *Explain how the domestic system usually worked and show clearly its advantages and disadvantages.*
3. *How far did the factory system already exist in the early 18th century.*
4. *On a map of England mark in the main industries in the first half of the 18th century. Indicate which of these were carried out on the domestic system and which in factories, or under factory conditions.*

4

The Iron Industry 1700–1800

The first step in the production of iron is smelting. This consists of heating iron ore until the metal itself melts and runs off. Up to 1700 charcoal was the fuel mainly used for smelting. It took almost half a hectare of woodland to smelt just one tonne of iron and by the beginning of the 18th century there was a serious shortage of the fuel in England. Areas like the Sussex Weald and the Forest of Dean, which had long been famous for producing iron, were desperately short of charcoal and the iron foundries were moving to regions like South Wales and the West Midlands where there was still ample woodland. The position was so serious that many iron manufacturers were having to import pig iron from Sweden.

Experiments had been made using coal instead of charcoal, but coal contains sulphur which makes the pig iron impure and brittle. Then in 1709 came a revolutionary change: Abraham Darby of Coalbrookdale in Shropshire was successful in smelting iron ore with coke.

Plate 5 shows how Darby used coke in his blast furnace.

Darby built up a successful business, and besides iron smelting, manufactured pots, iron pipes and grates. Both he and his son tried to keep their methods secret and the idea of using coke instead of charcoal was not generally known for some years. Abraham Darby's original furnace has been preserved by the Ironbridge Gorge Museum Trust and can still be seen at Coalbrookdale.

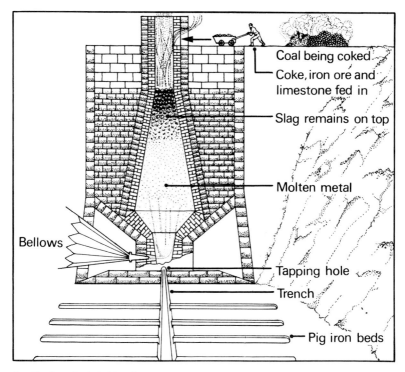

5 *Abraham Darby's blast furnace.*
The coal was coked by having gases and tarry substances removed and was then heaped near the top of the furnace. The furnace was lit and quantities of coke, ore, and limestone were taken along the bridge and emptied in. A terrific heat was created by the bellows which were worked by a water wheel. As the iron began to melt it ran through the slag, which remained in the cone, and formed a molten mass at the bottom of the furnace. When the furnaceman thought the metal was ready he ran it off and allowed it to solidify into pigs of iron.

11

6 *Iron Bridge, Coalbrookdale in Shropshire. This bridge which is part of the Ironbridge Gorge Museum Trust is visited by thousands of people each year.*

As the 18th century progressed the demand for iron increased and other ironmasters began to use coke. The most famous of them all was John Wilkinson who opened ironworks in South Staffordshire and Shropshire. "Iron-mad" Wilkinson was of great importance in the development of the industry. In 1774 he invented a new method of boring cannon. He followed this by supplying James Watt with the accurate parts he needed for his steam engine. Later Wilkinson in turn used Watt's steam engines to blow the bellows at his furnaces and to drive the hammers at his forges. His interest in iron was almost fanatical. He built the first iron boat in 1787, erected an iron chapel for his workmen, and insisted that he should be buried in an iron coffin. Wilkinson was also a businessman of outstanding ability, and in addition to owning a group of blast furnaces in the Midlands he controlled ironworks in France, which produced, amongst other things, waterpipes for the city of Paris.

Probably the greatest memorial to these Shropshire ironmasters is

12

the famous iron bridge spanning the River Severn at Coalbrookdale. (See Plate 6.) This was the first iron bridge ever constructed and was opened in 1779. It was actually built by Abraham Darby the Third after consultations with John Wilkinson. If you look at the photograph carefully you will see the enormous amount of iron used. It was built exactly as if it had been made of wood and even included vast dovetail joints!

The next major advance came in 1783 when Henry Cort took out a patent for puddling and rolling iron. Wrought iron was very important because it was malleable. It was particularly useful for the iron railings which the wealthy had round their houses and also for ornamental iron gates. At this time the only way in which pig iron could be converted into wrought iron was by hammering out the impurities while the metal was in a semi-molten state. Cort overcame this by designing the reverbatory furnace. (See Plate 8 *overleaf*.)

Although his inventions were of great benefit to the iron industry Cort, unlike Wilkinson, was not a clever businessman and made very little money out of his inventions.

These 18th century inventions transformed the iron industry and led to an enormous increase in output. The geographical situation of the ironworks changed considerably. The use of steam engines meant that water power was no longer necessary (notice how Darby's own works were still situated near water). The industry was able to move to the coalfields and in particular to the Black Country, South Wales,

7   *Shortages of copper coins from the Royal Mint provoked a spate of local minting of "trade tokens" in the 1770's. Minted by local merchants and industrialists, they were usually decorated with familiar industrial or commercial scenes (see Plates 4, 9, 14, 21). Wilkinson alone had the audacity to have himself portrayed, like a sort of local king (a George III penny is shown for comparison).*

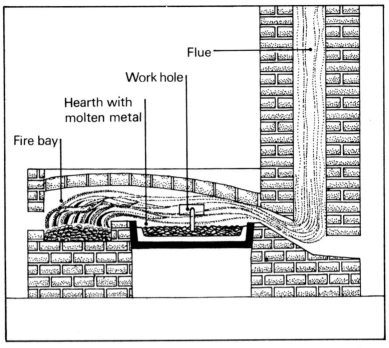

8 *Cort's puddling furnace.*
The heat was reflected from the roof and never actually touched the molten metal. The current of hot air passing over the molten metal oxidised the carbon impurities and turned them into carbon dioxide which escaped up the flue. Throughout the process the molten iron was continually stirred or puddled by a bar inserted through the work hole.

South Yorkshire, and Scotland. The smelting firms grew larger and began to control both coal mines and ironworks. Some employers, like Samuel Walker at Rotherham, Wilkinson at Broseley, Richard Crawshay at Merthyr Tydfil, and the Carron Works in Scotland, had hundreds of employees. The demands of the iron industry stimulated coal output and helped to make coal mining into a major industry. The production of cheap iron really made possible the machine age of the 19th century and played a major part in the Industrial Revolution.

Finally, reference must be made to the output of steel. Between 1740 and 1750 Benjamin Huntsman, a Sheffield watchmaker, devised a method of burning out the impurities of iron ore in a sealed crucible and then adding charcoal to harden the iron and make steel. However, the amounts made were small and generally used for such things as razors, expensive swords, and watch springs. The real development in steel manufacture was not to come until the 19th century.

Follow up Work

1. *a)* *Why did the iron industry move in the 18th century from the south and south-west of the country to the north?*
   b) *What contributions to progress in the iron industry did two of the following make:*
      1. Abraham Darby, 2. Henry Cort, 3. John Wilkinson.
                                   (Southern Regional Examinations Board, 1966)
2. *In what ways did the 18th century inventions transform the iron industry?*
3. *On a map of Britain indicate the main changes which took place in the 18th century in the location of the iron smelting industries.*

Coal Mining 1700–1815

As the map (Plate 10) shows, coal was being mined in many parts of Britain in 1700. Although there were already large pits in Durham and Northumberland, where in 1649 "one coal merchant imployethe 500 or 1000 in his works of coal", most of the coal mines rarely employed more than twenty men underground and were usually found in isolated country districts.

The workings were about 60m below the surface and ventilation was provided by a tall chimney, or, if the workings were not deep, by a shaft. By the early 19th century the coal was raised by a whim gin (Plate 9). These replaced the early cog and rung gins. Ropes were attached to the two pulley wheels and the circular drum. This drum was drawn by one or two horses and rotated round a vertical spindle. The coal was then taken away by packhorses or in carts.

By 1700 coal was used in brewing, pottery, brick making, and glass manufacture. As industry developed there was an increasing demand for coal, particularly for iron smelting and for steam engines. At the same time, as people became more accustomed to using coal, the domestic demand increased rapidly. Some idea of the growth of the industry is shown by the fact that in 1700 only $2\frac{1}{2}$ million tonnes of coal were mined, by 1800 10 million tonnes, and by 1815 the amount had jumped to 27 million tonnes. One important reason for this dramatic increase in output between 1800 and 1815 was the demand for iron and munitions during the wars against Napoleon.

Flooding and gas explosions made coal mining very dangerous, and these had to be overcome before there could be any great increase in the output of the mines. In small mines the water had either been baled out or run off by drainage channels. These methods were impracticable in deeper mines and flooding became a serious problem, causing many pits to close. It was largely overcome with the introduction of the steam engine, which was used for pumping water clear. During the 18th century Newcomen's and later Watt's engines were widely used in coal mines all over Britain (see Plates 15 and 16).

"Chokedamp" or carbonic acid gas had existed in many small pits. The presence of this gas was indicated by the flickering of the miner's candle, but it could usually be dispersed by "wafting" the miner's jacket. As the mines went deeper a new danger was met, "firedamp" or marsh gas. The miner's candle flame caused this to explode without warning and terrible accidents occurred. Numerous methods were tried in an attempt to overcome the problem of gas. "Firemen" wrapped in wet rags and holding a candle on a long pole would try deliberately to explode the gas. New methods of lighting were adopted such as the steel mill which sent out a shower of sparks and was only slightly less dangerous than the candle. Some miners even used rotten fish whose luminous glow gave out a tiny and almost useless light! Ventilation shafts were built and by lighting a fire in a special by-pit the air was driven round the mine workings. All too often the gas

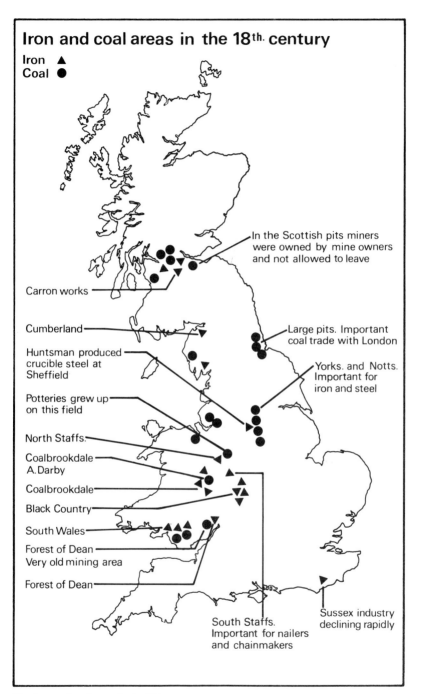

Iron and coal areas in the 18th century

Iron ▲
Coal ●

In the Scottish pits miners were owned by mine owners and not allowed to leave

Carron works

Cumberland

Large pits. Important coal trade with London

Huntsman produced crucible steel at Sheffield

Yorks. and Notts. Important for iron and steel

Potteries grew up on this field

North Staffs.

Coalbrookdale A. Darby

Coalbrookdale

Black Country

South Wales

Forest of Dean
Very old mining area

Forest of Dean

South Staffs. Important for nailers and chainmakers

Sussex industry declining rapidly

10   *Iron and coal areas in the 18th century.*

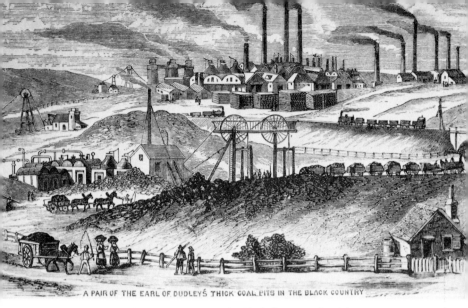

11 *An early 19th-century engraving of a Black Country industrial scene.*

was forced back towards the fire with disastrous results.

Finally in 1815 Sir Humphry Davy invented the safety lamp. Its design proved so sound that it has hardly been changed to this day, and some colliery men still carry them to detect gas. The flame of this lamp was encased inside a wire gauze. The gauze dispersed the heat of the flame so that the gas never became hot enough to ignite. Davy's lamp acquired almost immediate fame but unfortunately it enabled colliers to work in highly dangerous parts of the mines so that accidents did not decrease as quickly as they should have done.

The deepening of the pits also meant increasing difficulty in moving the coal from the face to the shaft. Previously the coal had been dragged on sledges, now rails were laid and wagons drawn by ponies or children were pulled along them (See Plates 54 to 58).

The development of canals in the 18th century provided a cheaper method of transporting coal. This led to an increase in the output of many inland coalfields. One very good example of the value of water transport to coal miners was the Manchester to Worsley canal which the Duke of Bridgewater had cut with the deliberate object of carrying the coal from his pits by barge, instead of by cart or packhorse. The price of coal in Manchester fell by almost one-half and there was a considerable increase in the amount used.

12   *A miner's oil lamp dating from the early 19th century.*
13   *An original Humphry Davy safety lamp. This particular one was used in the gaseous pits of the Northumberland coalfield.*

Follow up Work

1. *On a map of Britain mark in the coalfields which were worked in 1700.*

2. *Explain why the demand for coal rose from 2½ million tonnes in 1700 to 27 million tonnes by 1815.*

3. *"The people employed in the coal mines are prodigiously numerous, amounting to many thousands; the average earnings of the men are from one shilling to four shillings a day and their firing." (Arthur Young, 1790)*

   a) To which part of the country does this refer?
   b) What do you think is meant by "firing"?
   c) Write a description of the pit head of a small mine in the 18th century.
   d) What difficulties were the miners facing and how did they attempt to overcome them?

19

14

Steam Power 1700–1815

Some form of power has always been essential to industry. Men, dogs, and horses have been harnessed to machines, and when greater force was needed windmills and waterwheels were constructed. Waterwheels were generally the most successful of all these. They were used to grind corn and to power textile mills, they operated bellows and hammers in ironworks, and even worked pumps for draining floods.

Useful as water power was it had serious limitations, for it restricted industry to the sides of streams. Severe frost prevented the wheels turning and sometimes expensive reservoirs had to be constructed to provide water in case of drought. Some other form of power was essential before an industrial revolution could really take place.

Steam power had been known since ancient times but it was not used in this country until Captain Savery patented a steam engine in 1698. It was intended for pumping water out of tin and copper mines in Cornwall but it was not very powerful and had only limited success. Then in 1708, Thomas Newcomen, a Devonshire blacksmith, invented a much improved steam engine.

Newcomen's engine gained immediate popularity and hundreds of them were built. Most were used to pump water out of mines but some were erected to force water into canals and to supply towns with drinking water. The engine's greatest weakness was the amount of fuel needed continually to re-heat the cylinder; this problem was to be solved by the greatest of all the steam engine inventors, James Watt.

James Watt was born at Greenock in Scotland. His grandfather had been a teacher of mathematics and his father was an architect and shipbuilder. He was educated at the local grammar school and his natural mechanical and mathematical ability soon showed itself. Watt became a maker of scientific instruments and when he was twenty-one

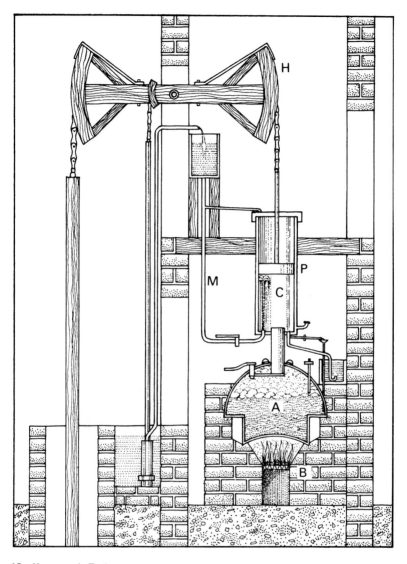

15 *Newcomen's Engine*
The boiler A was heated by the furnace B. The cylinder was at C and the piston at P. When the cylinder was full of steam the beam H was forced upwards. The steam was then condensed by cold water running from the tank, down the pipe M and into the cylinder. The condensing of the steam caused a vacuum in the cylinder and the beam came down again. Steam was then re-admitted into the cylinder and the piston was once again forced up.

was employed by Glasgow University. Here he met many leading scientists and widened his own scientific knowledge, including his understanding of steam power.

At the University he had to repair a model of Newcomen's engine and it was during this work that Watt began to think whether it would be possible to overcome the loss of power and waste of fuel occasioned by re-heating the cylinder. According to Watt himself he discovered the answer one Sunday in 1765 as he was walking across Glasgow Green. To prevent the cylinder losing heat the steam would have to be condensed in a separate chamber. Within a few weeks Watt had worked out his plans. Plate 16 shows how the principle of a separate condenser worked.

Watt had now to produce his machine commercially. This required far greater financial resources than he possessed. His first partner was John Roebuck, owner of the Carron ironworks. Using Roebuck's facilities, Watt made sufficient progress to take out a patent for his engine in 1769. However, the project was in its infancy, and in 1773, when the machine was still not working properly, Roebuck went bankrupt. At this point when it seemed as if Watt's invention was doomed to failure Matthew Boulton agreed to take over Roebuck's interest in the engine.

Matthew Boulton was one of the great businessmen of the 18th century. A highly intelligent, fair-minded man, he was the owner of the Soho works near Birmingham where he manufactured a variety of small metal goods like buttons, snuff boxes and watch chains. His factory depended on water power and Boulton saw a great future in Watt's invention. So it was that in 1774 the famous partnership of Boulton and Watt began.

Watt could now rely on Boulton's skilled men to make his engine parts. In 1774 John Wilkinson patented his cannon lathe and this meant that Watt could obtain accurate cylinders. By 1775 the first Watt engine was sold but although engines were being made it was

---

16 *Watt's Engine*

The steam comes from the boiler and passes through the steam valve A. The steam forces down piston P and the movement of the link bar B attached to the beam closes the steam and exhaust valves C and D and opens the central valves. The steam travels through these valves and this causes the piston to rise. This re-opens the steam and exhaust valves. The steam re-enters the cylinder again and forces down the piston. This time the steam in the cylinder is condensed to form warm water which returns to the boiler and needs less fuel to re-heat it.

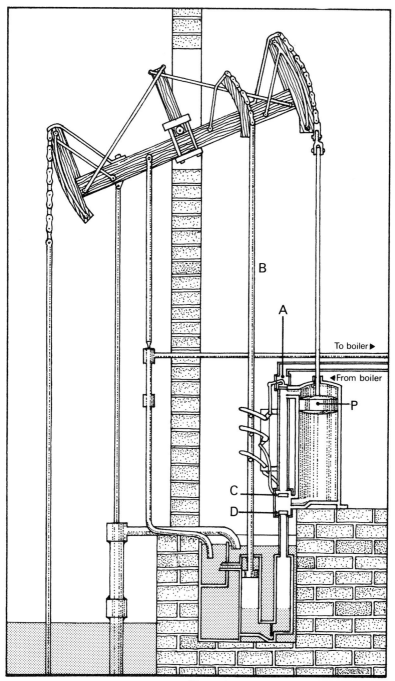

B

A

To boiler ▶

◀ From boiler

P

C

D

23

some years before the partnership became really profitable. In fact a series of unprofitable contracts, particularly with Cornish mine owners, brought them very close to bankruptcy. They managed to overcome these difficulties and in 1781 Watt took out his patent for a rotary motion, the "sun and planet" movement (Plate 17).

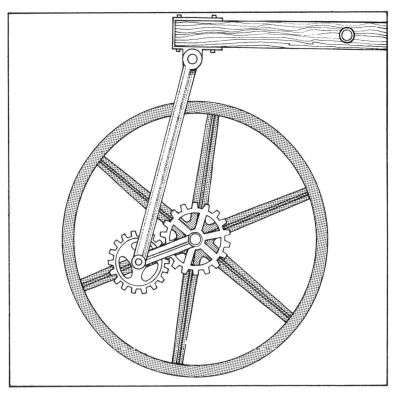

17 *The sun and planet movement. Watt's engine adapted to rotary motion. This relatively simple device now meant that the steam engine could be used for motive power, and it opened a whole new field.*

Watt's inventive. genius and Boulton's business ability produced a wonderful partnership and by 1785 they were highly successful. Their steam engines were used in the Cornish tin mines. They drove bellows and rolling mills in the iron industry. Cotton mills, distilleries, and waterworks were all being powered by them. It is no exaggeration to say that Watt's engine opened the way to the modern world. It meant that industry could grow up on the coalfields and it enabled large-scale production to take place. As steam power multiplied so did the output of iron, clothes, and countless other products. With the coming of the railways and steamboats in the 19th century it was to be applied to transport. The steam engine was one of the most important of man's inventions for without it the Industrial Revolution could never have taken place. Perhaps its importance was best summed up by Boulton himself when he said of his factory, ". . . We sell here, Sir, what all the world desires to have, Power."

Follow up Work

1. *a) Make a simple sketch of Newcomen's engine and explain briefly how it worked. Where were these engines mainly used and what was their greatest weakness?*

   b) Sketch Watt's engine, and make notes showing that you understand how it worked, and in what way it was an improvement on Newcomen's.

2. *Describe the parts played by James Watt, Matthew Boulton, and John Wilkinson in the development of the steam engine.*

3. *Why has it been said that Watt's steam engine was the most important invention of the Industrial Revolution?*

4. *Re-read the section on iron and then write a brief account showing the connection between the steam engine and the iron industry.*

18

Pottery 1700–1800

At the beginning of the 18th century the district now known as the Potteries gave little indication of its future greatness. The farmers of this sparsely populated area began to make pottery because of the suitability of the local clay, and because they needed to supplement the poor living they made from agriculture. Although the standard of the pottery produced improved after 1700 much of it was still coarse and heavy. There were about one hundred and fifty pot works in existence but many of them were little more than kilns attached to the thatch-covered cottages (once again, the domestic system). The potters themselves were poor and ignorant, living brutal lives in this small, isolated community.

It was here that Josiah Wedgwood was born in 1730, and before his death in 1795 this backward area had acquired international fame for the beauty of its products. Wedgwood came from a family of

19 *Josiah Wedgwood*

20 *This was Wedgwood's first factory before he opened up a larger works at Etruria. Eighteenth-century pottery works all began in small cottages in semi-rural surroundings.*

potters. His father, a small manufacturer, had died when Josiah was still young and then the boy had been apprenticed to his elder brother. When he was twelve he contracted smallpox which so weakened his leg that later in life he had to have it amputated.

Wedgwood was twenty when he set up as a manufacturer, at first with partners and later on his own. His artistic sense and scientific ability soon showed itself in the standard of the ware he was producing and by 1765 he had received a large order from Queen Charlotte, the wife of George III.

In 1769 he opened his works at Etruria. Named after the Italian province where Etruscan pottery had been made, this factory was to become the most famous of all pottery works. Here Wedgwood carried out countless experiments with clays and glazes. He produced beautiful pottery figures, delicate dinner and tea services, and the famous jasper ware. He employed the finest artists and craftsmen and trained his workmen so that they became specialists at one particular craft. His pottery became internationally celebrated and in 1774 he completed a dinner service for the Empress Catherine of Russia. It consisted of 952 pieces decorated with freehand paintings of 1,244 English scenes. The total cost was about £3,000 and many of the pieces still exist.

Wedgwood was not only a great potter, he was also an outstanding businessman. He was one of the first manufacturers to realise the value of the steam engine to power his machines. He bought a controlling interest in a Cornish clay company in order to ensure supplies of his raw material, and he was one of the originators and financiers of the Trent and Mersey Canal. It was this canal, engineered by James Brindley, which provided a cheap and easy way of carrying the raw materials to the factory and a safe means of transporting the finished pottery. Wedgwood wisely planned that his Etruria works would be built where he knew the canal would be cut.

A man of exceptional intelligence, a good but strict employer, Josiah Wedgwood stands out as one of the great figures of the Industrial Revolution. The firm which he founded still exists and it is probably the most famous pottery manufacturing company in the world.

Follow up Work

1. Write an account of Josiah Wedgwood's contribution to the pottery industry.

2. Show how Wedgwood profited from the discoveries and technological achievements of his time to establish a thriving and long-lasting business.

3 The Textile Industries 1700-1830

21

Silk

Silk manufacture was fairly widespread by the end of the 17th century. French Huguenots or Protestants who had fled from religious persecution had settled in Norwich, Spitalfields (London), and Coventry, and their skill had added considerably to the standard of English silk weaving. At the beginning of the 18th century silk became the first of the textile industries to change over to the factory system.

Behind the building of silk factories in England lay a rather strange story. It had been believed for some time that the Italians had invented silk throwing machines which removed the silk from the cocoon, but their secret was strictly guarded. In 1716 an Englishman, John Lombe, went to Italy to try to discover this secret. The journey was difficult and dangerous but he succeeded in finding out how these machines worked. He managed to get back to England but died soon after the first machine had been built (some said that the Italians had poisoned him). His brother, Thomas Lombe, went ahead with a factory at Derby and before his patent expired in 1732 he had made a fortune of £120,000. From then onwards factories employing thousands of workers were built at Stockport, Macclesfield and London. Despite these advances, however, silk never became a major industry partly because of the high cost of the raw material. The future lay with cotton and wool.

Cotton

Unlike woollen cloth, cotton cloth has only been manufactured in England since the 17th century. By about 1650 the industry had begun to grow up in South Lancashire, then a backward, sparsely populated region. This area had several advantages. Liverpool was developing

22 *An impression of the way the "outwork" system operated. Each task in the line would be subcontracted by the previous craftsman—often to members of his own family. So, the "fustian master" gave raw cotton to the weaver and paid him, the weaver paid for the spinner and the spinner paid for the thread to be carded.*

as a port and was well situated for the import of American cotton. The western slopes of the Pennines had a fairly high rainfall and cotton thread spinning needed a damp atmosphere. The hills also provided fast flowing streams suitable for water power. Agriculture was never prosperous on the high moorlands and farmers' families found a secondary living in cotton spinning and weaving.

In the early 18th century cotton manufacture was conducted on the domestic system and was controlled by merchants in a way similar to that of the clothiers of the West Country. The output was small at first, but even so the traditionally "national" woollen industry was alarmed and a number of Acts of Parliament were passed forbidding the wearing of cotton clothes. However, fustian, a mixture of cotton and linen, was allowed and this material became increasingly popular.

The rise in demand stirred the imaginations of inventors and the 18th century saw the appearance of a remarkable series of new machines. The first of these, John Kay's "Flying Shuttle" patented in 1733, was not really a machine but a device for speeding up the old-style weaving loom.

Kay was born in 1704 near Bury in Lancashire and worked for some time as a weaver for a Colchester clothier. He used a loom like that on page 29, but this had one great disadvantage: the weaver had to pass the shuttle between the long warp threads by hand from left to right. This meant that the width of material which a single workman could weave was limited by the length of his arms. In Kay's invention the shuttle was fitted with small wheels and set in a wooden groove. The shuttle was struck from one side to the other by small hammers which were worked by strings held by the weaver.

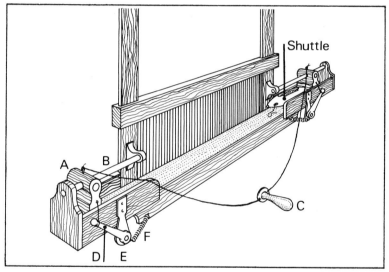

23 *Kay's flying shuttle.'The simple mechanism at D, E, F was operated by the picking stick C which drew back the picker A. When released, A ran along bar B and struck the shuttle. The same mechanism operated at both ends.*

This simple invention enabled broader cloths to be made much more quickly, but it met with immediate hostility. In Colchester the weavers accused him of destroying their livelihood. He moved to Leeds, but there manufacturers used his shuttle and refused to pay royalties. In Bury a mob attacked his house and Kay was forced to

31

flee. According to one story he only escaped hidden in a sack of wool, and in the end he was glad to live in France.

It was not until the 1760's that the "flying shuttle" was widely used and by then its real impact on the cotton industry was very apparent. The fact that it enabled weavers to work quicker led to an increased demand for spun thread. The spinners were unable to satisfy this demand, prices rose, and weavers were unemployed. Some form of mechanical spinning was desperately needed.

The Spinning Machine Inventions

Many attempts were made to create a workable spinning machine but the first really successful invention was James Hargreaves' "Spinning Jenny" in 1765. Hargreaves, a Blackburn weaver, was supposed to have had the idea for his machine from seeing how his wife's spinning wheel still turned after it had been accidentally knocked over. He may well have named the jenny after her. Plate 24 shows the simplicity of this machine.

Hargreaves' first machine had only eight spindles but this number was soon increased. It was not long before the hand spinners realised the competition this invention offered. In Blackburn workers broke into his house and destroyed his machines. He was forced to flee to Nottingham but he had already made the error of selling some of his machines before he took out his patent. For this reason manufacturers were able to use his machine without his permission. Although Hargreaves made over £4,000 from his invention this was only a fraction of its worth to the cotton industry. The spinning jenny spun a fine but weak thread. This was suitable for the weft (the cross threads) but not strong enough for the warp (the vertical threads). As it could easily be used in cottages it did not contribute to the change-over from the domestic system to factories.

The first important spinning machine to need considerable power to drive it was the waterframe patented by Richard Arkwright in 1769. Richard Arkwright, a Preston wigmaker, became one of the most successful businessmen of the 18th century. Plate 25 (*overleaf*) shows that the waterframe was a much heavier instrument than the jenny.

It was the waterframe which really heralded the textile factory age but it is doubtful how far Arkwright himself invented it. It seems very probable that he stole the idea from a number of sources, but if his ability as an inventor is questionable, as a businessman and organiser he was brilliant.

Arkwright entered into partnership with some wealthy Nottingham merchants and set up his first mill at Cromford in Derbyshire. Within a few years this mill had three hundred workers and Arkwright was building other factories in Derbyshire and Lancashire.

Although one of his mills at Chorley was burned to the ground by rioters, and his patent rights were attacked by other manufacturers, Arkwright went from strength to strength. At a time when workers were still unused to factory discipline, he organised and controlled

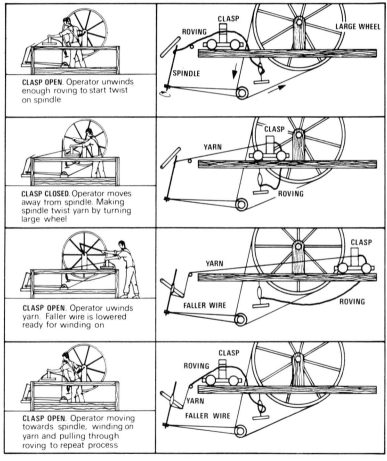

24 *The Spinning Jenny.*

25 *The raw cotton was held in the rovings at the top and drawn down through pairs of rollers, the second of which moved faster than the first so as to elongate the yarn. The rollers enabled a fine and strong thread to be spun. The roving continued to the spindles at the bottom, which were turned by belts attached to the pulleys. One extremely important fact was that these pulleys needed power to drive them. This machine was not suitable for use in cottages and its invention fostered the growth of spinning factories situated on the sides of fast-flowing streams. It is interesting to note that textile factories continue to be called mills even though they are no longer powered by water.*

34

thousands of employees. To do this he worked from five in the morning until nine at night and always travelled in a coach drawn by four horses to achieve the greatest possible speed. The "Bagcheeked, pot-bellied barber" as Arkwright has been described, eventually became high sheriff of Derbyshire, was knighted, and when he died in his palatial house at Cromford, left a fortune of £500,000.

The next important invention was also a spinning machine, the

26 *The thread was drawn between rollers similar to the waterframe and there was a carriage as in Hargreaves' jenny. The rollers could be controlled as the spindles were turning, and the speed of the carriage could be varied. It was the increased control which enabled the spinner to vary the type of yarn produced and made the mule capable of spinning finer and stronger threads than ever before in England.*

mule, invented by Samuel Crompton in 1779. Crompton's home was a lovely Tudor house called *Hall i' the Wood* near Bolton. (This house is now a museum and well worth a visit.) It was here that he began his experiments, and the fine threads which he was producing made it obvious to his neighbours that some new machine was being invented. To hide his invention Crompton often worked at night, and the strange noises coming from his house led to rumours that it was haunted. His final machine, the mule, as it was called, was a combination of the jenny and the waterframe. It was given the name "mule" because of the animal which is not a true breed but a cross between a horse and an ass. (See Plate 26.)

Crompton was completely unlike Arkwright. Although a brilliant inventor, he lacked business ability. He did not take out a patent, and failed in any way to protect his financial interests. Manufacturers who used the mule promised to recompense Crompton. The total amount he received was less than £100. Crompton was so bitter at this treatment that when he later invented a carding machine he deliberately destroyed it to prevent anyone gaining from it. The Government did eventually make him a grant of £5,000 in recognition of the importance of his work to industry, but even this he invested unwisely and died a poor man. His machine was at first used in cottages, but by 1790 it was being powered by water and thousands of mules were in operation in the growing factories.

In 1785 steam power was applied to spinning machines for the first time and factories could be built on the coalfields. This accelerated the growth of the great northern textile towns.

The Weaving Machine Inventions

In 1760 weavers had often found difficulty in obtaining spun yarn. The inventions of Hargreaves, Arkwright, and Crompton had reversed the position. There was now a great shortage of weavers. The wages of handloom weavers rose rapidly—some of them earned almost £2 a week in the 1790's when few skilled men earned as much as £1. Many weavers began to speak of their work as a "gentleman's trade". They strutted proudly around with their silver-topped canes, refused other workers admittance to their public houses, and on occasions put £5 notes in their hat brims as they strode through the streets. This prosperity was not to last for men's minds were occupied more and more with thoughts of a weaving machine.

Strangely enough the first weaving machine was produced by a clergyman, Edmund Cartwright, who, until he began his experiments had never seen a weaver at work. While on holiday in Matlock, Cartwright had met a group of cotton manufacturers who had told him that it was impossible to invent a weaving machine. Cartwright refused to believe this. He was a highly intelligent man and despite his lack of mechanical knowledge he set about the problem of producing a powerdriven loom. His first machine was patented in 1785 but it was too clumsy to be practicable. By 1789 he had improved on it sufficiently to open a factory at Doncaster, but like so many of the early inventors Cartwright was dogged by ill luck and lacked the necessary business ability. One factory at Manchester was burnt to the ground, probably by hostile handloom weavers. Cartwright himself made no money out of his invention and was ruined trying to put it into operation. Later, Parliament did make him a grant of £10,000 because, although numerous improvements were made to the original machine to make it practicable, the fundamental idea had been Cartwright's.

The power loom was slow to be adopted and by 1825 there were still many handloom weavers left. However, they were finding it impossible to compete with the power looms and by the 1830's the remaining handloom weavers were living in poverty.

Further Developments

The 18th century also saw important inventions in bleaching, dyeing, and printing. In 1774 Berthollet, a Frenchman, had discovered how to make chlorine bleaching powder and by 1798 Charles Tennant was producing the powder in large quantities in Glasgow. Many vegetable dyes were replaced by chemical products and in 1783 Thomas Bell invented a machine for printing patterns on cloth.

The 18th century had witnessed a series of inventions which were to transform the cotton industry. The first half of the 19th century was to see the domestic system almost completely disappear, and although some mills still remained on the banks of streams in lonely valleys, most had moved to the coalfields to be powered by steam.

It was in the 19th century that Lancashire was to grow into the great industrial area we know today and the cotton industry to reach its peak of greatness. An idea of the magnitude of this growth can be gained from these figures. In 1700 some 893 tonnes of raw cotton had been imported; by 1810 55,366 tonnes, and by 1880 765,134 tonnes.

Wool

As we saw in Chapter 2, although the woollen industry was spread over much of the country the three great centres were the West Country, East Anglia, and the West Riding of Yorkshire. The Industrial Revolution was to result in the famous wool towns of the past like Norwich, Colchester, and Tiverton, giving way to the Yorkshire towns of Leeds, Bradford, Halifax, and Huddersfield.

The woollen industry was slower than cotton to adopt the new machinery, being so scattered, older, and slow to accept change. Wool also was of a softer fibre than cotton and tended to break easily on the early machines.

Yorkshire took the lead in using the new machines. Here the industry was close to Lancashire and saw more clearly the value of these inventions. Once the machine age was accepted Yorkshire had other advantages. There were many rivers for water power and later the rich local coalfields were to prove invaluable for steam power.

By 1790 the flying shuttle and the jenny were common in Yorkshire but both these could be used in the domestic system. Factories were slow to develop. The first worsted mill was established in 1787 at Addingham on the River Wharfe. Leeds and Bradford began to grow rapidly during the 1790's and Crompton's mule was in common use in the factories there.

Spinning mills were important by 1800 but most of them were small. As late as 1840 handloom weaving still predominated and it was not until the second half of the 19th century that the factories really took the place of the domestic system in the woollen industry.

The Luddites

Although the introduction of powered machinery into the textile industries was ultimately to benefit everyone, it was bound to put handworkers out of work. In 1811 many textile workers were suffering from unemployment partly because the wars against France had disrupted trade, and partly because of the competition they were facing from machines. It was poverty and unemployment that led to the outbreak of the Luddite Riots. These attacks were named after a mysterious figure, Ned Ludd, who was said to have his headquarters in Sherwood Forest. No one has ever proved whether he really existed.

The Luddite campaign began amongst the Nottinghamshire stocking makers in the spring of 1811. Stockings had always been knitted on narrow frames as a complete article. Many masters had begun to use wider frames on which the stockings were cut out and sewn together. The result was that more stockings were made but that they were a far inferior product. To protect their livelihoods and their reputations the stocking knitters went from village to village smashing the wide frames. Before this outbreak of Luddism ended over one thousand frames had been destroyed.

In 1812 Luddite rioting spread to Lancashire and Cheshire where the handloom weavers began to destroy the power looms. High food prices also helped to cause mob violence and in the remote mining villages there were rumours of armed men being trained to fight.

In Yorkshire it was the shearing machines which were destroyed. The shearmen, highly skilled men who cut the nap off the woollen cloth, faced starvation when the machines were introduced. The Luddites smashed the machines with a huge hammer which they called *Great Enoch*. Their song spread fear amongst the manufacturers.

> *Great Enoch still shall lead the van,*
> *Stop him who dare. Stop him who can.*

The violence grew worse. On occasions, as with the attack on William Cartwright's mill at Rawsfold in Yorkshire, the outbreaks were carefully prepared. Cartwright had made plans to guard his mill and when the Luddites tried to smash open the doors they were met by musket fire. Two of the Luddites were wounded and as they lay dying it was said that Cartwright refused them a doctor at first because they would not divulge the names of their accomplices.

Fourteen men were hanged for this attack and later Cartwright, or "the Bloodhound" as he was called, was almost murdered near his own home. We must in fairness remember that Cartwright, like other manufacturers, believed that he had a right to use machines and it was the Luddites who were trying to destroy his business. During the attack on his mill one soldier had refused to fire at the Luddites. At a subsequent court martial he was sentenced to 300 lashes, but Cartwright managed to have this reduced to 25.

Over the whole country the Government took stern measures to check the outbreaks. Many men were to be hanged or transported before the violence subsided. The worst feature of the Government's actions was the use of *agents provocateurs* (spies who deliberately persuaded the workers to commit acts of violence and then reported them to the authorities).

The actual Luddite outbreaks soon ended. They had never had any real chance of success for their object was to prevent industry taking advantage of technological progress.

Follow up Work

1. *Why did the cotton industry grow up in South Lancashire?*
2. *Study the pictures of the machines carefully and read the lives of the great inventors. Then, without referring to the text, write accounts of John Kay, James Hargreaves, Richard Arkwright, and Samuel Crompton.*
3. *"Happening to be at Matlock in the summer of 1784, I fell into company with some gentlemen of Manchester, when the conversation turned on Arkwright's spinning machinery. One of the company observed that as soon as Arkwright's patent expired, so many mills would be erected, and so much cotton spun, that hands never could be found to weave it. To this observation I replied that Arkwright must then set his wits to work to invent a weaving machine. This brought on a conversation on the subject, in which the Manchester gentlemen unanimously agreed that the thing was impracticable."*
   a) *Who is speaking?*
   b) *What effect had the spinning of so much cotton on the handloom weavers?*
   c) *What is meant by taking out a patent?*
   d) *What did the speaker do to prove that a power loom was practical?*
   e) *How far was he successful?*
   f) *What happened to the handloom weavers as a result?*
4. *Why did the Industrial Revolution result in Yorkshire becoming the main woollen cloth producing area in Britain?*
5. *Write an account of the Luddite Riots.*

4 Agriculture in the 18th Century

Open Field Farming

Look carefully at Plate 27 (*overleaf*). It shows an open field village in 1700. The villagers' lands were not in compact holdings but were divided into strips scattered amongst the three great fields surrounding the village. The shaded strips show where one villager would have had his land. Each of these strips was about half a hectare in area, where possible 20m wide by 200m long.

The fields would have seemed strange to us for there were no permanent hedges or fences. Instead the strips were separated by grass balks or ridges. The three fields were used for arable farming, that is, for growing crops like wheat, oats, barley, peas and beans. Each year one of the three was left fallow because little was known about scientific manuring and the land was deliberately rested to enable it to regain its properties. Outside the three fields was the common land, where all the villagers pastured their cattle, sheep and geese. The woodland provided firewood and timber for building. The few houses on the edge of the woodland belonged to squatters who had been allowed to settle there but who had no village rights. The squire's land was in one enclosed area around his hall.

At the beginning of the 18th century most of East Anglia and the Midlands were farmed in this way. Much of the land in the West and North was unsuitable for open field farming either because it was too hilly, or too wet for wheat growing.

The open field method of farming had existed for centuries and it had the advantage that although the amount of land owned varied, nearly every villager had some on which he could grow crops. He was also entitled to graze his few animals on the common. However, there were many drawbacks to the system. A villager's strips might be a long way from his cottage, which meant a considerable waste of time walking and carting. It was very difficult to drain individual strips. Farmers

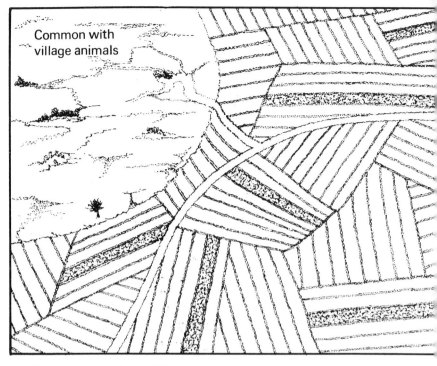

Common with village animals

27 *An open field village in 1700.*

suffered if their neighbours were idle and didn't weed their land. Land was wasted on the grass balks. The wheat stubble was left for autumn grazing which meant that winter crops could not be grown. This in turn meant that many cattle had to be killed off before Christmas, and fresh meat in winter was an impossible luxury. The fact that all the animals grazed together resulted in the unhampered and rapid spread of diseases, while selective scientific breeding was out of the question. The greatest drawback was that a man had to farm according to the custom of the village. Ploughing, sowing, and reaping were carried out when the majority of the village decided. This restricted any farmer who wanted to experiment with new ideas.

The open field system was wasteful and the antiquated ploughs and the broadcast sowing of seed were uneconomic. Obviously the crop yield was low but whilst the population only grew slowly it was adequate. However, the rapid growth in the 18th century created a much greater demand for food. New farming methods were urgently needed.

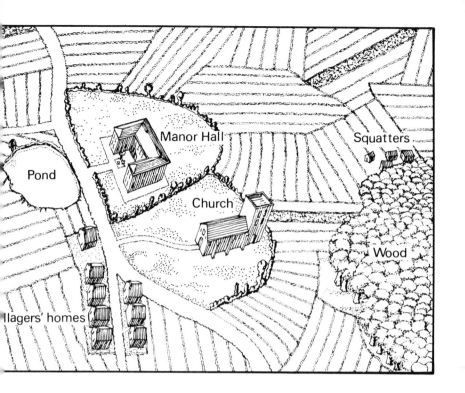

Pond

Manor Hall

Squatters

Church

Wood

llagers' homes

The Agricultural Revolution

Although a few men like Richard Weston in the 17th century had shown the value of clover for enriching grass and the use of turnips as a winter feed for cattle, any fresh ideas were exceptional. Most farmers kept to their traditional methods. Then in the 18th century there took place what has been called the agricultural or agrarian revolution. The word "revolution" is rather misleading for there was no sudden change. But there were extremely important advances both in farming itself and in the way the land was held.

The Agricultural Improvers

Jethro Tull (1674–1741)

Tull, a Berkshire farmer, was convinced that many of the farming techniques of his time were wrong. In 1731 he published a book in which he described the work he had carried out on seed drilling and hoeing. Tull believed that to sow seeds broadcast was wasteful for the crop could never be sowed evenly and birds could steal much of the seed. He insisted that his labourers should sow in regular channels and at a certain depth. The workers thought him a crank and went on strike. Tull's answer to this was to invent his famous seed drill shown in Plate 28.

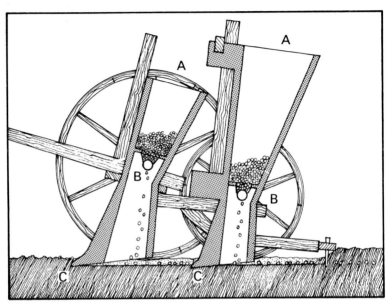

28 *Jethro Tull's seed drill.*
The seed was fed into the hoppers A A. From there it entered the funnels at B. The shares at C cut the furrow into which the seed fell and then the harrow at the back covered the furrows over with soil.

Crops sown with this seed drill grew in regular rows and Tull was able to hoe between the rows, keeping the land clear of weeds and letting the air and moisture get to the roots. Tull never fully understood the value of manure and sometimes sowed his seeds too thinly. Nevertheless his ideas on drilling and hoeing were to have a great influence on farmers in the future.

Viscount Townshend (1674–1738)

Townshend inherited large estates at Raynham in Norfolk. His land consisted mainly of marshes and sandy wastes where, it was said, "two rabbits struggled for every blade of grass". He improved this land by draining the marshes and mixing heavy marl or clay with his own light soil. Then, following Tull's ideas, he drilled and horse-hoed turnips instead of sowing them broadcast. His belief in the value of turnips as winter cattle feed earned him the nickname "Turnip" Townshend. Townshend also experimented in the rotation of crops for he believed that if the right crops were grown it would be unnecessary to leave land fallow. He popularised the famous Norfolk four course rotation of wheat, turnips, oats or barley, and clover. Townshend made a fortune out of his improvements and many Norfolk farmers followed his example. Outside his own county his ideas spread slowly for many farmers were still suspicious of change. Townshend's background was very different from that of Tull, as it was only during the last years of his life that he concentrated on his estates and farming. Until then he was a prominent political figure at home and abroad.

Robert Bakewell (1725–1795)

Robert Bakewell was twenty-five when he took over the management of his father's estates at Dishley in Leicestershire and began to concentrate on improving the breed of sheep and cattle. The leggy, goat-like creature shown in Plate 29 was typical of sheep in 1700. It was bred mainly for its wool, and as the flocks had to be driven a great distance to market along appalling roads, long legs were essential. One comment

29 *Some sheep typical of the flocks to be found in England before Bakewell began his breeding experiments. Compare these sheep with the one overleaf.*

about such sheep was "its skin could be said to rattle on its ribs like a skeleton wrapped in parchment". Bakewell began to breed sheep for mutton and the picture above of one of his "New Leicestershires" shows how successful he was. When Bakewell finished his experiments he had more than doubled the average weight of a sheep. People came from all over Europe to see his flocks. His methods of stock breeding were so successful that they have been followed ever since with most of the breeds of sheep kept today.

He was not successful with cattle as the breed he produced were not good milkers. But the Collings Brothers, who were also experimenting, eventually produced the Durham Shorthorns which were excellent for milk and meat. The disease-ridden cattle which had pastured on the commons were no bigger than donkeys and their meat was tough and stringy. At Smithfield Market the average weight of cattle more than doubled between 1710 and 1793.

Thomas Coke (1754–1842)

"Coke of Norfolk" inherited estates at Holkham in Norfolk when he was twenty-two. The soil was poor and the farmers backward. Coke adopted Townshend's methods and encouraged his tenants to do the same. He realised the value of crushed bones as fertiliser and also the need to sow good grass seed if the pastures were to be improved.

Each year he gathered the grass seeds he wanted and often persuaded local children to help him. Coke enriched his arable fields with marl and produced some of the finest wheat lands in England. He also experimented with breeding both cattle and sheep, and held an annual sheep shearing festival to which visitors from all over Europe came. His methods were so successful that he was able to increase the yearly rents from the farms on his estates from £2,000 in 1776 to £20,000 by 1816. His tenants, too, had obviously benefited from his methods.

Arthur Young (1741–1820)

Arthur Young played an important part in the story of agricultural improvement, for it was through his writings that farmers read of many of the new ideas. Travelling over England and noting the backward farming in many regions, he found that there were still farmers who regarded potatoes as food fit only for pigs and wasted valuable manure as fuel. Young saw that it was the wealthy farmers on the enclosed farms who were progressive and realised that the open field system would one day have to go. In 1793 he became Secretary of the Board of Agriculture and did much to improve farming during the wars against France when we needed to grow all the wheat we could.

These were the most important agricultural improvers, but there were many other farmers and landowners who wished to put the new techniques into operation. However, as Young had noted only too clearly, these techniques depended upon the land being enclosed and each farmer being allowed to practise as he wished.

The Enclosure Movement

In Plate 27 we saw a plan of an open field village in 1700. Plate 30 shows the same village in 1850. At some time in the intervening 150 years the strips of land were gathered into compact holdings surrounded by fences, the common land disappeared, and farmers built their houses adjacent to their own fields. This great change was the result of the enclosure movement which affected two and a half million hectares of land in Britain.

47

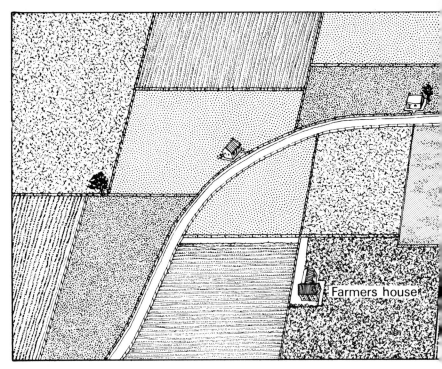

30 *This shows how the strip farming system shown in Plate 27 had changed by 1850. The manor house and church remain, but most farmers had their houses not in the village but among the fields. The villagers were mostly landless labourers working for other farmers.*

How the Enclosures were carried out

Enclosure of the village lands was usually the idea of the leading landowners. After 1774 notice of any decision to enclose had to be affixed to the church door so that all the villagers knew what was happening. A petition in favour of the enclosure was then taken out. If it was supported by the owners of three-quarters of the land (*not* three-quarters of the villagers) the petition was sent to Parliament. A private Bill was presented to Parliament but before it could be passed any of the villagers were entitled to put forward their objections. In practice this was almost impossible, for it took considerable courage and far more money than the small land holders could afford to appear before the House of Commons. As one politician of the time said, "The small man has little or no weight in regulating the clauses of the Act of Parliament."

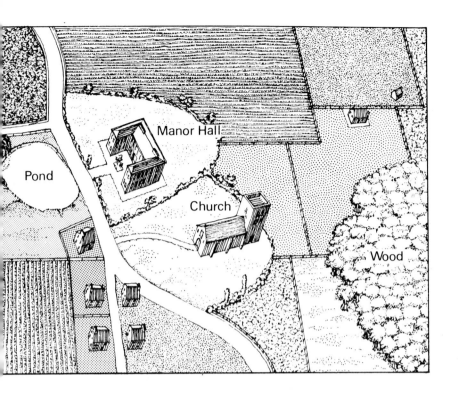

Once the Bill was passed three Commissioners were appointed and made responsible for checking all the villagers' claims and re-allotting the land amongst them. Many Commissioners did attempt to be fair but there is no doubt that in some cases they were the friends of the leading landowners and favoured them as much as possible. Although all the villagers with legal claims had to be given their rights, numerous villagers had held their land for generations but were unable to produce written evidence of their title to it. In some cases these people were to lose everything they had. Finally the Commissioners decided the cost of fencing, the rights of way across the fields, and the ownership of any woodland.

The enclosure movement progressed rapidly during the second half of the 18th century and continued into the 19th century. By 1850 most of the land had been enclosed. There is no doubt that economically these enclosures were necessary. If farmers were to attempt to improve their land, produce more food, and breed better animals, large compact holdings were essential. The enclosures hastened this progress, but even so in many areas improvement was to come slowly.

Some farmers adopted the new ideas but many were afraid to change, and backward methods were still used well into the 19th century.

The Effects of the Enclosure Movement

Wealthy landowners and large farmers definitely benefited by the enclosures while many of the smaller yeomen farmers found themselves better off, for the value of their land tended to increase. But in some cases, where their holdings were not large, these yeomen farmers were unable to compete and many sold out. Then they either rented farms or went to the towns and invested their money in industry.

To thousands of small farmers and cottagers, and to the squatters on the commons, the enclosures brought great suffering. Those villagers who could prove legal title to their lands were given their holdings. But even they had lost their rights to gather timber and graze their pigs in the woodlands, and to pasture their stock on the common land. To add to their burdens they were forced to share the full legal expenses of enclosure and the cost of surveying and fencing the land. This could be as much as £6 per hectare. Most of these villagers were forced to sell out and become landless labourers working for the large farmers. Some were even worse off. Those cottagers who had no written proof of ownership lost the land which they had always thought to be theirs. As for the squatters, a few were kindly treated, but most were driven from the commons and their houses destroyed.

It is not surprising that enclosure became a hated word throughout the Midlands. At Otmoor in Oxfordshire mobs tore down the fences and thrashed the squire's son when he threatened them with a pistol. In many other villages troops had to be used to quell threatened riots. Probably the clearest proof of the great suffering caused to the poor comes from Arthur Young. He always remained a great advocate of enclosures but as he toured the farming areas the appalling injustice was only too clear. He spoke to one destitute labourer about farming improvements. The pitiful reply was, "All I know is I had a cow and an Act of Parliament has taken it from me". In many villages Young found that the poor had lost even the ground on which a pig could be reared or a few vegetables grown. To them there seemed nothing left, and he wrote: "Go to an ale-house of an old-enclosed country and there you will see the origin of poverty. For whom are they to be sober? For whom are they to save? For the parish? If I am diligent shall I have leave to build a cottage? If I am sober shall I have land for a cow? If I am frugal shall I have an acre of potatoes? You offer

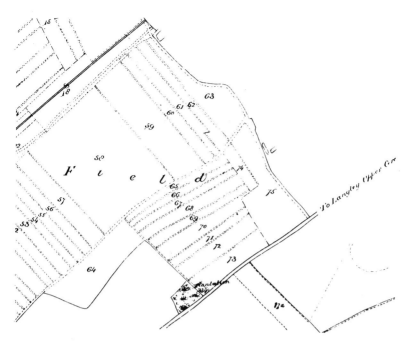

31 *Enclosure of commons land in the 19th century (Buckinghamshire). Above and below, the same area before and after enclosure.*

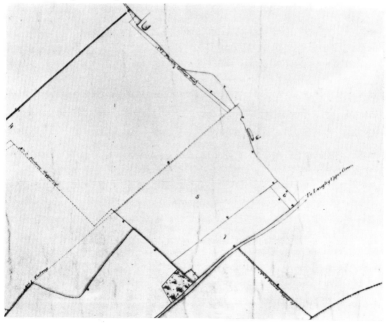

51

no motives, you have nothing but a parish officer and a workhouse. Bring me another pot."

The economic and social consequences of the enclosure movement were great. Economically enclosures were essential, and although improvements were bound to come slowly, the enclosed farms enabled new agricultural advances to take place during the 19th century.

The Poverty of the Agricultural Labourers

It is undeniable that enclosures caused much suffering but the poverty of the agricultural labourers at the end of the 18th century was due to more than just the enclosure movement. As the population grew many farm workers in the North drifted into industry. In the South, where there were no factories, the villages became over-populated. In addition their wives had been able to earn money by domestic work such as spinning. Now, however, spinning was rapidly becoming a factory industry.

Arthur Young was not the only observer to comment on the poverty of the farm workers. A village parson in Berkshire prepared a list of the weekly expenses of a man, his wife, and five children. Their diet was inadequate and monotonous, and at times they must have been very close to starvation.

	s	d	
Flour, $7\frac{1}{2}$ gallons at 10 d a gallon.	6	3	(31p)
Yeast to make bread $2\frac{1}{2}$ d; salt $1\frac{1}{2}$ d.		4	($1\frac{1}{2}$p)
Bacon, 1 lb. boiled with potatoes.		8	($3\frac{1}{2}$p)
Tea, 1 oz. 2 d, $\frac{1}{4}$ lb. of sugar 6 d, $\frac{1}{2}$ lb. butter 4 d.	1	0	(5p)
Soap, $\frac{1}{4}$ lb. at 9 d a lb.		$2\frac{1}{4}$	(1p)
Candles, $\frac{1}{3}$ lb. a week at 9 d.		3	(1p)
Thread and **worsted** for mending.		3	(1p)
	8	$11\frac{1}{4}$	(44p)

Rent, clothes, fuel and medicines cost another $13\frac{1}{2}$p a week so that the total expenses were $57\frac{1}{2}$p. The man himself could earn on the average 40 pence a week and his wife could usually earn another $2\frac{1}{2}$p. Their total income was 15p *less* than their expenses, which meant that unless the man was somehow able to make a few extra pence, "luxuries" like tea, bacon, sugar, butter and soap could not possibly be afforded.

The Speenhamland System

During the last years of the 18th century food prices were rising much faster than wages. In Southern England poverty had become a grave problem and death by starvation was not uncommon. In 1795 a group of well-meaning Berkshire magistrates tried to find a solution. They met in the *Pelican Inn*, Speenhamland, and it was there that the notorious "Speenhamland System" was worked out. It was decided that there should be an agreed minimum for wages, depending on the price of bread and the size of the family. Where a man's wages fell below this minimum he was to receive an allowance out of the local rates. The Speenhamland System was intended as a charitable scheme to be used in very bad years. When put into practice, however, its weaknesses were immediately apparent. By this system farmers could pay low wages and let the parish make up the rest. It also meant that there was no incentive for a labourer to work harder for he would be just as well off living off the rates. The wars against France from 1793 to 1815 provided work, for there was an increased demand for food and some of the surplus labour went into the army. As we shall see, though, in Chapter 13, the ultimate effects of the Speenhamland System were to be disastrous.

Follow up Work

1. *Draw a sketch map of a typical open field village. Write an account showing how farming was carried out in such a village. What were the disadvantages of this method of farming?*

2. *Read the following extract carefully.*
   "As I shall presently leave Norfolk it will not be improper to give a slight review of the husbandry which has rendered the name of this county so famous in the farming world. Pointing out the practices which have succeeded so nobly here, may perhaps be of some use to other counties possessed of the same advantages, but unknowing in the art of how to use them.

   From forty to fifty years ago, all the northern and western, and a part of the eastern tracts of the county, were sheep walks, let so low as from 6d to 1s. 6d and 2s an acre. Much of it was in this condition only thirty years ago. The great improvements have been made by means of the following circumstances.

   First.   By enclosing without the assistance of Parliament.
   Second. By a spirited use of marl and clay.
   Third.   By the introduction of an "excellent course" of crops.
   Fourth. By the culture of turnips.

Fifth.   By the culture of clover and ray grass well hand-hoed.
Sixth.   By landlords granting long leases.
Seventh. By the country being divided chiefly into large farms."
Answer these questions.

a) Give an approximate date for the extract.
b) Write a sentence saying what Young meant by enclosing.
c) Why was marl and clay put on some land?
d) What was the excellent course (rotation) of crops Young mentioned?
e) What were the advantages of growing turnips?
f) Why were clover and ray-grass grown?

(West Midlands CSE Board Specimen Paper, 1964)

3. A typical sheep of the early 18th century was described: "His frame large and loose, his legs long and thick, his chine as well as his rump as sharp as a hatchet, his skin rattling on his ribs like a skeleton covered with parchment."
   a) Give a brief account of farming conditions in the early 18th century which produced sheep like the one described above.
   b) What did the following contribute to farming methods in the 18th century: 1. Jethro Tull   2. Lord Townshend   3. Robert Bakewell   4. Coke of Holkham?

(Southern Regional Examinations Board, 1966)

4. "In 19 cases out of 20 the poor suffered by enclosure." Arthur Young.
   a) Explain fully how the enclosures were carried out.
   b) Why did the poor often suffer?
   c) In what ways did agriculture benefit from enclosures?
   d) Explain whether all farmers began to use new agricultural methods.

5. What was the Speenhamland System and why was it introduced?

6. Study the table of the Norfolk Four Course Rotation, and then answer the questions.

Year	Field 1	Field 2	Field 3	Field 4
1794	Wheat	Turnips	Barley	Clover
1795	Turnips	Barley	Clover	Wheat
1796	Barley	Clover	Wheat	Turnips
1797	a	b	c	d

a) What crops would appear in the spaces marked *a, b, c,* and *d?*

b) Who was the person who made this rotation of crops popular?

c) Name one advantage of this rotation over the older method.

d) What was one especial value of the turnips?

e) What purpose did the clover serve?

(Welsh Joint Education Committee CSE, 1966)

7. *Discussion Point:*

June 10th, 1784

"We had a very genteel dinner, Soals and Lobster Sauce, Spring chicken boiled and a Tongue, a piece of rost Beef, Soup, a Fillet of Veal rosted with Morells and Truffles, and a Pigeon Pye for the first Course, Sweetbreads, a green Goose and Peas, Apricot Pye, Cheesecakes, Stewed Mushrooms and Trifle. The ladies and Gentlemen very genteely dressed. Mr. Micklethwaite had in his Shoes a Pair of Silver Buckles which cost between 7 and 8 pounds. Miles Brandthwaite had a pair that cost 5 guineas."

(Parson Woodforde's Diary, 1758–1802)

Read this account written by a middle-class country parson in the South of England in the 18th century. Compare his diet with that of the labourer on p. 52. Work out how much of the "luxuries" mentioned on p. 52 the labourer's family could afford for the price of Mr. Micklethwaite's shoe buckles. Discuss with your teacher the great difference in living standards at that time.

5 Roads and Canals 1750-1830

The State of the Roads in 1700

At the beginning of the 18th century most parts of Britain were connected by roads but the majority of them were in an atrocious condition. Some of the surviving Roman roads were passable but even these had often had their stone slabs torn up for house building. The rest were far worse than present day farm tracks. Only a few carriages dared to use these roads and they jolted and lumbered along, often breaking wheels and axles in the ruts and deep holes.

The parishes were supposedly responsible for the upkeep of the roads in their own localities but they performed their tasks very badly. The most common method of repair was merely to fill in the holes with stones. These were soon dislodged and the surface was as bad as ever again.

Clearly, under such conditions, transport must have been extremely slow. There was a story told about this time of a man with a wooden leg refusing a lift because, he said, he could walk quicker. This may have been a joke but it was certainly no joke when the coaches to the Irish boat at Holyhead had to be taken to pieces at Conway and carried to the Menai Straits. Nor was Daniel Defoe, the author of *Robinson Crusoe*, joking when he wrote of Sussex in 1724: "A lady was drawn to church in a coach by six oxen, not for a frolic but because the way was too bad for horses."

Again, Arthur Young wrote:

"From Preston to Wigan, I know not in the whole range of the language, terms sufficiently expressive to describe this infernal road. To look over a map, and perceive that it is a principal one not only to some towns, but even to whole counties, one would naturally conclude it to be at least decent; for a thousand to one but they break their limbs by overthrows or breakings down. They will meet with ruts, which I actually measured four feet deep, and floating with mud only from a wet summer; what, therefore, must it be after winter? The only mending it received is the tumbling in of some loose stones, which serve no other purpose but jolting a carriage in the most intolerable manner."

How Goods were Transported

Under these conditions the most efficient method of transporting goods was by teams of sure-footed packhorses or mules. They walked in single file and were trained to follow one another. The goods were carried in big baskets which were strapped one on each side of the horse. But even the horses often stumbled and fell in the mud and on occasions died as they tried in vain to right themselves.

Most areas still have remains of the old routes and of the narrow packhorse bridges. Sometimes they have left traces in names such as Jaggers Clough in Derbyshire, named after a jagger or train leader. At other places, as in the Pennines, they can still be followed on foot over the moors.

There were also highwaymen lurking on Shooters Hill and Gads Hill on the old Dover Road, or Finchley Common and Hounslow Heath on the very outskirts of London.

Throughout the 17th and 18th centuries the amount of traffic and livestock travelling by road was increasing rapidly. Thousands of cattle were driven from Scotland and Wales to London, herds of pigs were a common sight and so, oddly enough, were vast flocks of turkeys and geese as they walked to the London markets. The roads, such as they were, were hopelessly inadequate to cope with this growing traffic, and various new ideas were put forward.

The Turnpike Trusts

The real answer to the problem lay in providing money to repair the roads properly. At that time this could only be obtained by turnpikes and toll roads. In 1706 Parliament created the first Turnpike Trust. This was a scheme whereby local leading citizens could set up toll gates and maintain the roads with the money received. Charges varied but were usually $\frac{1}{2}$p for a horse, $2\frac{1}{2}$p for a coach or waggon, $2\frac{1}{2}$p for a

32 *Just two of the hazards of travel in the age before the railway — bandits and bad roads. If you were not robbed then the chances were that your coach might be wrecked and you injured.*

score of cattle, and 1p for a score of pigs; foot travellers did not pay. Toll gates and turnpikes flourished throughout the 18th century and did not begin to die out until the coming of the railways.

Turnpikes were often unpopular. Local people objected to paying tolls and farmers did their best to avoid the gate-keepers. The Welsh drovers often avoided the turnpikes and cut through the fields, whilst young "bucks" amused themselves by leaping their horse over the gates. At times riots broke out, gates were torn down and gate-keepers assaulted. Perhaps the most famous of these outbreaks were the Rebecca Riots, when a party of rioters disguised as women, attacked the toll gates in the South Wales area.

Despite the opposition the number of turnpike roads continued to grow and by 1830 there were about 35,200km of them, of which about

one-half were said to be fairly good. The extent of the turnpike roads in the counties varied considerably. In 1829 Yorkshire had almost 2,400km, whereas Surrey had less than 483km.

The Stage Coach Era

The rapid increase in the number of turnpike roads after 1750 led to a considerable growth in the number of stage coaches. Stage coaches had been introduced in the middle of the 17th century. They were clumsy, uncomfortable vehicles, with wooden shutters for windows. They needed to be strongly made as they often had to go across country to avoid bad roads. Improved roads meant that coaches could be designed for greater speed and they were reasonably well sprung.

THE HIGHGATE ARCHWAY FROM THE TURNPIKE GATE AT HOLLOWAY.

33 *The turnpike (or toll road) was a way of paying for the upkeep of highways. This system is still used, for example on the Severn Bridge.*

The picture of a stage coach in Plate 34 shows that they were uncomfortable inside and passengers always complained of the jolting as the coaches became faster. Speed was the aim of most coach drivers. With great skill they handled their teams of horses, and by 1825 the famous "Wonder" could travel from London to Shrewsbury at an average speed of 16km/h, and its punctuality was legendary. The horses, however, were driven unmercifully and the speed of the coaches led to many accidents. The increase in speed is shown by the journey from Edinburgh to London. In 1760 it took 14 days, in 1830 the flying coaches took 40 hours. Fares were very high. Inside passengers paid about 1p a kilometre, outside passengers paid about ½p.

The stage coaches' greatest years were from 1820 to 1830, and by 1837 there were, 3,300 stage coaches, 30,000 employees, 150,000 horses, and hundreds of inns. By then, however, their end was in sight for already the railways had begun to take their place.

The improvements in the roads led to the use of coaches for carrying mail. During the first half of the century mail had been carried on horse-back, but in 1784 John Palmer of Bath persuaded the government to agree to his mail coaches. These were to be fast coaches protected by guards armed with pistols and blunderbusses. His system was an immediate success; by 1786 twenty Royal Mail coaches left London every evening and by the 1830's the number had increased still further. These coaches became so important that at the sound of the guard's horn in the distance the toll gates had to be thrown open, for any check could lead to a £2 fine.

34 *An 18th-century basket stage coach. The faster coaches were drawn by eight horses.*

35 *The commonest way to travel on the poorer roads was by slow heavy wagons. Journeys in these must have been tedious and extremely uncomfortable.*

The Great Road Engineers

John Metcalfe (1717–1810)

John Metcalfe was born at Knaresborough in Yorkshire. When only six he had been blinded by an attack of smallpox. Despite this disability "Blind Jack of Knaresborough" was an exceptionally able road engineer. He constructed his first road in 1765 and altogether built 270km of roads mainly in Lancashire, Yorkshire and the Peak District. Metcalfe overcame his blindness by prodding along the route with a stick and visualising in his mind the area which he was surveying. On the wet Pennine moors he ensured that his road surfaces were sufficiently convex to drain off the heavy rains (Plate 36).

Thomas Telford (1757–1834)

Thomas Telford was the son of a poor Scottish shepherd. He was apprenticed to a stonemason but his exceptional engineering ability soon showed itself. Later in this chapter mention is made of his outstanding work as a canal builder, but it is as a road and bridge engineer that he is perhaps best remembered. Telford's roads were made to last. Plate 36 will show you the strength of their foundations. A contemporary writer, Robert Southey, described how Telford built his roads: "The plan upon which he proceeds in road making is this. First to level and drain, then like the Romans to lay a solid pavement of large stones, the round or broad end downwards, as close as they can be set, the points are then broken off, and a layer of stones broken to about the size of walnuts, laid over them, so that the whole are bound together, over a little gravel if it be at hand, but this is not essential."

Telford constructed roads and bridges in the Highlands and Lowlands of Scotland but his most famous road was the one he built from London to Holyhead, now called the A5. Before it was constructed no mail coaches went further west than Shrewsbury and there was only one very poor road on Anglesey. Telford began this road in 1815 and it took 15 years to complete. Today this is still one of the main routes into North Wales, and travellers passing along the winding road down to Betws y Coed, up to Capel Curig, and through the wild Nant francon pass cannot help but be impressed by this fine piece of engineering. At the end of the run is the beautiful suspension bridge across the Menai Straits.

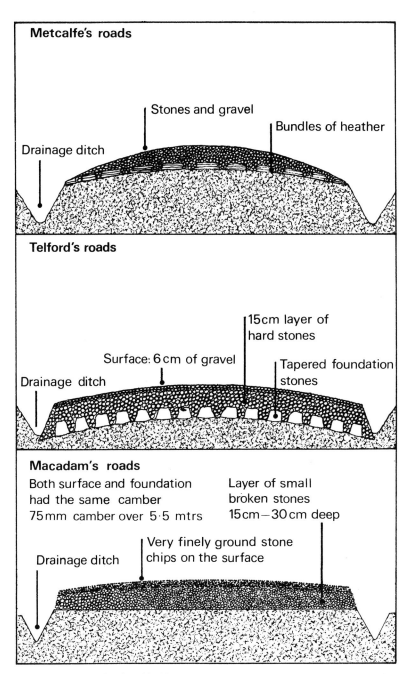

Metcalfe's roads

Stones and gravel

Bundles of heather

Drainage ditch

Telford's roads

15cm layer of hard stones

Tapered foundation stones

Surface: 6 cm of gravel

Drainage ditch

Macadam's roads
Both surface and foundation had the same camber 75mm camber over 5·5 mtrs

Layer of small broken stones 15cm — 30cm deep

Very finely ground stone chips on the surface

Drainage ditch

36 *Different methods of road building.*

Almost as beautiful is the other suspension bridge which Telford built at Conway. This has only recently been replaced by a wider bridge.

John Macadam (1756–1836)

John Macadam was also a Scotsman but spent most of his early years in America and did not return to Britain until he was twenty-eight. He carried out a number of experiments in road building and in 1816 he was made surveyor-general of the roads in the Bristol area. By 1827 he was the leading road engineer in the country.

Macadam's roads were not as strong as Telford's but they were cheaper to construct and this made them more popular with the turnpike trusts. As you can see, Macadam did not use foundation stones but laid a stone layer directly on to the subsoil. He maintained that it was the draining of the road that mattered, not its thickness and to make the surface waterproof the top surface was made as fine as possible. The powdered stone when mixed with rain water formed a type of cement. Much later, tar was used for the surfaces and this led to the expression tarmacadam or tarmac.

By 1830 much of Britain had a network of good roads, and the age of the commercial traveller began for it was much easier for firms to send out their representatives with samples. Business benefited from this and from the speedier transportation of goods along the improved roads. This extract from the *Huntingdon Gazette,* May 15th, 1830, gives some idea of the roads in their heyday. "It is calculated that a person has 1,500 opportunities of leaving London in the course of twenty-four hours by stage coaches, including the repeated trips of the coaches which ply the short distances. It is understood that about 300 coaches pass through Hyde Park Corner Turnpike daily. There are 40 Brighton coaches.

There are 84 coaches belonging to Birmingham of which 40 are daily, to Chester 19 of which 16 are daily, to Manchester 70 of which 54 are daily. In the year 1770 there belonged only two stage coaches to Manchester, one to London and one to Liverpool and they went only twice a week. Now twenty coaches pass backwards and forwards daily between these two places. There are 60 coaches belonging to Liverpool of which 56 are daily, to Preston 12, to York 18; to Hull 12, to Newcastle 6; to Glasgow 13; to Edinburgh 39 and to Inverness 3."

37 *Why, do you think, was the coach placed on a train for part of its journey?*

By then, however, the railway had already entered the scene. Plate 37, entitled *The last of the Coaches,* and dated 1845, shows the Louth-London mail coach being ferried for some of its journey by train—horses and all. The long distance coaches were vanishing for ever.

Follow up Work

1. *Describe the road conditions in 1700 and show how this affected the methods of transport used.*

2. *What were the advantages and disadvantages of the turnpike system?*

3. *Read the following quotation carefully, and then answer the questions:*
   "The roads can never be rendered perfectly secure, until the following principles be perfectly understood, that it is the native soil which really supports the weight of the traffic; that while it is preserved in a dry state it will carry any weight without sinking, and that it does in fact carry, the road and carriages also; that this native soil must previously be made perfectly dry, and a covering impenetrable to rain must be placed over it in that dry state." (J. Macadam)

a) What did Macadam consider to be most important in the construction of roads?

b) How did his method of road construction differ from the methods employed by earlier road builders?

c) What can you say about the size or weight of the stones which he used for surfacing his roads?

d) Why was Macadam's method cheaper than the methods of earlier road builders?

e) What name do we give to the organisations which were building roads at this time?

f) Name two other road builders who were working at much the same time as Macadam.

(Welsh Joint Education Committee CSE, 1965)

4. *Describe an imaginary journey by stage coach in 1800. Include in your account descriptions of the roads, the turnpikes and toll houses, the inns, the coaches, and the fares charged.*

5. *Write a full account showing the results of the improved roads.*

6. *Discuss with your teacher any local instances of old roads, bridges, packhorse routes, coaching inns etc., and put them on a local map showing their position in relation to well-known landmarks.*

7. *If you are observant you will often find old toll houses on main roads or interesting references to coaches in inn windows. The following can still be seen at Beaumaris on Anglesey:*

Reduced fares
From Holyhead to London

By the only four horse post coach which leaves Holyhead every evening immediately after the arrival of the packet boat.

The wonder fast coach
From Spencer's Royal Hotel, Holyhead

Fares

To **London**	*Inside £3*	*Outside £1. 10.0d.*
To **Shrewsbury**	,, *£1*	,, *10s.*

Time 26½ hours

1834. C. & R. Elliots
Sole Agents. Dublin

PLOUGH HOTEL COACH OFFICE, Cheltenham.

ROYAL MAILS AND LIGHT & ELEGANT POST COACHES
DAILY TO THE FOLLOWING PLACES.

LONDON MAILS every Evening at ¼ before Six o'clock, thro' Northleach, Burford, Witney, Oxford, Dorchester, Benson, Henly, Salt Hill, Maidenhead, & Hounslow.

LONDON The Retaliator Coach every Morning at Eight o'clock, through Northleach, Burford, Witney, Oxford, Tetsworth, Wycomb & Uxbridge.

LONDON The Two Day Coach every Morning at Twelve o'clock, (Sleeping at Oxford) through Henley.

OXFORD Coach every Tuesday, Thursday & Saturday, at Twelve o'clock, through Northleach, Burford, and Witney.

MILFORD every Morning at ¼ before Eight, thro' Gloucester, Ross, Monmouth, Ragland, Abergavenny, Crickhowell, Brecon, Trecastle, Llandovery, Llandilo, Carmarthen, St Clears, Narbeth, & Haverfordwest.

SHREWSBURY & HOLYHEAD every Morning, except Sunday, at Seven o'clock, through Tewkesbury, Worcester, Kidderminster, Bridgnorth, Cowbridge, Shrewsbury, Oswestry, Llangollen, Corwen, Capel Cerrig, Bangor Ferry, Gwyndu.

BIRMINGHAM every Morning except Sunday, at Seven o'clock, through Tewkesbury, Worcester, Droitwich and Bromsgrove.

BIRMINGHAM & MANCHESTER every day except Sunday, at Twelve o'clock, through Tewkesbury, Worcester, Bromsgrove, Birmingham, Wolverhampton, Stafford, Stone, Newcastle, Congleton, Macclesfield, & Stockport.

BIRMINGHAM & LIVERPOOL every day except Sunday, at ½ past one o'clock thro' Tewkesbury, Worcester, Bromsgrove, Birmingham, Wolverhampton, Stafford, Stone, Newcastle, Lawton, (Brereton Green) Holmes Chapel, Knutsford, and Warrington.

BIRMINGHAM Monday, Wednesday & Friday, at ¼ before Two o'clock thro' Evesham, Alcester & Studley.

WARWICK & LEAMINGTON Monday, Wednesday & Friday, at ¼ before Two o'clock, through Evesham, Alcester, Stratford & Warwick, & returns the following days.

BATH every morning, except Sunday, at Nine o'clock, through Gloucester, Rodborough, Petty France, to the York House, from whence Coaches leave daily, to Farrington, Wells, Glastonbury, Bridgwater, Taunton, Wellington, Collumpton, Tiverton, Exeter, Barnstaple, Plymouth, Devonport, Somerton, Longport, Chard, Ilminster, Crewkerne, Axminster, Lyme Regis, Honiton, Sidmouth, Charmouth, Weymouth & all parts of the West.

BATH every day, except Sunday, at Two o'clock, through Stroud.

BRISTOL every day, except Sunday, at Twelve, thro' Gloster & Newport.

GLOUCESTER Coaches at ¼ before Eight, Nine, Twelve & Three o'clock.

SOUTHAMPTON Monday, Wednesday & Friday, Mornings, at Seven o'clock, through Cirencester, Cricklade, Swindon, Marlborough, Burbage, Collingburn, Luggershall, Werhill, Andover, Werwell & Winchester, in Twelve Hours & Return the following days.

THE BERKELEY HUNT, NEW COACH TO LONDON,
every Morning at Six o'clock, through Henley & Salt Hill, to the Castle & Falcon, Aldersgate Street & Belle Sauvage, Ludgate Hill, in 10½ hours; arrives in London at half past Four to Dinner. This Coach leaves the above Houses, calls at the Old White Horse Cellar, & Dyson's Black Bear, Piccadilly, every Morning at half past Six & arrives at the Plough Hotel Cheltenham, at 5.

PERFORMED BY

JAMES NEYLER & Cº

S.Y. Griffith & Cº Copper Plate Printers.

THOMAS HAINES, JUN.

FLY WAGGONS TO LONDON,
FROM THE

Royal Hotel Yard,
every day except Sunday, through Northleach, Burford, Witney, Oxford & Wycomb, in two days,
TO THE

BLOSSOMS INN, LAWRENCE LANE,
Cheapside.

38 *A contemporary engraving which shows the ingenuity of the early canal pioneers.*

Water Transport

In the first half of the 18th century both the sea and navigable rivers were used for transporting goods and passengers. Sea-going ships were quite an important method of transportation, being particularly useful for carrying bulky goods, such as coal from Newcastle to London, cattle from Scotland to East Anglia, and timber from the forest of Dean to London. Navigable rivers were playing a vital part in inland transport. The Thames, Severn, Humber, Trent, Mersey and Dee, and the numerous rivers which flow into the Wash, were undoubtedly useful trade routes, and the value of river transport was realised sufficiently to cause the Rivers Aire and Calder in the West Riding to be made navigable. However, not only were rivers subject to floods and droughts but also large areas of the country had no suitable river transport. Thus, just on the eve of the Industrial Revolution, such important areas as the Black Country and most of Lancashire were without water transport.

The Canals

During the 18th century some better and cheaper method of transport than packhorse trains or waggons was urgently needed. There was an increased demand for coal both from the iron industry and from domestic users. Wedgwood had begun to create beautiful pottery which needed smooth transportation, and in Lancashire far more cotton was being carried. At the same time more food had to be brought into the towns to feed the growing population. Canals were to be the answer to the problem of internal transport.

James Brindley, Canal Builder (1716–1772)

The canal building era really began in 1759 when the Duke of Bridgewater, having been disappointed in love, devoted his energies to his coal mines at Worsley, 11km from Manchester. He found that transport costs were so high that he had difficulty in selling the coal, and so he decided to cut a canal as an alternative means of transport. The Duke employed James Brindley, an almost illiterate millwright, as his foreman-engineer, and paid him £1·05 a week. It is interesting to see how Brindley tackled some of the engineering problems. The first one was to ensure that the base of the canal did not allow the water to drain away. Before an amazed committee of the House of Commons he demonstrated that ordinary clay was porous but that clay and water puddled together would hold the canal water indefinitely. This simple process was adopted by all the canal builders. To support the banks when cutting through soft soil he often used long pieces of timber which he rammed into oak supports. On the canal from Manchester to Worsley he had to cross the River Irwell at Barton. He did this by means of an aqueduct, and the sight of boats high in the air caused amazement for many years. Finally there was the difficulty of passing through hilly country. He overcame this by locks which worked in the way shown in Plate 39. Despite his brilliance Brindley still had much difficulty in writing, as witness his notebook entry: "Ad a grate division of 127 Fort Duke." The completed canal, although only 17km long, made the Duke of Bridgewater one of the richest men in England, for the demand for coal, which he could now reduce in price by almost half, increased enormously.

In 1766 Brindley began the Grand Trunk Canal. This was the idea of a number of businessmen led by Josiah Wedgwood. Wedgwood was appalled by the losses his china suffered in transit and he thought of the idea of linking the Mersey and the Trent. In this way pottery could be transported to Liverpool or Hull, while raw materials could be brought in much more easily.

Although Brindley died before the Grand Trunk Canal was completed in 1777, he was responsible for others, including the Birmingham

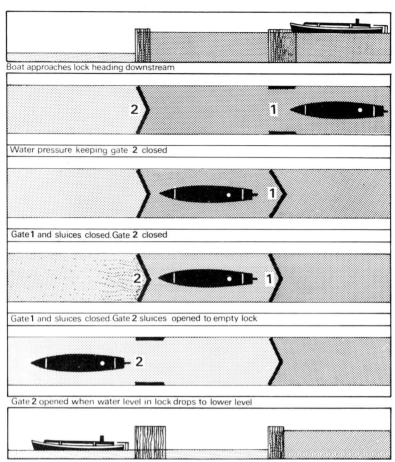

Boat approaches lock heading downstream

Water pressure keeping gate **2** closed

Gate **1** and sluices closed. Gate **2** closed

Gate **1** and sluices closed. Gate **2** sluices opened to empty lock

Gate **2** opened when water level in lock drops to lower level

Boat leaves lock heading downstream

39 *The system of locks used in the early canals.*

Canal, which in 1771 brought water transport to the heart of the Black Country, quickly benefiting two important industrial regions.

Other canal builders were greatly influenced by Brindley's engineering methods. His policy was to concentrate the locks together where practicable, and to have long, level routes between. He used earth banking as little as possible, and where he could Brindley deliberately followed the contours. For this reason many canals often take a winding course through the countryside. Brindley introduced the

70

practice of "legging" through long tunnels with the building of the Grand Trunk Canal. Harecastle Tunnel, which pierced the Pennines, was almost $2\frac{1}{2}$km long and only $2\frac{1}{2}$m high. Two leggers lay at each end of a plank across the front of the boat and pressed against the roof with their legs to push the barge through. It was extremely dangerous as one man, by a sudden movement, could throw the other in. Eventually separate boards were used. Legging was common on many later canals, including the tunnel at Standedge on the Rochdale to Huddersfield Canal which was almost 5km long.

Thomas Telford (1757–1834)

Amongst the canal engineers none were greater than Thomas Telford, the famous road builder. Telford was the engineer of the Caledonian Canal in Scotland. He also built some outstanding English canals, including the Ellesmere Canal with its magnificent aqueduct at Pont Cysyllte, and also the Birmingham to Liverpool Canal. One noticeable feature of Telford's canals was that they were usually more direct than Brindley's for as canal engineers gained experience they used deep cuttings and embankments instead of winding routes and numerous locks.

The Growth of the Canal Network

The last quarter of the 18th century saw a rapid spread of canal building. The Birmingham and Coventry Canal was begun in 1768, and the Oxford in 1769. Then with the building of the Grand Junction the Midlands had adequate canals linking Birmingham with London. London and the Bristol Channel were connected by the Thames and Severn Canal. On this waterway the 3km long Sapperton Tunnel had to be cut. Today this tunnel is no longer used but it is possible to visit it and to see exactly how the banks were strengthened and the tunnel itself lined.

The Results of Canals

For many parts of Britain the value of canals was inestimable in an age when roads as such were virtually nonexistent. They provided the cheapest transport system the country had ever known. The rate per tonne from Liverpool to the Potteries in 1777 was £2·50 by road and 65p by canal. For bulky goods they were much faster and surer than packhorse trains and it was the canals which enabled the South Wales coalfield to be exploited. Inland areas such as the Potteries and Birmingham derived great benefit from them. Birmingham was the centre of a network of canals which connected the town to the Mersey, the Severn and the Thames. The canals helped farmers by enabling fertilisers to be brought in more cheaply and agricultural products to be taken to the industrial towns. The port of Liverpool benefited from canals for they increased the area surrounding the town to which imports could be sent and from which exports could be drawn. The building of canals created those gangs of labourers called "navvies" who were to be so important in future railway development. In fact the term navvy is derived from "navigator" or canal cutter.

Reasons for their Decline

Although many canals were never profitable, particularly those passing through agricultural districts where there was less trade, it would be true to say that up to the 1840's canals as a whole experienced a "golden age". Then their prosperity began to wane.

There were a number of reasons for this decline. Some of the canals had been badly built and cost too much to maintain. Each company's canals varied in width, depth, and size of locks. This caused difficulties when barges had to travel over different canals. Where factories had been built on the banks it was almost impossible to widen the canals. Many canal companies took advantage of their local monopolies and charged exorbitant fares. But by far the most important reason for their decline was the coming of the railways which brought a quicker and more effective form of transport.

The canals struggled on throughout the 19th century, some just paying their way, others falling into disuse. Many came under the control of the railways which bought them out to prevent competition. If you walk along a canal side today, you will often find old notices giving rules and regulations, and signed, not by a canal company, but by the railway company which once owned the local railway.

Follow up Work

1. "James Brindley certainly deserves to be remembered as one of Britain's great engineers." Write a full account justifying this statement.

2. *In what ways did canals affect the economy of the country?*
3. *Study the map showing the main canals. Then, without referring to the map, answer these questions.*
   What goods were carried by these canals?
   (a) The Grand Trunk; (b) The Grand Junction;
   (c) The Birmingham and Liverpool; (d) The Leeds and Liverpool.
   Why were there very few canals in these areas?
   (a) The far north; (b) East Anglia; (c) Devon and Cornwall.
4. *It has been said that Telford was probably the greatest of all civil engineers. Consider this in the light of his work on roads and canals.*
5. *Canals in towns often pass through very interesting industrial remains. Take a sketch book and make notes and diagrams of such things as toll houses, locks, tunnels, old factories, wharves etc. Try to find out what any ruined factories were once used for. This will often give you a picture of the industrial history of your own district.*

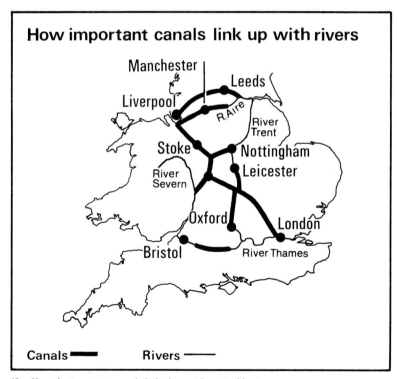

How important canals link up with rivers

Manchester
Leeds
Liverpool
R.Aire
River Trent
Stoke
Nottingham
River Severn
Leicester
Oxford
London
Bristol
River Thames

Canals ▬▬ Rivers ───

40 *How the important canals linked up with navigable rivers.*

6 Railways
1800-1860

"PUFFING BILLY," 1813.

At the beginning of the 18th century railways were being used to transport coal for short distances in South Wales and in the mining districts around Newcastle-on-Tyne. The tracks consisted of two parallel wooden rails along which trucks were usually pulled by horses, although in Neath, in South Wales, one ingenious mine owner fitted sails to the wagons so that the wind would blow them along. Obviously wooden rails soon wore out and later in the century with the development of the iron industry, iron tracks were in common use. At first these railways belonged to particular firms who used them for carrying their own products. It was not until 1801 that the first public railway, the Surrey Iron Railway, which ran from Wandsworth to Croydon, was opened, mainly to carry corn.

After James Watt had successfully improved the steam engine, men began to consider how steam could be used for locomotive power. In fact, in 1769, the year Watt patented his engine, a Frenchman, Nicholas Joseph Cugnot, caused considerable consternation with a steam carriage in the streets of Paris. A few years later, William Murdoch, one of Watt's associates, ran a model steam car in Cornwall. An amusing story is told of how, one evening, he terrified the local vicar, who, seeing this "fiery creature" charging towards him, thought it was the devil. The man, however, to whom we can really attribute the first successful railway locomotive was Richard Trevithick. In 1808 Trevithick took his locomotive to London and put it on a circular track inside a high fence. Then he charged 5 pence admission to see what he called his *Racing Steam Horse*. Trevithick did not proceed much further with his invention, but others did, including William Hedley who built the famous *Puffing Billy* shown at the beginning of this chapter.

The most famous of all the early inventors was George Stephenson. George Stephenson was the son of a colliery fireman in Northumberland. He grew up at a time when poor children rarely went to school and ·as a boy earned a few pence tending geese and cows. While still very young he went to work at the local pit and when he was fourteen he became an assistant fireman. He quickly showed an aptitude for anything connected with engines, an ability which was particularly useful at that time. Stephenson soon began to realise the disadvantages of being illiterate and so, even after a heavy day at the pit, he would walk over the hills to a village schoolmaster who taught him to read and write.

In 1812 he became engine-wright to the Killingworth Colliery, and in 1814 he built his first steam locomotive, the *Blücher*. He studied railway construction for some years and in 1821 was appointed engineer for a railway line from Stockton to Darlington. This line was only intended to take coal but it was important for two reasons. It was

41 *Richard Trevithick invited paying customers to see the early trials of his steam locomotive.*

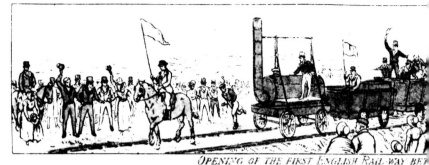

42 *Opening of the first English Railway between Stockton and Darlington, September 27th, 1825.*

the first line to use locomotives, although it was originally intended for horse-drawn trucks, and the gauge of 1·44m was later adopted for all our railways. In 1825 history was made when the Stockton-Darlington line was opened.

Although an outstanding landmark in the history of railways, this line was of minor importance compared with the Liverpool to Manchester line to which Stephenson was appointed engineer in 1826. This presented considerable engineering difficulties, particularly on the notorious stretch of swamp called Chat Moss. In places the mud was 9m deep and it was considered impossible to run a railway over it. Stephenson overcame this difficulty by laying his track on rafts of heather and brushwood, thus virtually floating it over. It took an enormous amount of brushwood to complete this work and in places the embankment over the moss was only just stable three years after they had begun. Despite the evidence of the Stockton-Darlington line the directors were still undecided whether to use locomotives or stationary engines. Such engines were placed at intervals along the track and pulled the train along by rope. Finally it was agreed that a competition should be held to settle the matter. Accordingly the Rainhill Trials took place in 1829 and were won by Stephenson's *Rocket* at the speed of 46½km/h. From the moment the *Rocket*, brilliantly painted in yellow, black and white, crossed the finishing line with its smoke stack red-hot, the future of locomotives was assured.

In the 1830's Stephenson was undoubtedly the leading railway engineer in Britain. He was the chief engineer of the London to Birmingham line along which he constructed the famous Kilsby Tunnel. As the tunnel was being bored, water burst through the roof and the workmen just managed to escape. It was believed impossible to overcome this water hazard, but Stephenson and his son Robert

STOCKTON AND DARLINGTON. SEPT. 27TH, 1825.

refused to be beaten. For 8 months, using 13 steam engines, they pumped out the water, and in the end through determination and skill they succeeded in roofing and bricking up the tunnel.

Stephenson will always be honoured as one of our greatest engineers. So too, will his son Robert, who, in addition to constructing many kilometres of track and developing engines, has left us two of our finest bridges, the tubular bridge across the Menai Straits, and the high level bridge across the Tyne at Newcastle.

Isambard Kingdom Brunel (1806–1859)

Another outstanding engineer in the early days of the railways was Brunel. Isambard Kingdom Brunel was appointed chief engineer to the Great Western Railway when only twenty-seven. He built the line from London to Bristol, probably the finest main line in Britain. It had a 2·1m gauge but unfortunately most of our railways followed Stephenson's 1·44m gauge. It has been generally agreed that the wider gauge was superior both for speed and comfort, but in 1892 the Great Western had to change over. Brunel also constructed a remarkable atmospheric railway in Devon. No locomotives were used, for the train was to be pulled by a piston being forced by air along a pipe. This meant that it would have been easier to climb steep inclines. Unfortunately leather flaps had to be used to seal the slot in the vacuum pipe through which passed the steel connection between the train and the piston. As the leather never lasted more than a year and its replacement cost was high, the project had to be abandoned. Brunel is also remembered for two very beautiful bridges, the Royal Albert Bridge over the Tamar, and the Clifton Suspension Bridge near Bristol.

77

43 *The Great Western broad-gauge railway.*

The Growth of the Railway Network

Businessmen and manufacturers soon realised the value of railways for carrying both goods and passengers. Railway companies were formed, routes surveyed, and Parliament approached for permission to lay the tracks over private land. Although landowners made the railway companies pay three or four times the value of the land before they would sell it to them, the railways still spread rapidly. In 1830 there were 110km of lines open, by 1840 there were 2,180km. Then in the 1840's there took place what has come to be called the "railway mania". All over the country railway companies were formed and people rushed to buy shares in them. In 1843 about 3,200km of track were open, and by 1848 nearly 8,000.

Objections to the Railways

There were many objections to the railways in their early years. It was natural that coaching companies and turnpike trusts should oppose them, for their coming meant the end of the long-distance

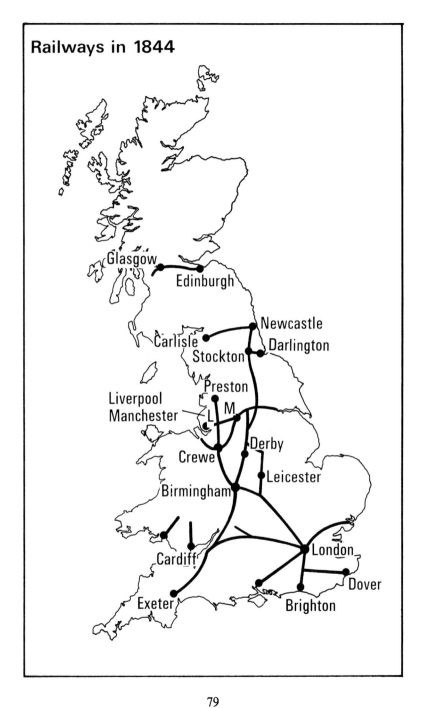

Railways in 1844

coaches. The canals also found it difficult to compete and many were bought up by the railways. Some grew sad over the passing of a more leisurely age. Other objections were less understandable. It was said in all seriousness that cows would stop milking, hens cease to lay, foxes and pheasants would not breed, and that the grass would wither and die. Probably the most ridiculous of all the objections was the statement that ladies would have to travel in tunnels with pins in their mouths to stop anyone kissing them. With so many objectors it is understandable that the surveyors often encountered trouble. Dogs were set on them and pitched battles with hired thugs occurred. Stephenson sometimes surveyed at night by lantern so that the landowners would not know. One amusing story is told of the clergyman who refused to allow his land to be surveyed. The engineer waited until Sunday morning, saw the vicar go to church, and promptly measured his field.

 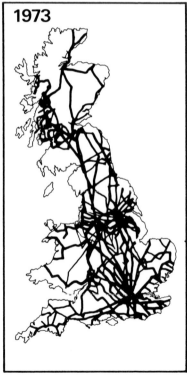

44 *Britain's railway network in 1836 and in 1973. How do you think it will look in AD 2000?*

There were even instances of towns not allowing the railways near to them. Northampton and the Potteries were guilty of this, but they were later to pay for this shortsightedness when they found themselves on branch lines instead of main routes.

Government Interference

Most of these objections were overcome as people realised how useful railways were. However, in the early days there were certain disadvantages. The railways were built by private companies and not by the Government and consequently there was no unified plan for the country as a whole. Parliament made some attempt to control railways and in 1844 tried to help poor passengers by ruling that every company had to run at least one train a day which stopped at every station and on which the charge was "one penny a mile".

Railway Amalgamations

In 1844 companies began to amalgamate with each other. It was clear that by forming large networks there would be less need for passengers to change trains or for goods to be transferred. The outstanding man in this movement was George Hudson, the "Railway King", as he was called. He organised the formation of the North Eastern Railway, thus beginning the series of amalgamations which resulted in the development of the Midland Railway, but he used fraudulent methods to get control of some of the companies and by 1849 these frauds were exposed and he lost the fortune he had made.

The Results of the Railways

By 1860 Britain had a considerable network of railway lines. The building of these lines was to have extremely important results. The railways provided a cheaper, quicker, and more reliable form of transport than had ever been known before. They were at least three times as fast as the coaches. In 1845 the journey from London to Exeter via Bristol took five hours by train, when it would have been nineteen by coach. The passenger rates had been 1p per $1\frac{1}{2}$km on top of the coaches; they were $\frac{1}{2}$p per $1\frac{1}{2}$km by train, third class. The canals were forced to reduce their fares by about one-third to compete with the railways. Although the coaches were put out of business and many canals badly hit, people as a whole benefited because fares generally went down.

The railways and the need for workers to operate them provided employment at a time in the 1830's and 1840's when there were many people without jobs. The railways called for a large amount of iron and this demand gave a considerable boost to the iron industry. The manufacture of rolling stock now became an important industry and helped to create skilled engineers, fitters and mechanics. Farmers gained for they were able to send their perishable produce to the towns more quickly. This in turn increased the variety of food the townspeople ate, and lowered its price. It meant too, that there was no longer any need to keep milking cows in the back streets of London. New towns like Crewe and Swindon grew up as railway centres. With the increase in travel facilities sea-side resorts like Blackpool, Llandudno, and Torquay began to flourish. Day excursions now became possible. In 1865 the Rochdale Co-operative Society was able to run a day trip to London for 30 pence return.

Finally the coming of the railways led to a greater mobility of the population.

Follow up Work

1. Look at the pictures on the following pages carefully. Using them write an account of an imaginary train journey in 1840.

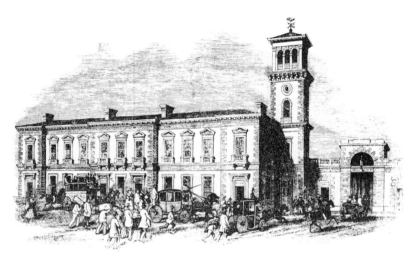

45   *The journey begins at the railway station.*

46   *The 1st class coaches were covered and had windows and some upholstery. The 2nd class had roofs but no windows. The 3rd class were just open boxes. These passengers had no more protection than the driver, the fireman, and the guard. None of the coaches had lights, corridors, or heating. Luggage was stowed on the roof.*

83

SECOND CLASS.

THIRD CLASS.

BIRMINGHAM—"ALL CLEAR."　　"SLACKEN SPEED—ENGINE."　　"CAUTION—RAILS."　　DOVER—CAUTION—RAILS.

THE TAMWORTH STATION.

JUNCTION SIGNAL POST.

LITTLEBURY TUNNEL.

THETFORD STATION.

THE BREAK OF GAUGE AT GLOUCESTER.

47 *The journey ends at the Great Western Railway terminus.*

2. *Imagine you were an engineer in 1840 and describe some of the difficulties involved in laying a track.*
3. *Read the following passage carefully and then answer the questions.*
   "Son of a fireman at Wylam, near Newcastle, he was employed as engine-man at Willington Ballast Hill in 1802. He became engine-wright to the Killingworth Colliery in 1812, and in 1815 designed safety lamps at the same time as Sir Humphrey Davy. He became engineer for the Stockton-Darlington railway which was opened in 1825, surveyed the proposed Liverpool-Manchester line which was opened in 1830, and won a prize with his Rocket *in 1829. His fame was now established and in 1838 he became vice-president, mechanical section, of the British Association. He did his best to check the railway mania of 1844, and became the first president of the Institute of Mechanical Engineers in 1847. He visited Belgium and Spain and was knighted by Leopold I in 1835, but refused British honours. He died at Chesterfield in 1848."*
   a) Which famous railway engineer is referred to in this passage?
   b) Write a few lines about his early life.

c) What was the Davy lamp?

d) What was the main purpose of the Stockton-Darlington line?

e) Why does it deserve to be remembered in history?

f) What was probably the greatest engineering difficulty in the Manchester-Liverpool line? How was it overcome?

g) At which trials did the Rocket win?

h) What was the railway mania of 1844?

i) George Stephenson's son was almost as famous as he was. Why was he famous?

4. Write an account of Brunel showing his importance in the history of railways.

5. This was one objection to railways written in 1841.

"Scarborough is but a small town, and except in the bathing-season, there is very little travelling from upon the road to York to this place; one coach, the mail, does the work for eight months in the year, and this coach, in the winter season, is very often not half filled, and I can see no very great advantage which our visitors would gain by a railroad from York to Scarborough in the summer season."

Any Yorkshire person knows now how ridiculous this objection was. Which of the other objections to the railways were reasonable and which were just foolish? Give your reasons.

6. Which do you think were the most important results of the railways? Why?

7. Without consulting your book write an outline account of the history of railways up to 1860. Illustrate it if you wish with maps or drawings.

8. Make notes of the railways in your own district. Show on a map where the track was laid and indicate any engineering difficulties which were met. Mark in the stations and any other interesting points. You should also show those parts of the district which began to grow up because people were able to travel in by train. Indicate also tracks which are now closed.

7 Trade Unions up to 1850

Today there are unions for almost every type of worker, and nearly 10,000,000 men and women are in the trade union movement. Whatever your occupation will be, whether you will become a factory worker or a film star, most of you will eventually be members of a trade union. The fact that unions exist to protect your interests is of great importance. It is something that should be valued, for as we shall see workers in the past fought a hard and often dangerous battle to build these unions.

Trade Union Origins

In the early 18th century labour organisations were local trade clubs, not national trade unions. The workers in different trades would form these clubs, partly to protect their own interests, and partly to have a cheerful evening in a public house. In fact some public houses with names like *The Jolly Potters* or *The Weavers' Arms* were so called after the clubs which met there. After 1750 these local clubs often joined together and a number of fairly powerful unions such as the Hatters and the Sailmakers emerged.

The Combination Acts

The employers began to look suspiciously at these unions and Parliament was already afraid of anything in this country which might resemble the French Revolution. In 1799, when the master millwrights of London complained that their men were forming a union, a nervous

Government passed the Combination Acts forbidding any combination of workmen trying to decrease hours or increase wages. Trade unions became illegal.

For the next twenty-five years trade unions were forbidden by law but the effects of the Acts on different unions varied. Many were driven underground and became secret societies meeting at night in lonely places. Some turned to violence, to acid-throwing as in Glasgow, and murder in Northumberland. There were prosecutions leading, among others, to the imprisonment of the *Times'* compositors in 1810. Yet at the same time many unions were allowed to survive and still negotiated with the employers.

The Repeal of the Combination Acts

The Combination Acts remained in force until 1824, and their repeal was the work of Francis Place, a London master tailor. Place, who had been brought up in the slums of London, had educated himself during spells of unemployment. He had led strikes and been black-listed by employers, and by sheer hard work he had built up a prosperous tailoring business. With the help of an MP, Joseph Hume, Francis Place conducted his case so adroitly that many MPs did not realise that the Combination Acts had been repealed until it was too late. Their repeal was followed by an outbreak of strikes and in 1825 Parliament passed another Act which introduced some restrictions. Despite this Act, trade unions remained legal.

The National Association for the Protection of Labour

After 1825 a number of unions came into being but the most interesting feature was the development of very large unions which aimed at merging a number of trades. The first of these was the National Association for the Protection of Labour, founded in 1830 by John Doherty. Doherty had already formed a Spinners' Union but now he wanted the potters, textile workers, and miners to join together in one body. By 1831 the Association was reputed to have 100,000 members and was publishing its own paper, *The Voice of the People*.

In spite of its large membership it was not well organised. There was ill-feeling amongst the branches and refusal to support the different sections' strikes. By 1832 the Association had collapsed and disappeared. It was followed by a great national union of builders but this was too weak to stand against the opposition of the employers. These unions were ahead of their time, for behind them lay more than the idea of opposing employers; their leaders saw in unions an opportunity to take over the factories and industries of the country and to do away with the profit motive. This was also the idea of Robert Owen.

Robert Owen, Social Reformer (1771–1858)

Owen was born in 1771 at Newtown in Montgomeryshire. He was apprenticed to a draper but by exceptional business ability he was soon managing his own spinning works. He married the daughter of David Dale, who owned large cotton mills at New Lanark in Scotland. By the time he was twenty-nine Owen was already controlling these mills and it was then that he tried to create a model factory and a model community. Owen firmly believed that employers had a duty towards their workers to treat them as human beings. He built pleasant houses for the workers and shops where they could buy good products at fair prices. Schools were provided for children and no child under ten was allowed to work in the mill. He paid higher wages than anyone else and when his mills were closed for four months because of lack of raw cotton he continued to pay his workers. His partners protested bitterly until they found that despite high pay and short hours the firm's profits increased. Owen had proved that it benefited both employers and employees if goodwill existed on both sides.

He tried to force other mill owners to restrict hours when he promoted the Factory Act of 1819 which, however, proved unsuccessful in practice.

Owen wanted far more than a model factory; he believed that men could only be really happy if they co-operated together instead of competing against one another. He began his first "village of co-operation" in America and called it New Harmony. Owen was a man of high principles and ideas, but too many of his villagers were not, and by their idleness and indifference destroyed his scheme.

Owen lost much of his fortune in America and in 1829 he returned to England. At this time co-operative societies in various forms were springing up everywhere, as groups of men strove to become independent of their employers. Owen conceived the idea of labour exchanges

48 *A labour note for 40 hours of work, signed by Robert Owen himself.*

by which exchange bazaars were to be set up. Workers would bring whatever they had made, deposit the products in these bazaars, and then were given labour notes in exchange. The labour notes were calculated according to the hours of work involved in the product. The worker would then exchange these notes for other goods at the bazaar. At first the scheme was extremely popular and the bazaars were flooded with goods. But the idea was to fail hopelessly. It was impossible to value the products and there was too limited a variety of goods deposited. By 1834 the labour bazaars were closing down.

The Grand National Consolidated Trades Union

It was at this time that Owen became interested in the trade union movement. Here, as in everything else, his ideas were vast in their scope. He saw in trade unions an opportunity to change the whole structure of society. In 1834 the Grand National Consolidated Trades Union was formed. This was a combination of a number of unions. The idea of this one great union spread rapidly. Within weeks there were 500,000 members from Exeter to Aberdeen, including such varied trades as miners, tailors, bakers and gas workers.

The employers saw the danger and began to resist. Many of them demanded that their employees sign the "Document" renouncing their unions. In Derby over 1,000 workers were locked out for refusing, and the Grand National made a levy of 5 pence a week on its members to help them. In London the gas workers and tailors struck, in Leeds textile workers, in Birmingham the builders. The Union was too weak to stand up to the pressure of so many strikes and then the Government stepped in. Many prosecutions took place but by far the worst was the tragedy of the Tolpuddle Martyrs.

The Tolpuddle Martyrs

Six villagers in the Dorset village of Tolpuddle had formed a union

CAUSE OF FREEDOM!

The LONDON CENTRAL DORCHESTER COMMITTEE feel great pleasure in informing their Fellow-Workmen and all Enemies to Oppression, that a

PUBLIC DINNER

WILL TAKE PLACE AT

WHITE CONDUIT HOUSE,

ON

Monday, April 25, 1836,

IN

CELEBRATION OF THE REMISSION OF THE SENTENCE

ON THE

DORCHESTER LABOURERS,

And in Commemoration of the Moral Power displayed by the Working Classes of London in their great Procession, April, 1834.

on the advice of the Grand National in an attempt to prevent their wages being reduced to the starvation level of 30 pence a week. The entrance fee was 5p and weekly contributions of $\frac{1}{2}$p were to be paid. Like many of these early unions they had an initiation ceremony. In front of a painted picture of a skeleton and with their hands on a bible they swore an oath never to divulge their union's secrets. This simple ceremony, carried out for the sake of their livelihood, was to be their undoing. As the villagers' union grew the authorities looked for some way to destroy it. They discovered a rarely used act which forbade illegal oaths. The six founders were charged with breaking the law. It was a minor offence but the Government saw a chance to strike at Owen's Grand National Consolidated. The labourers were found guilty. Their sentence—transportation to Australia for seven years. This savage punishment served its purpose. Thousands were frightened away from unions and although Owen fought desperately for the Tolpuddle Martyrs it was in vain. They were sent to Australia and it

CAUTION.

WHEREAS it has been represented to us from several quarters, that mischievous and designing Persons have been for some time past, endeavouring to induce, and have induced, many Labourers in various Parishes in this County, to attend Meetings, and to enter into Illegal Societies or Unions, to which they bind themselves by unlawful oaths, administered secretly by Persons concealed, who artfully deceive the ignorant and unwary,—WE, the undersigned Justices think it our duty to give this PUBLIC NOTICE and CAUTION, that all Persons may know the danger they incur by entering into such Societies.

ANY PERSON who shall become a Member of such a Society, or take any Oath, or assent to any Test or Declaration not authorized by Law—

Any Person who shall administer, or be present at, or consenting to the administering or taking any Unlawful Oath, or who shall cause such Oath to be administered, although not actually present at the time—

Any Person who shall not reveal or discover any Illegal Oath which may have been administered, or any Illegal Act done or to be done—

Any Person who shall induce, or endeavour to persuade any other Person to become a Member of such Societies,

WILL BECOME

Guilty of Felony,

AND BE LIABLE TO BE

Transported for Seven Years.

ANY PERSON who shall be compelled to take such an Oath, unless he shall declare the same within four days, together with the whole of what he shall know touching the same, will be liable to the same Penalty.

Any Person who shall directly or indirectly maintain correspondence or intercourse with such Society, will be deemed Guilty of an Unlawful Combination and Confederacy, and on Conviction before one Justice, on the Oath of one Witness, be liable to a Penalty of TWENTY POUNDS, or to be committed to the Common Gaol or House of Correction, for THREE CALENDAR MONTHS; or if proceeded against by Indictment, may be CONVICTED OF FELONY, and be TRANSPORTED FOR SEVEN YEARS.

Any Person who shall knowingly permit any Meeting of any such Society to be held in any House, Building, or other Place, shall for the first offence be liable to the Penalty of FIVE POUNDS; and for every other offence committed after Conviction, be deemed Guilty of such Unlawful Combination and Confederacy, and on Conviction before one Justice, on the Oath of one Witness, be liable to a Penalty of TWENTY POUNDS, or to Commitment to the Common Gaol or House of Correction, FOR THREE CALENDAR MONTHS; or if proceeded against by Indictment may be

CONVICTED OF FELONY,

And Transported for SEVEN YEARS.

COUNTY OF DORSET. Dorchester Division	C. B. WOLLASTON, JAMES FRAMPTON, WILLIAM ENGLAND, THOS. DADE. JNO. MORTON COLSON.	HENRY FRAMPTON, RICHD. TUCKER STEWARD, WILLIAM R. CHURCHILL, AUGUSTUS FOSTER.

February 22d. 1834.

G. CLARK, PRINTER, CORNHILL, DORCHESTER.

49 *Above and left, contemporary posters for and against the Tolpuddle Martyrs.*

was not until 1837, nearly three years later, that they were given a free pardon and returned to their homes.

As for the Grand National Consolidated, persecuted on all sides, struggling to finance strikes out of inadequate resources, it had collapsed by August 1834. Its failure destroyed the hopes of many British working men.

Follow up Work

1. *Explain how far trade unions had begun to develop before 1800.*
2. *Why were the Combination Acts passed and how strictly were they enforced? What part did Francis Place play in their repeal?*
3. *What was the part played by Robert Owen in early labour movements? Explain why his Grand National Consolidated failed.*
4. *Read the following passage and then answer the questions which follow it.*

   "From this time we were reduced to 7/- a week and shortly after our employers told us they must reduce us to 6/- a week. The labouring men consulted together what had better be done . . . They willingly agreed to form a Friendly Society among the labourers and shortly after two delegates from a Trade Society paid us a visit, formed a Friendly Society among the labourers and gave us directions how to proceed. That was in October, 1833.

   Nothing particularly occurred until February 21st, 1834, when placards were posted up, cautions from the magistrates threatening to punish . . . with seven years transportation any man who would join the union. On 24th February the constable said, 'I have a warrant for your arrest.' Accordingly I and my companions walked with the constables to Dorchester and were instantly sent to prison. As for the trial . . . the judge ordered us to be tried under an act for the suppression of mutiny among seamen . . . Two days later we were placed at the bar to receive sentence, when the judge told us that not for what we had done but for an example to others he considered it his duty to pass the sentence of 7 years transportation."

   a) *By what name have this group of men become known?*
   b) *What would we call a 'trade society' today?*
   c) *What does the sentence 'transportation' mean?*
   d) *What was the purpose of this severe sentence?*
   e) *What eventually happened to the seven men?*
   f) *Why were agricultural wages so low at this time?*
   g) *In what ways was it possible for these wages to be made up to a reasonable level at this time?*

h) *How did trade and friendly societies develop during the period*
1834–54?

(East Midlands CSE Board, 1966)

Chartism

The date was November 10th, 1838. In the town of Norwich a vast
crowd of men stood listening to the fiery words of the Reverend
Joseph Stephens, a one-time Methodist minister.

"Men of Norwich, fight with your swords, fight with your pistols,
fight with daggers. Women, fight with your nails and your teeth, if
nothing else will do!"

As he finished some of the audience roared their applause, and
banners with the words "Give us the Charter" and "We want the
People's Charter" were raised high in the air. Others shook their heads
for this was not what they expected from Chartism.

The People's Charter

This movement had begun in a much more peaceful atmosphere with
the formation in 1836 of the London Working Men's Association, a
group of skilled men led by William Lovett, a cabinet maker. These
men believed it wrong that the 1832 Reform Act had not given the
working class the vote. Their object was to get equal political and
social rights for all classes of society.

In May 1838, the Association published what it called "The People's
Charter" with its famous six provisions:

1. Universal male suffrage. All men, but not women, over the age
   of twenty-one to have the vote.
2. Annual Parliaments.
3. Vote by secret ballot.
4. Equal electoral districts. The country was to be divided into two
   hundred electoral districts, each about the same size.
5. Abolition of the property qualification for MPs.
6. Payment of MPs.

All these points were political but the real purpose behind the
Charter was to try to improve the social and economic conditions of
the workers by having their own MPs to represent them in Parliament.

95

The Causes of Chartism

Agents from the Association went to other towns addressing meetings and explaining the purpose behind the Charter. As the movement spread the attitude of the Chartists began to change. The members of the London Working Men's Association had been mainly well-paid and prosperous draftsmen who believed in persuading the Government by peaceful methods. But the dockers of East London, the nail makers of the Black Country, and the textile workers and miners of the North knew far more poverty and hardship. They had been embittered not only by the unfairness of the 1832 Reform Act. In 1834 the hated Poor Law Act had been passed. This had abolished outdoor relief and forced unemployed as well as aged workers into the dreaded work-houses. The agricultural labourers of the South, crushed by years of suffering, had accepted the Act, but in the Midlands and the North the industrial workers were openly hostile to it. Sir Charles Napier, who commanded the troops sent to control the Chartists, wrote of this incident in Nottingham.

"The poor in Nottingham resolved to die rather than enter the workhouses. I heard of an old man who being starved was told, 'Oh you can't have anything today, come again on Thursday.'

'But I have gone two days without food and shall be dead before Thursday.'

'We can't help that, you must weather the storm as others do.'

And he would have died if the Mayor had not fed him."

These were reasons enough for the popularity of Chartism but most important of all was the near starvation to which many workers were reduced in the 1838–39 trade depression. Their discontent had reached a pitch when they were ready to listen to talk of violence if necessary.

Feargus O'Connor and the 'Northern Star'

To them the tall, red-haired and silver-tongued Feargus O'Connor, an Irish journalist and brilliant orator, seemed the ideal leader. O'Connor had purchased a Leeds newspaper, the *Northern Star*, in 1837, and used it to spread his ideas on how the six points of the Charter could be obtained. This paper was widely read by working men and contained articles which were deliberately intended to arouse their anger.

This is one account taken from the *Northern Star*. "An inquest was held upon the body of a little girl aged five years who died from starvation on the roadside near Llangefni, North Wales, last week. It appears that her father was unable to procure employment and had applied to the relieving officer in the parish who gave him one shilling and told him to be about his business and not to trouble him again. The consequence was that the father had nothing to give his children, one of whom died for want of proper food."

Throughout the autumn of 1838 great Chartist meetings were held and thousands of workers listened to the vehement speeches of O'Connor and Stephens. On September 24th, at Kersal Moor near Manchester, a crowd of 50,000 heard O'Connor cry, "Soon we will turn to physical force for the people know they have borne oppression too long." Police spies in the audience hurried off to report and the Government sent in troops to the threatened areas of South Wales and Northern England.

In 1838, however, the Chartists were still using peaceful methods. They collected 1,200,000 signatures to a National Petition asking for votes for working men. But when the Petition was presented to Parliament in 1839 it was decisively rejected.

It seemed to many Chartists that the believers in peaceful methods had failed. Now the extremists began to take over the leadership. Although O'Connor opposed it the Chartists in South Wales planned a rising, and on a rainy night in November 1839, John Frost, a draper, led 4,000 miners against Newport. The whole revolt was ill-prepared and badly led. Some of the miners lost their way over the hills and when the main group reached Newport they were soon forced to flee by a handful of soldiers. There were no revolts in the rest of the country and the Government had little difficulty in imprisoning the leaders and transporting Frost to Tasmania for life.

In 1840 most of the Chartist leaders, including O'Connor, were in prison, but even so O'Connor was emerging in leadership. His writings, like his speeches, showed an almost unbelievable conceit, as when he finished one letter:

> *I am, my friends and brethren*
> *The tyrants' captive*
> *The oppressors' dread*
> *The poor man's friend and*
> *the people's accepted present.*
> **Feargus O'Connor.**

By now there was no doubt of O'Connor's leadership of the movement and when he was released from prison his audiences greeted him with this song.

> *The Lion of Freedom comes from his den,*
> *We'll rally around him again and again,*
> *We'll crown him with laurels our champion to be,*
> *O'Connor, the patriot of sweet liberty.*

The Plug Plots

Early in 1841 signatures were again being collected for another Petition and as a trade depression spread thousands of workers signed it. In 1842 when it was presented to Parliament it had over 3,300,000 signatures and was more than 9 kilometres long. It was said that the floor of the House of Commons looked as "if it had been snowing paper".

Once again Parliament rejected it overwhelmingly and a series of strikes broke out in the North of England. O'Connor spoke against violence and the strikes but in many industrial towns like Preston, Manchester, Stoke, and Blackburn, bands of angry workers destroyed factories and attacked the magistrates' houses. These strikes became known as the "Plug Plots" because in many mills the steam boiler plugs were knocked out to stop them working. The Government immediately sent troops to all the danger spots. By the end of September the violence was over, many of the strikers had been imprisoned or transported and the rest were forced back on the employers' terms.

The Fiasco on Kennington Common

The failure of the 1842 Petition and the collapse of the strikes was really the end of Chartism. Many thought that it would never be revived but in 1848 one last Petition was presented to Parliament. This was to be a monster affair of over 5,000,000 signatures which the Chartists thought Parliament would not dare to ignore. Plans were made for a great meeting on Kennington Common on April 10th. The Chartists were to form a vast procession to Westminster where the Petition would be presented.

For a moment the Government panicked. Queen Victoria was sent out of London and the aged Duke of Wellington was put in command of 100,000 troops and 150,000 special constables. Government buildings were barricaded and civil servants armed. Sandbags were piled up against the Bank of England and a cannon placed on the roof.

Then came the anti-climax. There were 20,000 people assembled on Kennington Common ready to march when the police warned O'Connor that if the procession took place it would be resisted by force. There was little the Chartists could do but to allow the Petition to be taken ignominiously by taxi-cabs. Once in the House of Commons the signatures were counted. Instead of 5,000,000 there were less than 2,000,000 and many of these were forgeries. On it were names like Flatnose, No Cheese, and Pugnose. The Duke of Wellington had signed it 17 times and even the Queen's name appeared.

The Reasons for the Failure of Chartism

Chartism had completely collapsed as an effective movement. A few of the leaders struggled to keep it alive but to most of the members it had obviously failed. There were a number of reasons for this failure. It had been a movement without proper leadership. O'Connor had been able to rouse his followers but he had no talent for guiding them. Worse still was the fact that he was unable to agree with the more level-headed leaders and there had always been dissension in the movement. Another reason for the failure had been the fact that many able men had joined other movements such as the Co-operative Societies and the Anti-Corn Law League. Most important of all, however, was the undeniable fact that economic and social conditions had greatly improved. As one Chartist leader said bitterly, "When times were bad the workers would join you in the demands for their rights. Now when times are good they are interested only in their pigeons and their dogs."

Yet although Chartism died on Kennington Common in 1848, today five of its original demands have become law. Annually elected Parliaments was the only one which was never accepted, and few people regard this as either sensible or necessary.

Follow up Work

1. *Read the chapter carefully and then, without referring to the text write down the six points of Chartism.*

2. *Explain fully why industrial workers were so discontented in 1840.*

3. *Feargus O'Connor has been called the evil genius of Chartism. What part did he play in the movement?*

4. *What were:*
    a) *The Newport Rising.*
    b) *The Plug Plots.*
    c) *The "fiasco on Kennington Common"?*

5. *Why did Chartism fail?*

6. *Discuss with your teacher what instances there were of Chartism in your own district and write an account of them.*

The Origin of the Co-operative Movement

On December 21st, 1844, a grocery shop opened for the first time in Toad Lane, Rochdale. There was nothing unusual about the building and the store was small and sparsely fitted out. Yet on this day history was made, for this was the beginning of the present co-operative movement.

For months previously twenty-eight poor workmen had saved their money until they had £1 each. With this tiny capital they founded the Rochdale Society of Equitable Pioneers, one of whose objects was "to establish a store to sell food and clothing". Some of these men had been Chartists, others had supported Robert Owen, most had suffered poverty through unemployment. They all knew how shop-keepers, by granting credit, could force people to trade with them and then sell inferior goods at high prices. These twenty-eight pioneers began their store as a deliberate attempt to help working people.

Nothing shows more clearly the humble beginnings of this great movement than the first stock order, "*Butter* 1 quarter 22 lb; *sugar* 2 quarters; *flour* 3 sacks at £1 17s. 6d., and 3 sacks at £1 16s.; *oatmeal* 1 sack; and 2 dozen *candles*." The total value was £16 11s. 11d. (£16·60). Most of this stock was sold out on the first night to the jeers of the local shopkeepers.

As the pioneers themselves did all the work the store only opened in the evenings. At first even the founders doubted if it would succeed, but at the end of the first year there were seventy-four members and the share capital had risen to £184. The store was prospering and as a celebration the directors decided to have an Anniversary Tea Party. They fixed the price of tickets for "gents" at 4p and for "ladies" at 3p. The pioneers showed their typical independence by saying that "No strangers were to address the meeting, the members would do it themselves."

The Growth of the Movement

By 1850 the Rochdale store had 600 members; by 1859 this figure had increased to 2,703 and the annual sales rose to £104,012. Now the other shopkeepers were clearly alarmed. Handbills were distributed in Rochdale with the words; "Will the shopkeepers still go on aiding the men who are fostering the system which is destined at no distant period to snatch their daily bread from their very jaws?"

It was not only the shopkeepers in Rochdale who had cause to worry, for by 1851 there were 150 co-operative societies with over 15,000 members. By 1880 almost 500,000 working people were trading with the co-operative shops in Britain.

The Reasons for its Success

One of the most important reasons for the success of the movement was the payment of dividends on purchases. The Rochdale Pioneers bought their goods wholesale and sold them at market prices. The surplus profit was then returned to the members according to the amount of their purchases. This was a clear incentive to buy more. At the same time they paid interest on share capital and encouraged their members not to draw out their dividend but to let it accumulate as shares. This meant that the "co-ops" always had money available to expand their business. To make sure that large shareholders could not control the Society the principle was adopted of allowing one member to have one vote only, regardless of the number of shares held. A second reason for the popularity of co-ops was the fact that their members were sure of buying pure food. It is a sad fact that in the 19th century the selling of adulterated food was common. Sand was mixed with sugar, chalk with flour, plaster of Paris put into bread, and rotten food disguised as good. Thirdly the co-ops were growing at a time, in the late 1840's and early 1850's, when trade was good and the workers of the North had more money to spend. Finally the Government had no cause to be hostile to the movement as it was to trade unions and Chartism.

Extension of Co-operative Activities

In 1863 the English Co-operative Wholesale Society was formed and then in 1868 the Scottish CWS was founded. This meant that the retail societies no longer had to buy from private wholesalers, for the CWS would supply them with most goods and pay each store a dividend on purchases in the same way as the stores paid dividends to their customers.

The next step forward was for the CWS to begin manufacturing its own products. It began in 1872 with the manufacture of biscuits at Crumpsall near Manchester. Soon both the English and Scottish CWS produced many of their own products including boots, clothes, tobacco and soap. The co-operative movement even formed its own bank and insurance society. The organisation which had begun so humbly had become one of the major businesses of the country.

The Rochdale Pioneers had thought of far more than business, however, for to them the co-operative society provided an opportunity for members to meet socially and to receive some education. The directors even went so far in 1845 as to decide that "the members who did not attend the annual tea party be either fined or charged the amount". In 1849 the top floor at Toad Lane was devoted to evening discussions and on Sunday it was used as a school. Between 1850 and 1855 members' children could receive instruction for 1p a month. By 1860 the library had 5,000 volumes and opened on Wednesdays and Saturday evenings. An early minute book records: "the librarian be provided with a pair of slippers owing to his noisy clogs".

In 1917, after much hesitation, it was decided to enter into politics with the formation of the Co-operative Party. This usually works with the Labour Party, and your own MP may be a Labour and Co-operative member.

Follow up Work

1. *Other co-operative stores had been tried before 1844 but they had all failed. Explain why the Rochdale Pioneers succeeded.*

2. *Show how the co-operative movement widened its activities after 1860.*

3. *In what ways did the early co-operative society attempt to provide for the social and cultural needs of its members?*

4. *Discuss with your teacher the part played by the CWS in retailing, and wholesaling, and manufacturing today.*

PROGRESS OF THE CWS—TRADE DEPARTMENT

YEAR	SHAREHOLDERS' MEMBERS	SHARE CAPITAL	NET SALES	CWS PRODUCTIONS	NET PROFIT BEFORE TAX
		£	£	£	£
1864	18,337	2,455	51,857	—	306
1865	24,005	7,182	120,754	—	1,850
1880	361,523	146,061	3,339,681	118,598	42,090
1890	721,316	434,017	7,429,073	341,277	126,979
1900	1,249,091	883,791	16,043,889	2,264,088	289,141
1910	1,991,576	1,740,619	26,567,833	6,581,310	462,469
1920	3,341,411	4,270,408	105,439,628	33,404,466	64,210*
1930	4,844,090	8,515,097	85,313,018	25,825,426	1,344,218
1940	7,078,362	15,859,540	142,593,952	46,297,545	4,740,388
1950	8,590,914	20,697,288	321,641,923	95,481,018	8,498,123
1951	8,633,242	20,811,953	359,141,772	106,820,059	8,667,954
1953	8,920,942	25,708,343	420,887,590	122,122,310	8,925,614
1954	9,220,970	27,481,064	410,552,832	128,609,025	9,696,538
1955	9,300,884	28,109,603	418,073,209	138,487,756	9,889,001
1956	9,415,062	28,743,473	444,285,406	142,832,603	10,036,486
1957	9,483,488	29,293,635	453,960,174	147,145,990	9,637,928
1958	9,695,545	30,117,392	463,274,603	146,798,765	9,514,857
1959	9,728,241	30,478,908	467,867,807	148,882,659	8,133,148
1960	9,780,279	30,797,349	475,565,896	143,870,416	8,078,099
1961	9,786,645	30,947,659	465,170,491	140,000,807	7,531,034
1962	9,806,838	31,489,353	479,749,123	145,126,063	7,485,504
1963	9,811,600	31,497,750	480,184,395	142,898,993	5,906,544
1964	9,820,151	31,500,019	488,496,661	146,606,750	5,760,979
1965	9,839,217	31,527,507	487,859,688	151,259,277	4,904,654

* Loss

50 *Why do you think membership increased significantly in the 1930's?*

8 Reforms in the Factories and Mines

Conditions in the Early Factories

Of all the evils which accompanied the early factories none were worse than the appalling conditions under which children and adults often worked. Study the picture (opposite) of pauper children scrambling for food which has been thrown into a trough for them. Pauper children, who were usually orphans with no one to protect them, were brought from all over the country and employed in the textile mills of the north of England. Ill-fed, badly-clothed, brutally beaten for the slightest offence, and working for as many as 15 or 16 hours a day, they spent their young lives in indescribable misery.

Plate 52 (on page 107) shows a group of "free" children at work. They were called "free" children because their parents were not compelled to send them to work in the mills. Frequently, however, the 15 or 20 pence which they could earn were desperately needed by the family. As this picture shows they were liable to be beaten and often had to crouch beneath the machines as they worked. It was not uncommon for them to work for as many as 16 hours a day and to spend their meal breaks cleaning the machinery.

Although conditions like these were sadly common, not all employers treated their workers cruelly. Some, like Richard Arkwright at Cromford, Samuel Gregg at Styal, and Robert Peel the Elder, whose cotton mills at Bury were earning him £50,000 a year in the early 1800's, provided reasonable houses and conditions for their employees. The outstanding mill owner was Robert Owen whose mills at New Lanark were mentioned in Chapter 7.

The First Factory Acts, and the Factory Reform Movement

It was men like Peel and Owen who were responsible for Parliament passing the Factory Acts of 1802 and 1819 which reduced working

51 *The horrors of child labour in 19th century England.*

hours for children in the cotton mills. Unfortunately no proper inspectors were ever appointed to enforce them and the Acts were unsuccessful as employers could easily evade them. For thousands of children there was to be little improvement during the next few years.

However, a movement for factory reform was growing. Three of the leaders of the movement were Michael Sadler, a Tory MP, John Fielden, a mill owner from Todmorden, and Richard Oastler, a land agent from Huddersfield. In 1830 readers of the *Leeds Mercury* were shocked to read this letter which Oastler had written.

"Thousands of our fellow creatures are at this very moment existing in a state of slavery more horrid than are the victims of that hellish system Colonial Slavery. These innocent creatures drawl out unpitied their short but miserable existences. The very streets of our towns are every morning wet with the tears of innocent victims at the accursed shrine of avarice, who are compelled not by the cart whip of the negro slave driver, but by the dread of the equally appalling thong or strap of the overlooker, to hasten half-dressed, but not half-fed, to those magazines of British infantile slavery, the worsted mills of the town of Bradford."

The Royal Commission's Report

Immediately there was an outcry as the manufacturers tried to deny these accusations, but the reformers had considerable proof available. Soon it became obvious that the evidence which they had collected could not be ignored. In 1832 Parliament agreed to set up a Commission to investigate conditions in the mills. The Commissioners toured the industrial towns and asked questions of numerous employees. Finally they prepared a report, some extracts from which are given here. They show clearly that children were terribly overworked, sometimes brutally beaten, and they reveal how young people were frequently crippled at the factories or grew up deformed because of their working conditions.

One witness named Samuel Coulson had two daughters. They worked at the mill because the family depended on their wages. These are some of the questions asked and the answers given.

"At what time in the morning, in the brisk time, did those girls go to the mills?"

"In the brisk time, for about six weeks, they have gone at 3 o'clock in the morning and ended at 10, or nearly half past at night."

"What intervals were allowed for rest and refreshments during those nineteen hours of labour?"

"Breakfast a quarter of an hour, and dinner half an hour, and drinking a quarter of an hour."

"What was the length of time they could be in bed during those long hours?"

"It was nearly 11 o'clock before we could get them to bed after getting a little victuals."

"What time did they get up in the morning?"

"In general me or my mistress got up at 2 o'clock to dress them."

A fairly wealthy man named Abraham Whitehead gave evidence of the cruelty he had seen in some mills. He spoke of having seen

52 *Notice how the girl is working under the machinery while it is still in motion.*

children thrashed with a leather strap and sometimes with an iron rod. On one occasion he saw an iron bar driven through the cheek of one young girl. Other children had died after having been thrashed.

William Cooper, a man of twenty-eight, who had begun work at ten, was only 1½ metres tall. This was because he had to work in a crouching position and his legs had grown twisted and deformed. A woman named Elizabeth Bentley had started to work when she was six. She had always worked bent under the machines until finally her shoulders were so deformed that she could no longer raise her head. Some witnesses gave evidence of seeing workers' arms and legs torn off by dangerous machinery and of children falling asleep and being killed by the machines they were tending.

When the Commissioners had gathered all their evidence they published a report showing what the working conditions were like in the textile mills. Public opinion was shocked at the facts revealed and many more people began to believe in the need for factory reform. Among the recruits who joined the reformers was Lord Ashley, better known by the title he later inherited, the Earl of Shaftesbury.

Lord Shaftesbury and the Factory Acts

Shaftesbury was one of the most humane men this country has ever known. Although he came from a wealthy family he devoted his life to helping the poor. Shortly after the Report was published Shaftesbury became the leader of the reformers in Parliament. Despite the clear evidence that children were being overworked there was strong opposition to shorter hours. Many mill owners refused to believe what Owen had proved, that shorter hours did not mean less profits. Manufacturers claimed that all their profits were made in the last hour of work and that in any case the Government had no right to interfere in the way they ran their factories.

However, the movement towards reform was too strong and in 1833 a Factory Act was passed. These were its provisions:

1. No children under nine to be employed.

2. Children between nine and thirteen not to work more than nine hours a day.

3. Young people between thirteen and eighteen to be limited to twelve hours a day.

4. Government inspectors to be appointed. (This was very important for it ensured that the Act was obeyed.)

Shaftesbury and his followers were far from satisfied with this Act. They had long advocated a ten-hour working day and they continued their demands for this. In 1844 Sir Robert Peel the Younger was Prime Minister and despite the fact that his government would not accept the ten-hour day another important Act was passed. Women's hours were reduced to twelve a day and although children were allowed to begin work at the age of eight instead of nine, their hours were reduced to $6\frac{1}{2}$ a day. Then in 1847 Shaftesbury persuaded Parliament to pass the Ten Hours Act. This limited the working hours of all young people under eighteen and of women to ten a day. Unfortunately this Act did not benefit men at first for the employers made the women and children work shifts and in this way there were always some present to help the men, no matter how long they worked.

By these Acts the conditions of the textile workers were gradually improved and as the century progressed Parliament became more willing to help other factory workers. Then in 1878, a Factory Act was passed which applied to most industries, and thus the majority of workers became protected by law.

53 *Malnutrition was common among the children of the labouring poor, as this print shows.*

Conditions in the Coal Mines

However, before 1840, as Lord Shaftesbury knew, it was not only in the factories that children were suffering. In the coal mines, colliers and their families were working under the most brutal conditions. Frequently, mining villages were so isolated that little was known of the pit workers, but in 1840 Shaftesbury persuaded Parliament to set up a Royal Commission to inquire into the lives of the miners. In 1842 their Report was published and its contents shocked the country.

54 *This was seen in a coal mine in Halifax. The girl had a belt around her waist with a chain running between her legs. She had to drag a wagon containing up to 250kg of coal from the coal face to the shaft, a distance of about three hundred metres. She did this for as long as twelve hours a day.*

The following are just a few of the statements in the Report. Sarah Gooder, who was eight years old, was a trapper. She opened the wooden trap doors when the coal carts came along the gallery. This door was essential for it prevented vital air from escaping from the pit face. This is what she said:

"I'm a trapper in the Gauber Pit. It does not tire me but I have to trap without a light and I'm scared. Sometimes I sing when I have a light, but not in the dark. I dare not sing then. I don't like being in the pit."

55 *The trapper (see the account of her work above).*

Another witness was Margaret Leveston. She was only six years old and yet she had to carry coal on her back up the shaft. She told the Commissioners that she worked with her sister Jesse and her mother. She didn't know how long she worked. It was dark when she came to the pit and dark when she left.

As in the textile mills brutality was common. James Robinson who was fourteen told how the collier, for whom he and his younger brothers worked, often kicked them to the ground and flung lumps of coal at them. Sometimes they were so badly beaten that they could hardly get home, but they dared not complain in case they lost their jobs.

The Commissioners reported that young boys were often responsible for the engine which raised and lowered the miners. On one occasion a boy of nine had been distracted by a mouse, the engine went out of control and four other boys were sent crashing to their deaths.

These were the conditions in many mining areas and although

56 *Pictures like this in the Royal Commission's Report awoke public opinion to the horrors of the mines.*

miners were not badly paid compared with other workers some of the mine owners were making enormous fortunes. For example, in the 1820's the Earl of Lonsdale received £4,000 a week from his pits in Whitehaven.

It was obvious to Parliament that something had to be done. In 1842, despite opposition from the mine owners, Peel's government

57 *Women carrying heavy baskets of coal to the pit surface.*

passed the Mines Act. These were its provisions:

1. No women or children to work underground in the mines.
2. No child under ten to be employed at all.
3. Boys not to be employed as engine-men until they were 15.
4. Inspectors were to report on the miners' conditions.

Thus as we have seen, by 1850 great progress had been made towards improving conditions in mines and factories, particularly for children and women.

Lord Shaftesbury's Other Work

Meanwhile Lord Shaftesbury continued his efforts to help the poor. It was largely due to him that in 1864 Parliament forbade the use of "climbing boys" to sweep chimneys. This had been a terrible task and numerous boys had been burned to death or suffocated inside the chimneys. Shaftesbury also helped to improve lunatic asylums. In many asylums mentally sick people had been loaded down with chains and treated like animals. He supported Florence Nightingale in her campaign for better nursing facilities and encouraged Dr. Barnardo in the founding of his famous homes for destitute children. In addition Lord Shaftesbury himself was one of the main workers behind the Ragged School Union. This was an organisation founded to provide free education for children whose parents were too poor to send them to school (see Chapter 12). Countless children were to benefit from the help which Shaftesbury gave them.

Despite the great sympathy he always felt for the poor and the work he did for them, Shaftesbury was a strong Tory and, to the end of his life, remained opposed to any form of socialism in politics.

For your amusement . . .

These regulations were in force in a cotton mill office in Burnley in 1852:
1. Godliness, cleanliness and punctuality are the necessities of a good business.
2. This firm has reduced the hours of work, and the clerical staff will now have to be present between the hours of 7 a.m. and 6 p.m. on weekdays.
3. Clothing must be of a sombre nature. The clerical staff will not disport themselves in raiment of bright colours nor will they wear hose unless in good repair.
4. Daily prayers will be held each morning in the main office. The clerical staff will be present.
5. Overshoes and top-coats may not be worn in the office but neck scarves and headwear may be worn in inclement weather.

"The sketch here given is intended to represent Ann Ambler and William Dyson, hurriers in Messrs Ditchforth and Clay's colliery at Elland, in the act of being drawn up cross-lapped upon the clatch-iron by a woman. As soon as they arrived at the top the handle was made fast by a bolt drawn from the upright post; the woman then grasped a hand of both at the same time, and by main force brought them to land. The corve on these occasions is detached from the hooks to render the load lighter."•

58   *The pit head. How do miners get to the surface today?*

6. A stove is provided for the benefit of the clerical staff. Coal and wood must be kept in the locker. It is recommended that each member of the clerical staff bring 4 pounds of coal each day during the cold weather.

7. No member of the clerical staff may leave the room without the permission of Mr. Rogers. The calls of nature are permitted and the clerical staff may use the garden below the second gate. This area must be kept in good order.

8. No talking is allowed during business hours.

9. The craving of tobacco, wines and spirits are a human weakness and as such is forbidden to all members of the clerical staff.

10. Now that the hours of business have been drastically reduced the partaking of food is allowed between 11.30 a.m. and noon, but work will not on any account cease.

11. Members of the clerical staff will provide their own pens. A new sharpener is available on application to Mr. Rogers.

12. Mr. Rogers will nominate a senior clerk to be responsible for the cleanliness of the main office and private offices, and all boys and juniors will report to him 40 minutes before prayers and will remain after closing hours for similar work. Brushes, brooms, scrubbers, and soap are provided by the owners.

13. The new increased weekly wages are hereunder detailed: junior boys (up to 11 years) 1/4, boys (to 14 years) 2/1, juniors 4/8, junior clerks 8/7, clerks 10/9, senior clerks (after 15 years with the owners) 21/-. The owners recognise the generosity of the new labour laws but will expect a great rise in output of work to compensate for these near Utopian conditions.

Follow up Work

1. *What were the pauper children? Explain fully whether there is any truth in this statement which has been made about them: "Their young lives were spent at best in monotonous toil, at worst in a hell of human cruelty."*

2. *Look at the picture of the "free" children and read the quotation from the 1832 Commission. Then write an account of the life of a young child in one of the worst types of cotton mills.*

3. *What part did Robert Owen play in the factory reform movement?*

4. *Write down in note form the provisions of the 1832, 1844, and 1847 Factory Acts. Then learn these provisions.*

5. *Look at the pictures and read the quotations from the Mines Commission. Imagine you were a child in a coal mine in 1840. Write an account of your experiences.*

6. *Learn the provisions of the 1842 Mines Act.*

7. *In what ways did Lord Shaftesbury help the poor during the 19th century?*

8. *Read the following quotation carefully, and then answer the questions that follow:*

"*In conclusion, then, it is proved, by a preponderance of seventy-two witnesses against seventeen, that the health of these employed in cotton mills is nowise inferior to that in other occupations; and, secondly, it is proved by tables drawn up by the secretary of a sick club . . . that the health of the factory children is decidedly superior to that of the labouring poor otherwise employed.*"

(From the Factory Report, 1844)

a) *Was this passage quoted by a supporter or by an opponent of reform?*

b) *What bad effects did the conditions in the factories have upon the children working in them?*

c) *Who do you think opposed reform and why did they do so?*

d) *Name two Acts which had already been passed to improve factory conditions, and give their dates.*

e) *What regulations had been laid down by the most successful Factory Act which had already been passed?*

(Welsh Joint Education Committee, CSE, 1966)

9 Shipping
1800-1939

Steam Power

In March 1802 spectators on the Forth-Clyde Canal watched a tiny steam tug, the *Charlotte Dundas,* tow two 70 tonne barges. For 30 km the little steamer chugged against a head wind so strong that no other boats were launched. Six hours later the barges were drawn into Port Dundas dock at Glasgow. William Symington, the builder of the *Charlotte Dundas*, had proved that a steamer could be driven by paddle wheels (Plate 59).

Symington hoped that his steamboats would be used regularly by canal companies, but the directors of the Forth-Clyde Canal, fearing that the wash from the steamers would damage the canal banks, banned them. The Duke of Bridgewater, the famous "Canal Duke", gave Symington permission to try steamers on his canals, but unfortunately the Duke died before the tests could take place. No one else

59   *A cutaway view of a paddle steamer.*

60 *Henry Bell's steamboat the* Comet.

in Britain showed any interest in Symington's steamboat and despite his importance in shipping history, he died almost penniless.

Meanwhile Robert Fulton, an American who had watched the *Charlotte Dundas* being used, designed a vessel of his own, the *Clermont*. In 1807 the *Clermont* sailed 240 km up the Hudson River. As the boat steamed noisily along, a newspaper reporter noted the amazement shown by the other sailors. "They saw with astonishment that it was rapidly coming towards them, and when it came so near that the noise of the machinery and paddles was heard, the crews, in some instances, shrank beneath their decks from the terrific sight, or left their vessels to go ashore, whilst others prostrated themselves and besought Providence to protect them from the approach of the horrible monster which was marching on the waves and lighting its path by vomiting fire."

Henry Bell

In Britain, Henry Bell built the *Comet*, a steamer which was designed to carry passengers along the Clyde from Glasgow to Greenock. In August 1812 Bell advertised in the *Glasgow Chronicle*.

"The steamboat *Comet* between Glasgow, Greenock, and Helensburgh. For passengers only. The subscriber, having, at much expense,

117

61 *The arrival of the* Great Western *steamer at New York in 1838.*

fitted up a handsome vessel to ply the river Clyde from Glasgow, to
sail by the power of air, wind, and steam, intends that the vessel shall
leave the Broomielaw on Tuesdays, Thursdays, and Saturdays, about
mid-day, or such hour thereafter as may answer from the state of the
tide, and to leave Greenock on Mondays, Wednesdays and Fridays, in
the morning to suit the tide.

The elegance, safety, comfort, and speed of this vessel require only
to be seen to meet the approbation of the public and the proprietor
is determined to do everything in his power to merit general support.

The terms are for the present fixed at 4 shillings for the best cabin
and 3 shillings for the second."

The *Comet* was the first of many steamboats which were later to
be built on the Clyde (Plate 60).

Steamboats were soon crossing to Ireland and France and then in
1819 an American steamboat, the *Savannah,* crossed the Atlantic.
Most of the voyage was by sail and the engines were only used for
part of the time. It was a Dutch boat, the *Curacao,* which in 1827
made the first Atlantic crossing using steam only.

118

Brunel

During the 1830's a number of steamships crossed the Atlantic, and in 1838 Brunel's *Great Western* was launched. He visualised his Great Western Railway being linked at Bristol with ships which could sail to New York, and had begun to build a 1,300 tonne paddle steamer—the *Great Western*. Shipping companies saw this as a challenge and two other trans-Atlantic steamers were planned. In April 1838 a small boat, the *Sirius*, sailed from London to New York by way of Cork. Four days later the *Great Western* left Bristol. Both ships met heavy seas but the *Great Western* rode them with ease. The *Sirius* on the other hand was in great danger and at one point her captain, Lieutenant Roberts, had to threaten his crew with a pistol to suppress a mutiny. Slowly the *Great Western* overhauled her rival but it was the *Sirius* which arrived first, just a few hours before Brunel's ship. The really important fact was that Brunel had proved that his ship could carry adequate fuel, for when she docked there were still 200 tonnes of coal left. The *Sirius* on the other hand had almost exhausted her fuel and had been very close to drifting helplessly in the open sea.

119

To the crowds who gathered to see the *Great Western* dock, it was obvious that here was a steamer which offered a fast and safe way of crossing from the Old World to the New. Next day the American paper the *Morning Herald* reported the scene. "The approach of the *Great Western* to the harbour and in front of the Battery was most magnificent. The sky was clear—the crowds immense. The Battery was filled with the human multitude, one half of whom were females, their faces covered with smiles, and their delicate persons with the gayest attire. Below, on the broad blue water, appeared this huge thing of life, with four masts and emitting volumes of smoke" (Plate 61).

During the years that followed several famous steamship lines were established in Britain, including Peninsular and Orient (P & O) and Cunard. Brunel himself continued to design boats and in 1845 he built the *Great Britain*. This boat was made of iron and the paddle wheels were replaced by a screw propeller. The *Great Britain* crossed the Atlantic in $14\frac{1}{2}$ days, but in 1846 by an unfortunate navigational error she ran aground off the Irish coast. Later she was re-floated and used for many years on the Australia run.

Despite the progress that had been made, steam did not rapidly replace sails, as you can see from the table on page 122. Steamships were not always reliable and their high consumption of fuel meant that cargo had to be sacrificed to carry coal and extra fresh water for the boilers. The early steamships had also to face competition from the clippers, the finest sailing ships of all time. These beautifully built boats with vast sails, raced home from China to Britain with the first of the tea crop. The most famous of them all, the *Cutty Sark*, has been preserved at Greenwich. This boat in 1888 reached a speed of 17 knots and overtook the P & O's fastest steamship.

Fine ships though they were the clippers were fighting a losing battle. Rapid strides were made in marine engineering and steamships became increasingly efficient. In 1854 John Elder's compound engine made it possible to economise on fuel. By Elder's method steam drove one piston and then passed to another cylinder to drive a second piston. The saving in fuel meant that more cargo could be carried. The opening of the Suez Canal in 1869 was a very important factor in the struggle between steam and sail. Unreliable inland winds made the canal unsuitable for sailing ships and the clippers were compelled to use the longer and more expensive route round the Cape of Good Hope.

62 *The* Great Britain *at her launching by the Prince Consort in 1843.*

A development of marine engineering also meant that more power-ful steamships could be built. In 1853 Brunel began the *Great Eastern*—208m long with cargo capacity of 18,000 tonnes. The *Great Western* which he had designed less than 20 years before could only take 1,300 tonnes. Brunel intended the *Great Eastern* to be the finest boat of all time. She was to be driven by paddles, a screw propeller, and even sails if they were needed. Her interior was to be luxurious, and there was accommodation for 4,000 passengers. The building of the *Great Eastern* was an immense task and at times it seemed doubtful if the ship would ever be completed. After months of delay she was ready to be launched in 1857. The launching of this huge ship, which should have been an occasion, turned out to be a fiasco. The ship stuck fast as she slid into the water and despite every effort nothing could move her. It was not until the flood tides some months later that she finally launched herself. The *Great Eastern* was an excellent passenger ship, but despite all the comforts she offered there were never enough passengers to sail in her. Each voyage lost her owners money and eventually she had to be withdrawn from service. As a great liner she was a disastrous failure but she later performed an invaluable service, for she was the only boat large enough to carry, and lay, the telegraph cable between Europe and America.

In 1856 Bessemer invented his converter and in 1866 Siemens perfected his open hearth process of making steel. These inventions led to a much greater output of cheap steel and after 1880 the ship-building industry benefited considerably, for steel boats were lighter and stronger than iron. The general speed and efficiency of ship's engines was further improved when Charles Parsons invented the turbine in 1897. The turbine was a type of rotary engine with a number of blades which were driven by steam. Parsons waited for the annual naval review at Spithead to show how efficient his turbine engine was.

Ships registered in Britain

	Sailing Ships	Steam Ships	Motor Vessels
1820	21,935	34	...
1830	18,876	298	...
1840	21,883	771	...
1850	24,797	1,187	...
1860	25,663	2,000	...
1870	23,189	3,178	...
1880	19,938	5,247	...
1890	14,181	7,410	...
1900	10,773	9,209	...
1910	9,090	12,000	...
1920	6,309	12,307	...
1930	5,098	9,729	3,237
1938	4,019	7,441	5,789

As the Lords of the Admiralty inspected the assembled warships they were amazed to see a small boat speeding rapidly amongst the fleet. Naval vessels tried to intercept it but Parsons's *Turbinia* could travel at 35 knots, 5 knots faster than any other boat. The naval officials were sufficiently impressed to order these new engines and, in addition, large shipping companies soon saw the value of turbines.

In the early years of the 20th century some magnificent ships were built. Probably the greatest of these was the *Mauretania* which was launched in 1907. For nearly twenty years this beautiful boat held the Blue Riband of the Atlantic, the trophy given to the ship which could make the fastest crossing. The *Mauretania* and her sister ship, the ill-fated *Lusitania*, brought a new standard of luxury to trans-Atlantic liners.

63 *The* Queen Mary, *now a floating museum and amusements centre in the USA.*

One of the largest of these liners was the 50,000 tonne *Titanic*, which began her maiden voyage in 1912. It was claimed that she was unsinkable and insufficient lifeboats were carried. A radio message was received that there were icebergs in her path but an error was made and the captain was not informed. The great vessel steamed through the night directly into an iceberg. Of the 2,200 passengers on board, only 700 were saved.

When motor vessels began to be used in the early 1900's oil was too dear to replace coal but gradually the number of motor ships increased and by the 1930's more motor ships were launched than steam. Britain, however, did not take full advantage of these new developments and although in 1939 we still had the largest merchant fleet in the world, other countries were catching us up. In the building

64 *The* Queen Elizabeth II, *launched in 1967.*

of vast liners, Britain still led the world. The 81,000 tonne *Queen Mary* was launched in 1936 and the 85,000 tonne *Queen Elizabeth* in 1940. With the overwhelming competition from aircraft it seems improbable that ships quite so large will ever be built again, though the new *Queen Elizabeth II,* launched in 1967, is a notable exception.

The second half of the 19th century saw many improvements in passenger travel but at first conditions for merchant seamen were appalling. Not only were the crew's quarters atrocious but there existed what were rightly called "coffin ships". These were boats which were heavily insured and then sent to sea overloaded and in poor condition, with no regard for what happened to the sailors. Samuel Plimsoll, the "Sailors' friend", fought against this in the House of Commons, and in 1876 Parliament made the load line, the Plimsoll line as it was called, compulsory. From then on ships have had a line painted round their hulls, and it has been illegal to load ships beyond the point where the line is beneath the water.

Follow up Work

1. *What major developments took place in marine engineering during the 19th century?*
2. *What part did Brunel play in the progress of steamships?*
3. *a) What were "coffin ships"?*
   b) Who was Samuel Plimsoll, and what did he do?

10 Public Health 1815-1950

Conditions in the Large Towns

Plate 65 shows a picture of a Glasgow close in the 19th century. It could have been Leeds, Bradford, Manchester, Liverpool, or a score of industrial towns, for this was typical of the manufacturing towns of the North, many of which had more than doubled their populations between 1800 and 1830.

65 *It was a long time before people realised that such filth and open cesspools helped the spread of dreadful diseases, such as cholera.*

As the people flocked into the towns and the populations grew, builders rushed up houses to accommodate them. There was no planning and no control. Flimsy houses were built back to back, or in tiny, cramped alleys. They were built without water supply, drains, or sewers. One pump often supplied water to 50 houses, or, as in parts of Manchester, there was only one toilet (a hole in the ground) to 215 persons. In most towns only the main streets were swept, and these not often enough. One visitor to Manchester wrote, "A few streets are cleared once a week, the second class once a fortnight, the third class once a month, while the courts and alleys never." In these industrial towns refuse was often dumped anywhere and rivers and brooks were sometimes the only sewers. In some districts of Newcastle "a mass of filth constitutes the streets", and one official writing from Glasgow could not believe that "so large an amount of filth, crime, misery, and disease existed in one spot in any civilised country".

Water was often desperately short. Only a few towns like Preston had a good supply as did Nottingham, although it had, at the same time, some of the vilest slums in the country. In other towns water was frequently bought from carriers who toured round the streets. It varied in price. In Bradford $13\frac{1}{2}$ litres cost $\frac{1}{2}$p, while in Carlisle it was 36 litres for half a penny. Even when water could be bought it was probably drawn from polluted wells or from streams into which sewage had been emptied.

To the horrors of filth were added the evils of overcrowding. Whole families occupied a single room or even shared it with others. When people could not find houses they lived in cellars without light or heat. In Liverpool alone there were 39,000 living in this way.

The First Reports

It needed a serious outbreak of cholera in 1832 to waken the authorities to the appalling conditions of the towns. 18,000 people died, mostly in the slums, where the disease spread through unclean drinking water. In 1837 fever was rife in the East End of London where thousands of people were crowded together in incredible squalor and space was so scarce that sometimes the dead rotted at home for days through lack of cemeteries. In one graveyard bodies were piled on top of one another and a sudden flood washed away the soil to reveal the arms and legs of the newly buried. The seriousness of the fever outbreak frightened the Government and led to a report by Dr. Southwood

Smith describing the terrible slums of Bethnal Green and Whitechapel.

This is only one extract from the report:

"Bethnal Green. Punderson's Gardens.

Along the centre of the street is an open, sunk gutter, in which filth of every kind is allowed to accumulate and putrefy. A mud bank on each side commonly keeps the contents of this gutter in their situation; but sometimes, and especially in wet weather, the gutter overflows, its contents are poured into the neighbouring houses, and the street is rendered nearly impassable."

It was reports like this that really woke the Victorians to the filth around them. Then in 1842 Edwin Chadwick, the Secretary of the Poor Law Board compiled his *Report on the Sanitary Condition of the Labouring Population of Britain* which covered most of the country.

Today it is almost impossible for us to believe how terrible these conditions were but this extract is one of many later reports from towns all over Britain.

"Few of the streets in the working class area of Bradford are paved at all, none of them properly. In some streets a piece of paving is laid half across the street, opposite one man's tenement, whilst his opposite neighbour contents himself with a slight covering of soft engine ashes, through which the native clay of the subsoil is seen protruding and pools of slop water and filth are visible all over the surface. The dung heaps are found in several parts of the town and open privies are seen in many directions. . . . From the sewers the stench is sometimes very strong and fevers prevail all around. Taking the general condition of Bradford, I am obliged to pronounce it the most filthy town I visited." (James Smith, 1843)

The Public Health Acts

Chadwick was convinced that effective drains, sewers, and water supplies were the main answers to the problem, and when in 1844 a Royal Commission on the State of Large Towns issued its report, it was only too clear that something would have to be done. The Government now had considerable evidence available but it still needed yet another outbreak of cholera in 1847 to compel it to act. In 1848 the first effective Public Health Act was passed. A National Board of Health was to be set up, and included amongst its members were Chadwick, and Lord Shaftesbury. This National Board was given power to create local boards of health in places where conditions were very bad. Unfortunately the Board met immediate hostility. Chadwick himself was unable to tolerate any form of inefficiency and soon made enemies. The owners of slum property opposed the Board in every possible way and the influential *Times* newspaper began a campaign objecting to Government interference. One article spoke of Britain as suffering from a "perpetual Saturday night" and made it clear that cholera was preferable to loss of liberty. The Board of Health only lasted until 1854 by which time it had succeeded in creating local boards of health over less than half the country.

In 1866 there was another cholera epidemic which killed 20,000 people. Partly as a result of this a Sanitary Act was passed by which local authorities had to appoint sanitary inspectors and control obvious dangers to health. Progress came faster now. A Local Government Board was set up and made largely responsible for public health in towns. Then in 1875 a comprehensive Public Health Act was passed. By this all local authorities had to appoint Medical Officers of Health and to ensure that reasonable standards of sanitation and cleanliness were maintained.

There were, however, other factors detrimental to people's health which needed government action. One of these was the sale of adulterated food. The Co-operative Societies owed part of their successful growth to the fact that they only sold pure foodstuffs, but some private manufacturers were deliberately treating their products with injurious chemicals either to make them more presentable or because it was cheaper. It was not until the Sale of Food and Drugs Acts that such actions were effectively made illegal by the appointment of public analysts.

Housing Improvements

The question of slum housing was one which had to be tackled as part of any campaign to improve public health. During the 19th century the demand for houses was far greater than the supply and in many towns terrible slums had developed. These problems were extremely difficult but by the Artisans Dwelling Act, 1875, the government did empower local authorities to demolish slums and re-house the slum dwellers. Some cities like Liverpool made determined attempts to improve housing but over the country as a whole progress was

Board of Health, Winterbourn.

CHOLERA.

THE

CHIEF SYMPTOMS

OF THIS FATAL MALADY ARE A

Relaxed & Disordered State of the Bowels,
PURGING, VOMITING.

Cramp, and Great Coldness.

Any Persons in this Parish taken with the above Symptoms are requested to send *Immediately* either to MR. HAY, or MR. DAY, the Medical Men appointed by the Board of Health established in this Parish in conformity with an Order of the *Privy Council.*

T. WHITFIELD,
Chairman of the Board of Health.

Winterbourn, Sept. 1st. 1832.

WANSBROUGH, Printer, (Albion Office,) Redcliff Street, Bristol.

66

slow and in parts of London tenement flats were incredibly squalid. It would be true to say, however, that by 1900 the general standard of workers' houses had improved considerably and although there were all-too-many black spots there were also privately planned towns like Cadbury's Bourneville and Lord Leverhulme's Port Sunlight where conditions were probably the best in the world.

The Beginning of the Welfare State

After 1850 the Government took more and more interest in the health of the people. Cholera and smallpox had almost disappeared by 1900, but unfortunately widespread poverty and malnutrition still caused tuberculosis to be a dreaded disease. Attempts were made to improve children's health and in 1907 free medical inspection for school children was made compulsory. This was an important step in preventive medicine and the result of these measures was shown by a rapid fall in the death rate for children.

Probably the greatest departure from the attitude of *laissez-faire* (government non-interference) came with the reforms introduced by the Liberal Party between 1906 and 1911. In 1908 they brought happiness to hundreds of thousands of retired people when, for the first time, old age pensions were introduced. It was only 25 pence a week but even this small sum lifted them out of destitution. In post offices all over the country old people wept as they received their first pension. In 1911 the Liberals passed the National Insurance Act. This provided that there should be compulsory health insurance for all manual workers and all non-manual workers who earned less than £160 a year. The employee had to contribute 4d. (1½p) a week, the employer 3d. (1p), and the state 2d. (1p). The workers then became one of a doctor's panel or list of patients and received free medical treatment (though medicines still had to be paid for). For the first time millions of workers no longer lived in dread of being ill. The doctors also benefited for they now received a regular basic income. We can say that although poverty was still rife and slums existed in most of our large towns, the welfare state had, in a sense, begun.

Public Health 1918–1950

The years between the wars saw many more people provided for by national insurance. Even so by 1939 only half the adult population was covered by national health insurance and although our welfare service was far ahead of most countries there were still improvements to be made. Hospitals still depended on flag days and voluntary contributions for many necessary improvements. It was not until the National Health Service Bill of 1946 that the entire population was provided for by the state. By this Act, medical service, prescriptions, dental treatment, and spectacles were to be provided free of charge.

67 *School medical examination, early 1900's.*

In addition all hospitals were to be taken over and administered by the new National Health Service. Since the Act was passed many minor changes have been made and, of course, the weekly contributions payable by individuals have increased, but the main idea of a state medical service remains.

National Assistance

Although the general standard of living rose in the 1920's and 1930's there was still considerable poverty. Surveys were conducted in various towns and results varied. It was found that probably 20% of the population were living in poverty. Much of this was due to the unemployment which prevailed in many areas, but some was caused by low wages, or by sickness. As part of our welfare state an attempt was made to combat this poverty by setting up a National Assistance Board in 1948. Its main object was to supplement the earnings of

131

people who were in real need. We also regard a high level of employment as something to be deliberately aimed at by the Government.

The Housing Problem 1918–1950

In 1918 housing conditions like those shown on Plate 65 remained, and although the position was not as acute as in the 19th century many slums still existed as the following accounts show:

"One family which I visited lived in an odd little house consisting of one bedroom, one ground-floor room; and a basement kitchen opening into a high-walled yard . . .

In the bedroom the bugs were crawling on the walls and dropping on to the beds. "We have tried everything," our hostess explained, "but as fast as we get them down, they come in fresh from houses on either side."

Father, mother, and the two youngest children slept in this room. Three girls slept in the ground-floor room and the two boys in the kitchen."

(*Life's Enchanted Cup*, by Mrs. Peel, Bodley Head 1933)

Or this account of South Wales in 1936:

"Many of the houses in Merthyr Tydfil contained only two rooms, one up and one down, joined by a rickety wooden staircase rotting into holes. The ceilings of the lower rooms are simply the loose floorboards of the upper. Windows are small and low, and at two in the afternoon it is dark inside these houses. Ramshackle sheds in cobbled yards, shared by several cottages, are the only sanitation. There are few back doors, and when I touched the back walls my hand came away, not merely damp but wet, although it was not raining. Rents for these hovels vary from 5/- to 6/6 a week." (Dudley Barker, *Evening Standard*, 1936)

Overcrowding was common in most large cities and in many working class areas bathrooms were a rarity. Almost every large town had slum areas where the houses were unfit for habitation.

In the 1930's, however, slum clearance was tackled in earnest. All over the country new council houses were built and although it was estimated in 1939 that there were still over $\frac{3}{4}$ million houses which were unfit to live in, many of the really bad slum areas had been demolished.

Since the end of the Second World War the housing shortage has always been a major problem. The fact that many war-damaged

132

houses had to be repaired made things even more difficult. Over the years the problem has become less acute, but even today there are large areas in many towns where slums or poor housing remain.

Many other factors played their part in improving the general health of the people. By 1939 almost 12 million workers were entitled to holidays with pay, whereas in 1918 this had been an uncommon luxury. More and more people began to take seaside holidays. Butlin opened his first camps, and resorts all over the country competed to attract workers who once could never have afforded a holiday. People also found it easier to escape into the countryside at week-ends, and youth hostels were built for hikers and cyclists.

Today, although there are groups of people, such as old age pensioners, who live on the edge of poverty, most people enjoy the benefits of an affluent society. Food, housing and public health have all improved, and have played their part in increasing general happiness.

68 *Leeds in 1885.*

The Welfare State

In 1942, when the Second World War was at its height, a committee set up by the Government under the chairmanship of Lord Beveridge, published what became known as the Beveridge Report. The report was in fact a plan to find a solution to the poverty of pre-war days. Beveridge proposed State insurance covering unemployment, sickness, old age, widowhood, and the payment of children's allowances. It was hoped to "make want under any circumstances unnecessary."

Until the war ended little effective action could be taken but the first Act, the National Insurance Act 1946, came into effective operation on July 1st, 1948. All persons over school-leaving age were insurable, the money to pay the "welfare" benefits coming from weekly contributions by insured people and employers, and partly from taxation. At the same time the National Health Service Act provided free medical treatment to all who wished to receive it.

Britain's welfare system was for many years the envy of the world; it has since been copied by many countries and bettered by some.

Follow up Work

1. *"All the streets and dwellings in this ward are stated to be more or less deficient in sewerage, unpaved, full of holes, with deep channels formed by the rain intersecting the roads and annoying the passengers, sometimes rendered untenable by the overflowing of sewers and other more offensive drains, with ash-holes exposed to public view and never emptied; or being wholly wanting, as is frequently the case, the refuse is accumulated in cellars, piled against the walls, or thrown into the streets." (Health of Towns Committee, 1840)*

   a) *Name some of the towns in which conditions like these existed.*

   b) *What caused the Government to have investigations carried out?*

   c) *Name two of the men who carried out these investigations.*

   d) *Apart from filth what other evils were there in these growing industrial towns?*

   e) *What actions did the Government take in 1848 to combat conditions like those in the passage?*

   f) *Who opposed these Government measures? Why?*

2. *What attempts were made during the 19th century to improve housing conditions?*

3. *"Between 1906 and 1911 the Liberals began the welfare state." Explain fully what is meant by this statement.*

4. *What has the Government done since 1918 to combat sickness, poverty, and slum housing conditions?*

5. *Consider your own district and make notes of any parts where slums developed during the 19th century. Try to find out when they were demolished and where new estates were built to re-house the people. Also make notes of any other municipal facilities which improved people's lives and when they were built. This will include schools, public baths, parks, hospitals, libraries, etc.*

6. *Discussion Point:*

   You have read of the improvements which have taken place in the last 150 years. Discuss with your teacher how you think public health and safety can be·further improved today.

11 Medicine 1800-1950

Operations in the 18th Century

At the same time as improvements were taking place in public health, medical knowledge was advancing, and the two together opened the way to the conquest of many of the most feared diseases. At the beginning of the 19th century, despite the work of outstanding men like Jenner who had discovered a vaccine against smallpox, the public generally had a poor opinion of doctors and surgeons. To a certain extent this was unfair, for although there were many quacks there were also some fine surgeons who had performed extremely difficult operations. External growths had been removed and many complicated amputations successfully carried out. In London and Edinburgh there were surgeons who had made a scientific study of human anatomy and who were fully qualified to operate. One of them, Sir Benjamin Brodie, was earning as much as £10,000 a year in 1820. The real obstacle to the progress of surgery was the lack of proper anaesthetics. At times alcohol or opium were used to lessen the pain, and on occasions patients were hypnotised in the hope that they would not be conscious during the operation. Frequently, however, the only recourse was for the patient to be strapped down and for the surgeon to work as quickly as possible. Some surgeons were so dexterous that they could amputate a limb in less than a minute, but the patient must have suffered terrible agony.

The First Anaesthetics

As early as 1798 Humphry Davy, who invented the miners' safety lamp, discovered the value of nitrous oxide, or "laughing gas" as it was called, because of the pleasant sensation it gave. Even so it was not until the 1840's that nitrous oxide was deliberately used by an American dentist to deaden the pain when extracting teeth. More important than laughing gas was the use of ether by another American dentist, William Morton. Ether was so successful as an anaesthetic that it was soon being used for many surgical operations. Then in 1847 James Simpson, a Scottish surgeon, experimented with chloroform on himself and two colleagues. This was a more efficient anaesthetic than ether and after Queen Victoria had been given chloroform at the birth of Prince Leopold it was soon in general use.

Louis Pasteur (1822–1895)

The dreadful sufferings of the past had been removed from operations but almost half the patients still died through their surgical wounds festering and poisoning the blood stream. Although no one realised it germs and bacteria were carried from one patient to another by surgeons in blood-stained clothes and using unsterilised instruments. Louis Pasteur proved that bacteria could be carried in the air or on hands and clothing.

Louis Pasteur was born in a small French village in 1822. His parents made considerable sacrifices to send him to university and by the time he was thirty, such was his outstanding ability that he was made a Professor of Chemistry. In this position he had many research facilities at his disposal and was able to carry out numerous experiments. Through his researches he discovered that if bacteria got into wine vats they could damage the wine. He found that the remedy was to heat the wine to a temperature which would kill any contaminating bacteria. This discovery was most important to a wine-producing country like France, but it was equally as valuable elsewhere for the process, known as pasteurisation, could be applied to milk. Pasteur also saved the French silk industry from a disastrous pest, but a far greater triumph was his discovery of a vaccine against anthrax, a terrible disease which killed 90% of the cattle and sheep in parts of France. Then came what was probably his most famous discovery, a vaccine for rabies. People contracted rabies, a disease which drove its victims insane before they died, through being bitten by mad dogs and wolves. Today it has been eliminated in Britain, and to prevent any risk of it being re-introduced, all animals coming from abroad are put into quarantine for a lengthy period before they are allowed into the country.

Joseph Lister and Antiseptics

It was Pasteur's work on bacteria which led Joseph Lister, a British surgeon, to experiment with the use of antiseptics when operating. In 1865 Lister used carbolic acid as an antiseptic. In his early attempts, although the carbolic acid killed the germs it burned the patients and caused considerable discomfort. Lister diluted the acid and found that it still served its purpose. Even then his operating theatre was sometimes so full of fumes that the doctors and nurses choked and coughed throughout the operation.

69 *1965 stamps commemorating Lister. Left, his carbolic spray.*

X-Ray and Radium

In 1895 the German scientist, Wilhelm Röntgen, discovered X-rays, which were invaluable for revealing broken bones and also for locating tuberculosis in the lungs. Unfortunately the Röntgen rays were in use for some years before it was realised that they could cause skin cancer. Many doctors and nurses died until adequate protection was adopted. Mass X-rays are now carried out all over this country so that tuberculosis can be discovered before it has become serious. In 1898 Pierre and Marie Curie discovered radium which is now used for treating some forms of cancer and is also part of radiotherapy treatment.

Progress in Medicine

Progress in surgery was accompanied by developments in medicine generally. Although the idea of blood letting for almost any complaint was dying out, some of the prescribed treatments were farcical. For example in the middle of the 19th century as a perfectly serious cure for ear-ache it was recommended that the ear should be rubbed hard for fifteen minutes, then a hot onion put inside it, and tobacco smoke blown around the ear drum. One suggested remedy for depression was a quick rub down with a bunch of stinging nettles. Some idea of the stupidity shown even by educated men is indicated by this extract from a country parson's diary.

"The stiony on my right eye-lid still swelled and inflamed very much. As it is commonly said that the eye-lid being rubbed by the tail of a black cat would do it much good if not entirely cure it, and having a black cat, a little before dinner I made a trial of it, and very soon after dinner I found my eye-lid much abated of the swelling and almost free from pain. Any other cat's tail may have the above effect in all probability, but I did my eye-lid with my own Tom Cat's tail..."

Despite the ignorance shown by many doctors considerable research went on. Terrible diseases such as cholera, diphtheria, tuberculosis, tetanus, and polio, have all been overcome, but one of the greatest medical advances in this century was the discovery of penicillin by a Scots bacteriologist, Alexander Fleming.

Alexander Fleming and Penicillin

To a certain extent this discovery was accidental, for one day in 1929 Fleming saw that dangerous bacteria, which he was deliberately cultivating in his laboratory, were being killed by a fungus which could only have come in through the open window. There the accident ended for Fleming was a highly trained scientist. He realised that whatever was killing the bacteria could be of fundamental importance to the study of medicine. In the weeks that followed he concentrated on this strange substance which he called penicillin. Carefully he tested it over and over again, checking which bacteria it killed and how it affected the human blood cells, until he was satisfied that penicillin would really benefit mankind.

The production of the drug proved a great problem and by 1939 the output was still very small. The outbreak of war compelled scientists to search for increased quantities of the fungus which was eventually found to grow in larger amounts on rotten melons. Fleming's discovery saved the lives of thousands of wounded servicemen, for it killed the germs which had infected their wounds. After the war it was produced for civilian patients and has become of inestimable value in treating infections and diseases. Penicillin was the first of the *antibiotics*, that is, substances produced by fungi which will kill other bacteria. Today many other antibiotics are in use, including streptomycin and terramycin, but a danger which scientists must always guard against is the development of bacteria which can resist these drugs.

The Nursing Profession

One other development in the history of medicine which should never be overlooked is that of the nursing profession. At the same time as surgery was progressing and hospitals were being built in many towns, the nursing profession was being transformed. Charles Dickens in *Martin Chuzzlewit* held nurses up to ridicule with his characters Sarah Gamp and Betsey Prig. Drunken, dirty, and ignorant, these two women typified professional nurses at the time. In this passage Dickens explains how Sarah Gamp treats an old man who has complained of feeling ill.

"Mrs. Gamp took him by the collar and gave him a dozen or two hearty shakes backwards and forwards in his chair, that exercise being considered by the disciples of the Betsey Prig school of nursing as exceedingly conducive to repose and highly beneficial to the performance of the nervous functions. Its effect in this instance was to render the patient so giddy and addle-headed, that he could say nothing more; which Mrs. Gamp regarded as the triumph of her art.

'There,' she said, loosening the old man's cravat, in consequence of his being rather black in the face, after this scientific treatment. 'Now, I hope, you're easy in your mind. If you should turn at all faint we can soon revive you, sir, I promise you. Bite a person's thumbs, or turn their fingers the wrong way and they comes to wonderful, Lord bless you.'"

Florence Nightingale (1820–1910)

It was largely due to the efforts of Florence Nightingale that nursing became a respected and respectable profession.

Florence Nightingale came from a wealthy family. An intelligent and strong-willed woman she wanted an independent career, and it was a desire to break away from her Victorian home that led her to think of nursing. She overcame considerable family opposition and by 1853 she was caring for sick gentlewomen in London.

During the Crimean War against Russia in 1854 she became famous. The *Times* newspaper had printed the despatches sent by its correspondent showing the appalling conditions of the military hospitals. The reports led to a public outcry and Sidney Herbert, the Secretary of War and himself a friend of Florence Nightingale, took the unusual step of asking her to lead a party of nurses to the Crimea. She went with a party of thirty-eight nurses to the military hospital at Scutari. The conditions were more horrifying than she had been led to believe. One part of the hospital was over the town's open sewer. There were few surgeons, no bandages, poor food, and inadequate beds. The wounded frequently lay on the floor with their injuries scarcely attended to. Many of them died of gangrene or hospital fever and the organisation was so chaotic that nothing seemed to be done for them.

Florence Nightingale began by forcing the Government officials to provide her with medical equipment. She had the floor of the hospital scrubbed, the men's clothes washed, the beds cleaned and changed. By working for twenty hours a day and personally supervising every part of the hospital, Florence Nightingale transformed the conditions at Scutari. Then "when her administrative and clerical duties were done, before retiring to such rest as she allowed herself, it was her custom to make a last tour of the wards". This was how she gained the immortal title, "The Lady with the Lamp".

When she returned to Britain in 1856 she was acclaimed by the whole nation. Fifty thousand pounds were raised for her services in the Crimea and with this money she founded the Nightingale Home for Training Nurses at St. Thomas's Hospital. It was her school and its methods that really laid the foundation of a nursing profession that could be trusted and admired. Many years were to elapse before nurses were accorded the respect we give them today, but from the time of Florence Nightingale the vision of nurses as gin-sodden old women had vanished for ever.

Follow up Work

1. Why were operations dreaded at the beginning of the 19th century?

2. Describe Florence Nightingale's work under the following headings:
   a) the Crimea,

b) the improving of army medical conditions after the war,
c) the improved training of nurses.
(Metropolitan Regional Examinations Board CSE, 1966)

3. Show how the work of the following medical scientists has benefited mankind:
   a) James Simpson,
   b) Joseph Lister,
   c) Louis Pasteur,
   d) Alexander Fleming.
   (West Yorkshire and Lindsey Regional Examinations Board, 1971)

4. The following are important medical terms: 1) Vaccination 2) Antiseptics 3) Anaesthetics 4) Inoculation 5) X-ray photography.

   In each case write an account of the work of the men who made the most important discoveries in each field, naming the diseases which they hoped to overcome, or the medical problems they were solving, and the extent of success.
   (West Midlands CSE Board, 1966)

5. In 1970 the disease cholera reappeared in the Middle East and in some parts of Eastern Europe. The last cholera epidemic in England was in the 1840's.
   a) Describe the conditions of living in England in the 1840's which encouraged the epidemic.
   b) Explain what steps were taken by the Public Health Act of 1848 to try to prevent another outbreak.
   (Associated Lancashire Schools Examining Board, 1971)

Population 1850–1950

Improved public health, greater medical knowledge, and more scientific care of young children were amongst the most important factors causing an increase in the population from 18 millions in 1851 to almost 45 millions by 1951. In Chapter 1 we saw that the main cause of the population rise from 1700 to 1850 was a fall in the death rate; after 1850, however, the reasons for the increase were more complicated.

The birth rate began to decline in the last quarter of the 19th century. In 1880 it had been over 30 in 1,000, by 1914 it had fallen to almost 20, and by 1939 it was below 15. It is always interesting to find out how far your own families followed this pattern.

There were a number of reasons why parents chose to have smaller families. The Education Act of 1876 made school attendance compulsory and thus children became an expense instead of an additional source of income. Towards the end of the 19th century many people were beginning to enjoy a higher standard of living. They wanted bicycles and later cars, pleasanter houses and wireless sets, and they found it easier to afford these when they had fewer children. In fact during the 1930's it became quite common for parents to have only one child.

Since 1945 the birth rate has been rising. Family allowances and higher wages have all meant that two or three children could be afforded without seriously affecting living standards.

The death rate, which had fallen during the 18th century, rose between 1830 and 1870. This rise occurred mainly in the large towns where living conditions were extremely unhealthy. As we have seen these conditions began to improve after 1870 and then the death rate fell. It fell even more rapidly after 1900 when increasing care was taken of children. Cholera, diphtheria, and later, tuberculosis were almost eliminated and the death rate fell from over 20 in the 1,000 in 1870 to 12 in 1939.

Between 1850 and 1914 almost 2 million people emigrated from Britain, most of them going to Canada, Australia and New Zealand. Since 1945, although emigration has continued, we have had a large number of immigrants from the Commonwealth.

There has also been a noticeable re-distribution of population. People have continued to move from the countryside to the towns but in addition there has been a drift to the prosperous South East from some of our older Northern industrial areas. This has accentuated the housing shortage and urban sprawls around London.

Population 1950–1970's

During the 1960's government statisticians forecast a population explosion even greater than that of the 18th century. By 1975, however, it was clear that the birth rate was falling and that future population figures would have to be completely revised. The original forecast for the year 2000 was 63 millions, now it is calculated at about 60 millions in 2011. It must be stressed that it is impossible to prophesy whether the birth rate will begin to rise again.

12 Education

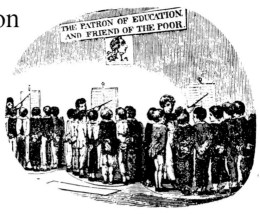

At the beginning of the 19th century there was no organised system of education in England and Wales as there is today. Education was not compulsory and although most upper and middle class children received some teaching, the majority of the working class were either illiterate or could barely read and write.

Public Schools

The children of the upper classes were usually educated either at home or at one of the public schools like Eton, Shrewsbury, or Winchester. In the early years of the 19th century most of these schools offered a very poor education. Little was taught except Latin and Greek and the boys spent hours memorising passages which frequently they did not understand. Food was poor and bullying an accepted feature of school life. Discipline was at times brutal and boys were flogged for the slightest offences. Dr. Keate, one of Eton's headmasters, once birched a group of boys sent to him as confirmation candidates because the list of candidates was on a sheet of paper the same size and shape as a punishment slip. When we consider that the school was so seriously understaffed that the headmaster himself had a class of over 150 boys, it is hardly surprising that he had to exercise such control. In other schools even flogging failed. At Rugby and Winchester the boys mutinied and troops had to be called out to suppress riots.

Many parents were taking their sons away and the public schools were declining rapidly. However, a number of outstanding headmasters began to raise the standards of their own schools and compelled others to follow their example. At Shrewsbury, Samuel Butler broke away from tradition and taught modern subjects as well as classics. He also encouraged boys to take up hobbies and leisure interests. At Rugby, Thomas Arnold adopted similar ideas, playing a most important part in moulding his pupils' characters and in setting an outstanding example to other schools. Thomas Hughes's famous novel, *Tom Brown's Schooldays,* is based on life at this school.

Throughout the 19th century the general standard of the public schools rose rapidly. They became increasingly popular, for there were many wealthy merchants and manufacturers, in addition to the traditional aristocracy and county gentry, who wanted a good education for their sons and were able to pay for it.

Middle Class Education

There were the old-established grammar schools and numerous small private schools for the middle classes who could not afford to send their children to the public schools. By 1800 many of the ancient grammar schools had fallen into disrepute. At Leicester Grammar School in 1820 there were four pupils whereas fifty years before there had been three hundred. At Berkhampstead two clergymen drew an income of £3,000 per annum from money which had been left to the school, and yet neither of them had taught for years. Examples like

70 *Upper School, Eton, 1816. Note how different classes were held in the same hall. Compare this with Plates 71, 73.*

these were common and even when the schools still actively existed, their curriculum, like that of the public schools, was restricted to the classics. In some areas, particularly the North, attempts were made to introduce subjects more suited to an industrial age. Leeds Grammar School attempted to broaden its curriculum but Parliament interfered, ruling that Latin and Greek must be taught first. It was not until after 1850 that the grammar schools really began to break away from the past and to offer a greater variety of subjects.

As for the small private schools, only a few offered a good education and some were atrocious places. In *Nicholas Nickleby* Charles Dickens caricatured one of these schools, when Nicholas meets Wackford Squeers, the headmaster of Dotheboys Hall. "We go upon the practical mode of teaching, the regular education system. C-l-e-a-n, clean, verb active, to make bright. W-i-n, win, d-e-r, winder, a casement. When a boy knows this out of a book, he goes and does it."

Working Class Education

Upper and middle class children were badly taught, the poor were hardly taught at all and at the beginning of the 19th century only one out of every thirty working class children received any education. A few charity schools survived from the 18th century and in some of these the teaching was quite good. There were also the Sunday schools founded by Robert Raikes in 1780. These had spread rapidly in some large towns for in addition to Divinity they gave instruction in the "3 R's". Most common were the dame schools where young children were looked after by old women for a fee of about $1\frac{1}{2}$p a week. Many of these schools were unbelievably bad but some of these old "schoolkeepers" did manage to teach the children to read and write.

Read this eye-witness account of one such school. "In one of these dame schools I found 31 children, from 2 to 7 years of age. The room was a cellar, about 10 feet square and 7 feet high. The only window was less than 18 inches square and not made to open. It was a hot August day and the room was close and miserable. The children sat crammed near to the foot of the old woman's bed. There were no books and insufficient light to read by had books been placed in their hands. The only instruments of instruction were a glassfull of sugar plums and a cane by its side. Every point in instruction being secured by the good old rule of mingling the useful with the sweet."

When the children were too old for the dame schools they would sometimes go on to what were called "common day schools". In these they paid 2½p to 4p a week for which they received very little tuition. Anyone could start a school and it did not matter whether the teacher himself was educated. It was not unusual for people who were themselves only just literate to set up schools of their own.

The Monitorial System

In the early years of the 19th century, schools for the poor were begun by two religious societies: the British and Foreign Schools Society founded by Joseph Lancaster for Noncomformists, and the National Society founded by Andrew Bell for members of the Church of England. Both these Societies used the *Bible* as a textbook and also taught reading, writing, arithmetic. Plate 71 shows what one of these schools would have looked like. All the pupils were in one room, crammed together on narrow benches, and divided into groups. There was only one teacher who taught the school monitors a set of questions and answers. These monitors then taught the other pupils the same questions and answers. Every now and then the master would silence the room and test individual pupils. This method was cheap for it meant that very few teachers were paid. In Manchester there was a school with one thousand children and only three teachers. Obviously such education was very limited and there was much pointless memorising, as this passage shows.

Monitor	"You read the sentence 'the enamel is disposed in crescent shaped ridges.' What is the enamel?
Boy	The hard shining part of the tooth.
Monitor	What do you mean by disposed?
Boy	Placed.
Monitor	The root of the word?
Boy	Pono, I place.
Monitor	What is crescent-shaped?
Boy	Shaped like a moon, before it is a half moon.
Monitor	What is the root of the word?...."

However, these religious schools did ensure that many working class children were at least literate. Even so there were still large numbers who never went to school and in 1830 over 30% of the men and 40% of women still signed the marriage register with a cross.

146

71 *A Lancasterian school. Monitors, standing, are teaching their groups. "Rewards for Good Boys" hang from the ceiling.*

The First Government Grants

The Industrial Revolution created a demand for more skilled workers which meant that a higher standard of education was essential. In 1833 the Government made its first grant to education, £20,000, to be divided between the two religious societies. In the same year some £70,000 was spent on the Royal kennels and stables at Windsor.

After 1840 the Government steadily increased its grant and by 1858 it had risen to £900,000 per annum. Despite this, educational progress was still very slow. Most of the schools were in poor buildings, there were inadequate books, and the teachers were ill-paid and often unqualified. Also in many industrial towns like Birmingham and Manchester only half the children actually went to school.

The Ragged Schools

Although a few more schools now existed many children were unable to attend school because of lack of suitable clothes. This passage is an extract from a report by the Secretary of the Sunday School Union in the 1820's.

"There are an amazing number of children in the Metropolis who are prevented from attending any school whatever from the absolute

72 *Ragged school children in London in the early years of this century.*

want of decent clothing. In Southwark there are at least 2,000 like this. I know of one family of six children where there is only one suit of clothes and each child is obliged alternately to use this when going into the street."

It was partly to combat this that John Pounds, a Portsmouth cobbler, started the Ragged Schools. Lord Shaftesbury became President of the movement and by 1850 there were over 80 ragged schools with more than 8,000 pupils.

Payment by Results

In 1860 Robert Lowe, the minister in charge of education, introduced "payment by results". By this scheme the amount of money a school received from the Government depended upon the number of children on the register, and how well they did in an annual examination in Reading, Writing, and Arithmetic. Each year inspectors tested the children and naturally the teachers tried every subterfuge to ensure that the correct answers were given. Nothing was taught except the facts required, and these were often learnt parrot fashion. The idea appealed to Victorian businessmen who believed that everything should be assessed by the profit shown, and undoubtedly the Government saved considerable money by this method. In practice the scheme had many grave drawbacks for although it ensured a knowledge of the 3 R's it meant that any really intelligent children were never taught anything but the elementary work which the inspectors tested.

73 *A London Board school. The whole school assembled for lessons in one hall under the headmaster's supervision. Later on classes were partitioned or built off the hall.*

The Board Schools

Despite the progress which had been made, education in England

149

was inferior to that of France or Prussia. This was serious, for although Britain was still the leading industrial nation in the world other countries were catching her up. If she was to improve her methods of production more workers would have to be educated.

In 1867 the second Reform Act was passed which gave the vote to the working class in the towns. As Robert Lowe said, "We must educate our masters," for now the workers could choose their own MPs.

In 1870 Forster's Education Act was passed. These were the main provisions of this Act.

1. The schools founded by the two religious societies were to continue and their grants were doubled.

2. In districts where no such schools existed, locally elected School Boards were to be set up. They were to organise Board Schools paid for partly out of the local rates and partly by a government grant. In these schools religious instruction was to be undenominational.

The 1870 Act was an extremely important educational advance. However, education was still not compulsory and at first parents had to pay a weekly fee of one or two pence. Education was made compulsory in 1876 for boys and girls from five to ten years of age. In 1891 elementary education was made free and in 1899 the school leaving age was raised to 12. In these Board Schools the payment by results system continued until 1900, although many areas allowed subjects other than the 3 R's to be taught.

Local Education Authorities and Modern Education

The beginning of the 20th century saw another great educational advance with the passing of the Balfour Act in 1902. This abolished the School Boards set up by the 1870 Act, and replaced them with Local Education Authorities. It gave these the power to provide secondary schools. At first these schools charged fees but they soon began to offer free places to children who were clever enough to pass what was called a scholarship examination. Unfortunately there were still many intelligent children whose parents had to send them to work because of the money they could earn. Nevertheless, by 1913 there were many pupils being educated free of charge at grammar schools.

In 1918 the Fisher Act raised the school-leaving age to 14. The Government tended to economise in education between the wars but an increasing number of pupils gained scholarships to grammar schools. By 1939 it was a common thing for intelligent working class children to go to a grammar school and although still far too few went on to universities, opportunities for children from poor homes were very much better than at any other time.

In 1944 the Butler Act was passed raising the school-leaving age to 15. The same Act provided secondary education for every child.

Since the early 1950's there have been far-reaching changes in the educational system. The most significant are, probably, the move away from selection at 11-plus in favour of comprehensive schooling and the introduction of non-streaming.

The raising of the school-leaving age in 1972 to 16 was much criticized in some quarters, but the general opinion was that this was long overdue.

Follow up Work

Before attempting to answer these questions you must read the chapter and look at the pictures carefully.

1. *Write an account of the public schools in 1800. What attempts were made to improve these schools during the 19th century?*

2. *Write an account of the work of Lancaster and Bell in the founding of the National and British Schools in the early 19th century.*

   Imagine you were a pupil in one of these schools. Describe what your school was like.

   In what other types of school was it possible to receive some education in the early 19th century?

3. *Show how the state educational system has developed, using the following as a guide.*

   a) The 1833 Grant   *b) "Payment by Results"*
   c) Forster's Act 1870 *d) Balfour Act 1902*
   e) Fisher Act 1918   *f) Butler Act 1944*

4. *Discuss with your teacher the development of education in your own district.*

13 Agriculture in the 19th Century

The Years of Distress, 1816–1836

During the Napoleonic Wars farming prospered, but by 1814, even before the Battle of Waterloo, a depression had set in. Wheat prices suddenly slumped and in an attempt to help the farmers Parliament passed the Corn Law of 1815, prohibiting the import of cheap foreign grain when English wheat was below £4 a quarter (350 kg).

This protection did little to prevent the depression which was to continue from 1816 until 1836. Prices of agricultural products fell and many farmers were unable to sell even at a loss. 1821 was a year of very low prices when it was hardly worth taking animals to market to sell them. To add to the difficulty of falling prices was the fact that during the war years farming had prospered and many farmers had borrowed money at high interest rates to buy land and re-build farmhouses; now they had difficulty in repaying their debts. Between 1815 and 1830 many small farmers were ruined.

The Effects of the Speenhamland System

Farm workers had suffered during the Wars for although their wages had risen, prices had increased far more. However, their time of real distress began after 1816. By then the development of enclosures meant that most of them were landless. At the same time discharged soldiers were returning to their villages, and the population continued to increase (see the graph on p. 1). In Southern England agricultural wages were the lowest in the land. Labourers were dependent on the Speenhamland System (see Chapter 4), and the terrible results of this System were now becoming apparent. The very fact that wages were to be subsidised out of the poor rates meant that farmers could get cheap labour. There was no incentive for labourers to earn money, for if they did they lost their allowances, while any villager who owned a

The *Blessings* of *Peace* or the *Curse* of the *Corn Bill*.

cottage was ineligible for poor relief and was compelled to impoverish himself. The labourer was demoralised for it scarcely mattered whether he worked or not. The parish overseers for their part used various methods to make the poor work and thus reduce the allowance paid. In some places they were forcibly auctioned off to farmers who wanted cheap labour, in others they were set to breaking stones for the roads. In many parishes they were sent "on the rounds". This meant going from farmer to farmer, each being compelled to employ them for a short time. This roundsman system was used at Kibworth Beauchamp in Leicestershire. There the householders who employed the labourers had to feed them and pay them 2½p a day. To this the parish added 1½p which gave a man 25 pence a week out of which to feed and clothe his family and pay his rent. As if this acute poverty was not enough the overseers frequently made conditions as unbearable as possible for the poor. One of the most degrading tasks imposed was that of harnessing men and women to the parish cart and forcing them to drag it like horses.

The appalling conditions under which the labourers were living is shown very clearly by William Cobbett who toured England in the

1820's and wrote a book called *Rural Rides*. He described the villagers at Cricklade.

"Their dwellings are little better than pig-beds and their looks indicate that their food is not equal to that of a pig. In my whole life I never saw human wretchedness equal to this, not even amongst the free negroes of America who do not work one day out of four." The labourers' cottages in Leicestershire were "Hovels made of mud and straw, bits of glass, or of old cast-off windows merely stuck in the mud walls. Enter them and look at the bits of chairs and stools, the wretched boards tacked together to serve for a table, the floor made of pebbles or of bare earth."

The labourers lived mainly on bread and cheese, and often the only meat they tasted came from poaching. This was highly dangerous for by the Game Laws of 1816 poachers could be transported. When starving villagers still defied the law landowners introduced spring guns and man traps to kill or maim trespassers. By 1827 so many innocent farm workers had fallen victim to these vicious objects that they were made illegal.

The Labourers' Revolt

The bitterness and hate of the starving labourers grew until in 1830 a series of revolts broke out in Kent, Sussex, and Essex, and spread almost over the whole of the South and South-West. Bands of labourers marched around the countryside destroying machinery, burning ricks, and demanding a minimum wage of $12\frac{1}{2}$ pence a day. Farmers and landowners received threatening letters signed by a mysterious "Captain Swing". Workhouses were destroyed, and some unpopular overseers bundled head-first into manure carts and driven out of the parish. For a few months the labourers controlled Kent and Sussex but there was no proper organisation behind the revolt and when the Government sent in soldiers the outbreak collapsed. Although there had been many threats there had been little actual violence and even some of the farmers had sympathised with the workers. But the ruling class was determined on revenge. A special Commission of Assize was set up to try the labourers and the villagers of the South listened in horror when the savage sentences were read. Nine men were to be hanged, four hundred and fifty-seven men and boys transported. One of those hanged was nineteen; he had knocked the hat off a wealthy farmer's head.

This was the last labourers' revolt. The law had destroyed any spirit the countryman had left. He could now only wait and see what the future offered him.

Follow up Work

1. *Why was there an agricultural depression after 1815? What attempts, if any, did the Government make to help the farmers?*
2. *Explain fully the chief causes of poverty amongst the agricultural labourers between 1815 and 1830.*
3. *Read the text carefully, then write a full account of the life of the farm labourers in Southern England during these years of distress.*
4. *Write an account of the Labourers' Revolt of 1830.*

The Golden Years, 1837–1873
The Poor Law Amendment Act, 1834

By 1837 the worst of the agricultural depression was over and a period of prosperity, sometimes called the "Golden Years", began. A number of factors contributed to this prosperity. The Speenhamland System had not only degraded the labourers, it had led to a considerable rise in the parish poor rates. By 1830 the ratepayers in country districts were paying out £6 million in poor relief. This situation had become intolerable and in 1834 the Poor Law Amendment Act was passed. By this Act all outdoor relief ceased except for the old and sick. Instead the poor had to enter workhouses where conditions were made as unpleasant as possible. Families were separated, workhouse uniforms had to be worn, and silence was compulsory at mealtimes. People grew to hate the "Bastilles", as they were called, and to detest the name Edwin Chadwick, the Secretary of the Poor Law Commission and the man mainly responsible for carrying out the Act. This was unfair, for Chadwick was only performing his duties and was far from inhumane. The Act was intended to be harsh. Its object was to prevent people seeking relief and to deter them from entering the workhouses. Lifting the burden from the poor rates helped ratepayers in the country and restored some self-respect to the labourers by forcing them to look for work. However, there is no doubt that there was still much suffering in many country districts.

Technical Progress

Another factor benefiting farmers at this time was the coming of railways. They were to prove of great value to farmers, providing, as they did, a cheap and convenient form of transport. Food and livestock could be sent to market more easily and fertilisers and heavy machinery brought to the farms. The droving of vast herds of cattle from Wales and Scotland ceased, and the lowing of milk cattle was heard no longer in the back streets of London.

After 1850 rising standards of life in the towns led to greater demands for food and this further stimulated the use of improved farming techniques. Machinery was growing in popularity. Ploughs were improved, reaping and threshing machines more widely used, and steam engines were to be seen in the fields. At the Crystal Palace Exhibition in 1851, British agricultural machinery had an honoured place among Whitworth's great industrial machines and many other achievements of the age (Plate 75).

Land drainage became much more scientific. James Smith of Perthshire drained his land using trenches filled with stones, and then John Read produced a cylindrical clay tile similar to those used today. These methods replaced the old idea of building the land up in ridges and letting the water drain off by furrows.

Once the land was drained it paid to manure it more extensively. In 1840 a German scientist named Liebig published a book showing how plants benefited from certain chemicals in the soil. Soon afterwards a factory was built at Deptford to manufacture superphosphates. At the same time Peruvian guano was coming into the country. This guano was the droppings of sea birds which had accumulated in vast deposits off the coast of Peru. It was exceptionally rich in chemicals, and today is still one of Peru's main exports.

When the Corn Laws were repealed in 1846 many farmers prophesied the ruin of British agriculture. They were too pessimistic for as yet Britain did not import large quantities of foreign wheat. It was not until after 1875 that agriculture felt the full impact of foreign competition.

Backward Methods

There is no doubt that despite a few bad harvests these years were generally very prosperous. Technical progress was made but there

74 *The beginning of the machine age in agriculture.*

were still some farmers who, either through ignorance or lack of capital, failed to make any real advances. For example when steam ploughs and modern reaping devices were in use on some farms there were many areas where the scythe and sickle were still used, while in Sussex and Gloucester ox teams had not completely disappeared. The fact that women and children could be paid low wages and employed in gangs discouraged some farmers from buying machinery.

The Farm Labourers

As for the farm workers their average wages rose by almost 40% but at the same time prices were also increasing. Wages tended to vary over the country. In North Devon they were still as low as 35 pence a week. In some areas rural housing was appalling whereas landlords like the Duke of Bedford were building model houses. Although farm workers were gradually improving their conditions, generally speaking these were not golden years for them.

75 *The Great Exhibition of 1851. Notice the many different machines, both industrial and agricultural.*

Follow up Work

1. Why was the Poor Law Amendment Act 1834 passed? What were its provisions and what were its results?

2. What technical progress was made in agriculture between 1850 and 1875?

The Great Depression, Cause and Effects

The "Golden Years" were not to last; their end came suddenly in 1875. A depression in industry caused a fall in demand for many agricultural products. This was serious but not unusual. Then nature began to add to the farmers' burdens. From 1875 to 1883 almost every spring and summer was cold and wet, and in 1879 and 1882 heavy rain lashed the growing crops and the sun scarcely shone. In the Midlands and the East wheat crops were mildewed, potatoes rotted, and the pastures were ruined by floods. Foot and mouth disease broke out amongst the cattle and liver rot killed over three million sheep.

Farmers lost heavily, but these catastrophes could have been over-come if it had not been for a far worse disaster. The 1870's saw the beginning of intense foreign competition (1875 was the year in which German iron production exceeded the British for the first time). Railways had opened the North American prairies and the steamships meant that wheat could be carried cheaply and rapidly. In 1877 wheat was selling in Britain at £2·85 for 12½kg; by 1894 the price had slumped to £1·15. At the same time wool was being imported from Australia and New Zealand, and the price of British wool fell heavily. Then refrigerated ships were invented and in the 1880's frozen meat and mutton was being brought from New Zealand, Australia and the Argentine. From 1870 to 1890 the price of English beef fell almost continuously, but as many people preferred fresh meat our cattle producers were never quite as badly affected as our wheat growers.

For years the depression dragged on and although the Government twice set up Royal Commissions to consider the problem there was very little it could do to bring back prosperity. It may be wondered why import duties were not charged on imported food and the Corn Laws re-introduced. The fact that England was now an industrial country meant that a large proportion of the people lived in towns and benefited from cheap food. Also manufacturers were afraid that if

159

tariffs were imposed on food, the food producing countries would restrict their own purchases from us.

It was not until 1896 that agricultural prices slowly began to rise. By then many farmers had been ruined, farm rents had fallen by one half, and almost 200,000 farm labourers had deserted the land. However, bad as the depression was, it had not affected the whole of Britain equally. It was the wheat lands of Lincolnshire and East Anglia which were hit worst of all. In the west, where pasture land was more important than arable, conditions had not been as bad, for the demand for dairy produce and fresh meat had continued to grow, except when industry was also depressed.

Agricultural Changes

Everywhere farmers began to adapt themselves to the changing conditions. Fruit growing developed rapidly in Kent, Worcester, and Cambridge, and market gardening spread, especially in the Vale of Evesham and near to London. These years saw the building of a great number of glasshouses, particularly close to London, and the English tomato, which had been rarely eaten in 1870, became common.

One important social movement was the creation of smallholdings. It was believed that if men were given plots of land of about 6 hectares they would be encouraged to remain in farming. After 1892 a number of Acts were passed allowing the acquisition of such smallholdings, but the scheme was never really successful. It was found that farming such small amounts meant very hard work while the returns were usually only small.

The Agricultural Picture, 1870–1914
(Figures in 000,000's)

	1870	1900	1914	
Arable	5·9	4·9	4·4	*Hectares*
Pasture	4·4	6·1	6·4	*Hectares*
Wheat	1·3	0·7	0·7	*Hectares*
Cattle	4·3	5·6	5·8	*Numbers*
Sheep	21·6	19·2	17·2	*Numbers*
Pigs	2	2·2	2·4	*Numbers*

By the outbreak of war in 1914 farming as a whole had made a timely recovery from the depression. Although agriculture was not prosperous many farmers had been able to establish themselves on a sound basis once more.

Follow up Work

1. *"Many farmers had prophesied the ruin of British agriculture in 1846. In fact, there followed the Golden Years, but these were not to last . . . their end came suddenly in 1875. The condition of industry, nature itself, but most of all, overseas development, ruined British farming."*

   a) *Explain why many farmers had prophesied the ruin of British agriculture in 1846.*

   b) *Give reasons why "there followed the Golden Years".*

   c) *Explain in detail why British farming was ruined by the factors suggested in the extract.*

   (East Anglian Examination Board, 1970)

2. *Why was the Western side of England less affected than the Eastern by the depression?*

3. *How did farmers attempt to combat this depression?*

14 Foreign Trade and Free Trade 1800-1970's

Throughout the 18th century the ports of London, Bristol, Newcastle, Liverpool, and Hull bustled with trade as our imports and exports increased rapidly. From the countries bordering the Baltic Sea ships brought timber, iron, hemp and flax; the ships of the great East India Company unloaded tea and spices from the Orient; West Indian sugar and rum were imported; and as the century progressed an increasing number of ships came through the Mediterranean with cotton from the Levant. Our exports were even greater than our imports. Into the holds of the outgoing ships went quantities of woollen goods, and by 1800 almost as many cotton products. Hardware, cutlery, and pottery were exported all over the world, and before the end of the century large amounts of British coal were being sold abroad.

The growth of marine insurance, and particularly the development of Lloyds at this time, shows clearly how important foreign trade was becoming. Lloyds began in a coffee house where merchants met to transact business. Today it is the largest marine insurance group in the world.

The Slave Trade

One of the most lucrative forms of foreign commerce in the 18th century was the slave trade. English slave trading began with John Hawkins who in the 16th century had taken captured negroes from West Africa to the Spanish colonies in the West Indies. The trade had grown and during the 18th century thousands of pounds were invested in ships leaving Liverpool and Bristol.

The trade was triangular. A ship would leave Liverpool or Bristol with cloth, trinkets, and alcoholic spirits, and sail to Africa. There these goods were exchanged for hundreds of negroes who had been captured by slave traders or by enemy tribes. The negroes were herded into the holds of the ships and taken on the Middle Passage to the

162

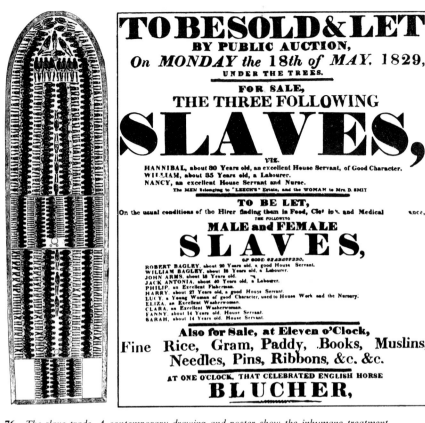

76 *The slave trade. A contemporary drawing and poster show the inhumane treatment of slaves.*

West Indies or to American colonies like Virginia. This passage was horrifying. The negroes were chained in the holds with barely enough room to turn around. If the sea was calm they were taken out in groups and exercised once a day. The exercise gave the crew a chance to wash out the filth from the holds, but even this was rarely done for it was said that slave ships could be smelt from 5 kilometres away. Crowded in these appalling conditions, fed on little else but beans, it was common for as many as a quarter of the slaves to die on the voyage. To the owners of the ships these losses were not excessive since they normally wrote them into the costing of the voyage, and the slaves who survived were sold at enormous profits. In the West Indies the ship was loaded with such goods as rum, sugar, or tobacco to be brought back to England.

163

The slave trade was extremely profitable and the merchants had influential friends in Parliament. Although public opinion was shocked by accounts of the ships and of the lives of the slaves on the plantations, it was years before slavery was abolished. The leader of the abolitionists was William Wilberforce, a wealthy Hull merchant. Wilberforce and his supporters found many who favoured their cause, but Liverpool slave traders exercised all their political influence. The slavers did their best to show how essential slaves were and how valuable the plantations were to Britain. They even tried to maintain that the slave ships helped to train seamen but this theory was completely false for conditions on these ships were so bad that it was said that the sailors rarely sailed on them twice. Wilberforce and his supporters fought a long and difficult battle. Finally in 1807 they succeeded. A law was passed abolishing the slave trade in British ships. Even so it was not until 1833 that slavery itself was abolished in the British Empire.

The Mercantile System

Throughout the 18th century all our foreign trade and our growing Empire were subject to very strict government control under an economic policy known as mercantilism. This policy had definite objects. One of its main purposes was to protect British industry. For this reason the export of machinery and the emigration of skilled artisans was forbidden. At the same time the Government deliberately restricted the cotton industry so that it would not harm the old-established and privileged woollen trade. Another aim of mercantilism was to strengthen the navy. This was one reason why, in 1651 and 1660, the Navigation Acts had been introduced. These enacted that only British ships could trade between Britain and her colonies, and that, in addition, goods coming from a foreign country had to come either in British ships or in that country's own boats. Thus a French ship could not trade between Spain and Britain. It was believed that these Acts would strengthen our merchant navy and in this way provide sailors for the Navy if necessary. Under a mercantilist policy the colonies were very rigidly controlled. The main purpose of all colonies was to supply Britain with raw materials and to buy our manufactured goods. For this reason the West Indies with their sugar were highly prized. Finally one very important feature of mercantilism was that tariffs should be used as much as possible both to protect home industries and to raise revenue. This led to the list of import duties growing so large that it was almost impossible to administer the system. At one time there were even duties on bullrushes!

Such heavy duties were bound to lead to smuggling. Certain places like the Isle of Man, Romney Marsh, and Cornwall became notorious for smugglers' hideouts. In some villages even the squires and the parsons received contraband goods (see p. 175). The ill-paid revenue officers were terrorised by gangs of smugglers and frequently the Government officials themselves connived at the trade. (The great Sir Robert Walpole himself had smuggled while Chancellor of the Exchequer!) The only effective way to prevent this large-scale smuggling was to change the whole mercantilist approach to duties.

Free Trade

By the middle of the 18th century it was clear that mercantilist ideas were becoming less popular for they restricted the development of commerce and business. Industries were growing rapidly, new overseas markets were needed, and manufacturers wanted raw materials like cotton to be imported as cheaply as possible. As the Industrial Revolution gathered momentum industries no longer needed the protection offered by mercantilism.

Then in 1776, Adam Smith, a professor at Glasgow University, wrote his famous book *The Wealth of Nations*. In this book he tried to show that both buyers and sellers would benefit if the tariffs and restrictions were replaced by free trade. In other words countries should import each others' goods without paying duties and then there would be far more bought and sold. This book was widely read and its ideas were to have a great influence in the future.

The first move towards free trade was made when William Pitt the Younger became Prime Minister in 1783. Pitt believed in Adam Smith's ideas, and as part of a movement towards free trade the Eden Treaty with France was signed in 1786. By this treaty the duty on French wines was reduced and in return the French imported British woollens and hardware at lowered tariffs. Unfortunately war broke out between Britain and Revolutionary France in 1793 and the first move towards free trade ended.

It was in the 1820's that the movement towards free trade began in earnest. By then British industries were generally prosperous and manufacturers had no reason to fear foreign competition. In 1823,

William Huskisson, MP for Liverpool, became President of the Board of Trade (he was later to have the macabre distinction of being the first man to be run over by a railway train). Huskisson began a policy leading towards free trade. He revised the Navigation Acts and got rid of many of the old restrictions. Even then most of the Empire's trade remained confined to British or colonial ships and it was not until 1849 that this part of the Navigation Acts was finally repealed. Huskisson also introduced a detailed scheme whereby many of the customs duties were reduced. The maximum protective tariff on manufactured goods was 30%, and the import duties on many raw materials were abolished. In an attempt to help the colonies he introduced a system of colonial preference. Indian silk and Australian wool were charged lower duties than French silk and Spanish wool.

Imports and Exports
(in thousands of £)

	Imports	Exports	Re-Exports
1700	5,840	3,731	2,081
1725	7,095	5,667	2,814
1750	7,772	9,474	3,225
1775	13,550	9,723	5,478
1800	30,571	24,304	18,848

Sir Robert Peel (1788–1850)

Throughout the 1830's the Whig government made little progress towards free trade but when Sir Robert Peel became Prime Minister of the Tory Party in 1841 the free trade movement really gathered force. Sir Robert Peel was the son of the cotton millionaire who had introduced the Pauper Apprentices Act in 1802. Like his father, Peel was interested in social improvements. As Home Secretary he had reformed the penal code in 1823 and abolished the death penalty for over one hundred minor offences out of approximately 230 capital offences. In 1829 he had founded the Metropolitan Police. This was the first police force and the 3,000 top-hatted, blue uniformed members performed an important service in London. It was not long before they were nicknamed "bobbies" or "peelers" after their founder. It was Peel who, in 1836, proved to the Tories that although they should conserve what was good they should reform abuses and wrongs: this

166

77 *Peelers in Hyde Park, 1848, awaiting the Chartists.*

led to the change of the name from Tory to Conservative. In Chapter 8 we saw the part his government played in the reform of the mines and factories.

Peel now began to use his great abilities in the movement towards free trade. Knowing that any reduction of duties would cost money he provided for an alternative source of revenue by re-introducing income tax at 7d. (3p) in the £ on all incomes over £150 a year. Then he began reform of the tariff in 1842. The maximum duty on all imported raw material was to be 5%; on partly manufactured goods 12%; and on fully manufactured goods 20%. At the same time he abolished all export duties on British manufactured goods. Later, in 1845 and 1846, he reduced import duties even further until the duties on 600 articles had been abolished altogether and those on another 400 had been drastically reduced. His reforms meant that manufacturers and consumers could obtain raw materials and food much more cheaply.

The Repeal of the Corn Laws

Then Peel took another, and this time very difficult step, towards free trade. He planned the repeal of the Corn Laws. To understand what these Corn Laws were we need to go back to 1815. During the wars against Napoleon, farmers and landowners had generally prospered and food prices, particularly wheat, had been high. When the War ended agriculturists feared that imported cheap foreign wheat would ruin them, and to protect both landowners and farmers Parliament passed the 1815 Corn Law. By this law no foreign wheat could enter the country when British wheat was less than 80 shillings a quarter (£4 for 12½kg). The law was amended in 1828 and a sliding scale of duties was introduced. By this scale the duty varied according to the price of English wheat.

Throughout the 1830's hatred of the Corn Laws grew. The landlords and the Tory Party supported them because they protected agriculture but the manufacturers maintained that if they were repealed people would get cheaper bread and that countries from which we bought wheat would in turn buy our industrial products. As Britain changed from being an agricultural to a manufacturing country these arguments became more important. In 1839 the Anti-Corn Law League was formed. The League was an organisation with which the manufacturers set out to defeat the landlords. Brilliantly led by two Lancashire manufacturers, Richard Cobden and John Bright, cleverly organised and well financed, the Anti-Corn Law League became a powerful force in the early 1840's. The manufacturers spent hundreds of thousands of pounds employing professional writers and issuing almost 9 million pamphlets. They made great use of "the penny post" which had been founded by Rowland Hill in 1840, and their speakers were able to travel widely on the growing railway network.

The League's arguments were strong and in the House of Commons Peel faced a dilemma. His Tory Party consisted largely of landlords although he himself was a manufacturer. He knew that they would oppose any repeal of the Corn Laws and until 1845 he was able to resist the demands made by Cobden and Bright. In that year nature took a hand. Heavy rain fell throughout the summer and the wheat would not ripen. Then from Ireland came news of a terrible crisis. The Irish depended on the potato crop and all over their country a blight had struck the plants. As the peasants dug up the rotten crop, starvation faced them. The supporters of the League began the cry of "Open the ports", for it was obvious that unless cheap wheat was allowed in countless Irish people would die. As Parliament debated, the Irish starved, until eventually almost one million of them were dead.

Peel became determined to repeal the Corn Laws even though many of his own party opposed him. In 1846, with the help of the Whigs

BOY AND GIRL AT CAHERA.

78 *1845. While Parliament debates the Corn Laws the Irish starve.*

and some Tories, he repealed the Corn Laws. Three days later, despised by many of the Tory Party, he resigned. Robert Peel never returned to political power. He died four years later when he was thrown from a horse. He had been an outstanding politician and few men in the 19th century did more for their country.

The Zenith of Free Trade

The policy of free trade was completed in the 1850's by another outstanding politician, W. E. Gladstone. By 1860 he had abolished the duties on almost all imported food and in that same year Richard Cobden, the anti-Corn Law leader, helped him to negotiate the Cobden-Chevalier treaty, with France. By this treaty Britain also abolished all duties on manufactured goods imported from any country. As was said at the time, "Britain had reached the zenith of free trade."

The Workshop of the World

From 1850 to 1875 Britain was exceptionally prosperous. This was the time when she really was the "workshop of the world". Her

169

industries developed, her population grew, and, with free trade, imports and exports expanded rapidly. In those twenty-five years imports rose from £130 million to almost £300 million and exports from £100 million to over £250 million. Cotton, wool, wheat and timber came into the country in increasing quantities, and coal, cotton and woollen cloth were being sent all over the world. This was the hey-day of Victorian prosperity when it was almost impossible to disagree with the policy of free trade. This does not, of course, mean that free trade was the only cause of our wealth. During those years powerful industries had developed which could withstand any competition; a free trade policy took advantage of this position.

Exports in £000,000's

	1830	1840	1850	1860	1870	1880	1890	1900	1910
Cotton goods	19·4	24·7	28·3	52	71·4	75·6	74·4	69·8	105·9
Woollen goods	4·9	5·8	10	15·7	26·7	20·6	24·5	20·2	31·6
Coal	0·2	0·6	1·3	3·4	5·6	8·4	19·0	38·6	37·8
Machinery	0·2	0·6	1·0	3·8	5·3	9·3	16·4	19·6	29·3

Imports in tonnes

	1850	1860	1870	1880
Cotton	368,200	423,600	680,300	765,100
Wool	42,500	74,650	137,100	216,500
Flax	78,330	78,670	118,300	95,980

It was obvious, however, that Britain's industrial supremacy must eventually be challenged and by the end of the 19th century she was already losing her lead. Germany and the USA had become dangerous rivals in the old industries like coal, metals, and textiles, while in such infant industries as the car and electrical engineering industries they were well ahead of us. Even France was outpacing us in motor vehicle production. These countries had all introduced tariffs to protect their industries and by 1900 Britain was the only major industrial power which still retained free trade.

The Departure from Free Trade

In 1903 came the first important movement towards a re-introduction of tariffs when Joseph Chamberlain formed the Tariff Reform League. Chamberlain was a firm believer in the unity of the British Empire. He advocated a system whereby tariffs should be re-introduced to protect our own industries against foreign competition while products coming from the Empire should only be charged low duties. By this scheme our manufacturers would be protected and at the same time our colonies and dominions would be given preference over other countries.

79 *An election poster of 1906 warned that the end of free trade would mean the end of cheap food and high wages.*

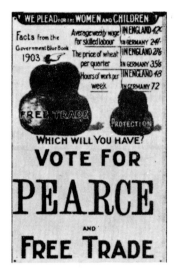

Many businessmen supported Chamberlain's ideas and tariff reform became an important issue at the 1906 elections. However, there was one great weakness in Chamberlain's scheme. If imperial preference was introduced this would necessitate tariffs on food imported from foreign countries. In the early years of the 20th century food was extremely cheap and working people were wholeheartedly opposed to any increase in the cost of living. Election posters like the one in Plate 79 proved extremely effective and the Tariff Reform League was defeated.

Britain continued her non-tariff policy. In 1915, during the First World War, the McKenna Duties were introduced to prevent luxuries being imported when there was a shortage of ships, but it was not until after the war that any real deviation from free trade began. Then, when trade was bad and our manufacturers were finding foreign goods, especially from Japan, being "dumped" in Britain, the Safeguarding of Industries Act 1921 was introduced. This imposed duties on a large number of imports and was deliberately protective.

The real departure from free trade came in 1932 in the midst of a terrible slump with over three million men unemployed. The Government introduced the Import Duties Act 1932 which provided for a general 10% duty on most imports, including some raw materials and food. This Act did not apply to Empire products and in 1932 the Ottawa agreements provided a policy of definite colonial preference. Thus the idea of free trade had ended. Britain had returned to protective tariffs.

The Common Market

Since the Second World War there has been a movement towards a return to free trade. In 1947 a treaty called the General Agreement on Tariffs and Trade (known as GATT) was signed. This was an agreement between a number of countries throughout the world and its object was to work towards a lowering of tariff barriers.

Far better known, however, is the European Economic Community (EEC), generally called the Common Market. This began with the Treaty of Rome in 1957. Six countries—Belgium, the Netherlands, France, West Germany, Italy, and Luxemburg, agreed gradually to reduce all the customs duties then in force.

Originally Britain was invited to join the Common Market. At the time we felt that it would adversely affect our trade with the Commonwealth. Instead we formed the European Free Trade Association, known as EFTA. This is an association between Britain, Austria, Denmark, Norway, Sweden, Portugal, and Switzerland. Gradually opinion in this country has turned towards membership of the Common Market. It has become increasingly apparent that Europe offers prosperous markets for many of our most important exports. Also many economists now believe that in the future our closest ties will be with European countries.

In 1963 and again in 1967 Great Britain applied for membership of the Common Market, but on both occasions President de Gaulle of France vetoed the application. It was clear, however, that Britain was wanted as a member of the Community and, when negotiations were reopened in 1970, de Gaulle was dead and his successor M. Pompidou was prepared to accept Britain's application. However, as the discussions between British representatives and the Six advanced, a political uproar broke out at home. The Conservative Party clearly favoured membership but many members of the Labour Party maintained that the terms of entry were unfair.

The greatest fear of the anti-marketeers was their belief that entry into the Common Market would mean great increases in the cost of living. Pro-marketeers, however, maintained that membership would raise the standard of living as it had in other countries within the EEC. Bitter arguments for and against entry (including demands for a referendum) divided both the House of Commons and the House of Lords, but in November 1971 Parliament finally voted in favour of joining Europe, linking our future with the larger community of nations. The Labour Party always maintained that when they were returned to power a referendum would be held giving the British people the chance to decide whether to remain in the Common Market. This referendum was held in June 1975 and resulted in a decisive "Yes" vote.

Two other members of EFTA, Norway and Denmark, applied to join the European community. In September 1972, however, a Norwegian referendum decided against entry. A few weeks later Denmark voted overwhelmingly in favour.

The decision to join Europe was of major economic and political importance for Great Britain that it is worth considering some of the changes it brought.

1. Workers and Jobs

From January 1973 British nationals have been able to look for work in any of the other Common Market countries without many of the previous restrictions. Workers who can obtain higher wages in Europe might think it worth moving abroad. Conversely, it also means that nationals of the Common Market countries can qualify for jobs in Britain.

2. Tariffs

On entry into the EEC Britain began to abolish all industrial tariffs existing between her and the Common Market countries. By 1978 there should be no tariffs in force. This means that British manufacturers will not have to pay duty when exporting to other members, but it also means that imports from Common Market countries will be allowed into this country without paying duty. This should mean lower prices for many imports. Our ability to compete successfully both abroad and in the home market will depend on the adaptability and efficiency of British manufacturers.

3. Fishing

Britain's inshore fishermen were strongly opposed to entering the Common Market because they feared competition from European ships fishing near to the British coast. They complained, quite understandably, that the French, who have overfished their own seas, would send their fleets towards Britain. It has been agreed that no foreign fishing ships shall be allowed into British coastal waters until 1983. This time may be extended.

4. The Commonwealth

One of the major obstacles to Britain joining the Common Market was her wish to maintain traditional ties and trade preferences with the Commonwealth. After long negotiations it was agreed that New Zealand butter and cheese would continue to come to Britain for at least five years, paying reduced tariffs, and that the interests of small, sugar-producing countries would also be safeguarded.

5. Food

Before Britain's entry food prices were kept low by the Government paying subsidies to farmers and by Commonwealth preferences. When Britain joined the Common Market these subsidies and preferences were largely abolished, and there is no doubt that the price of food has risen. This is a major concern to the British people already faced with growing inflation and rising prices. Increased industrial output could lead to higher wages which would alleviate this increase in the cost of living.

Follow up Work

1. On a map of the world mark the areas from which we imported timber, flax, tea, sugar, and cotton during the 18th century. Mark in also the "Slave Triangle".

2. *Write an account of the slave trade and show the part played by Wilberforce in its abolition.*

3. *"March 29th, 1777.*

    Andrews the Smuggler brought me this night about 11 o'clock a bagg of Hyson Tea 6 lb weight. He frightened us a little by whistling under the Parlour Window just as we were going to bed. I gave him some Geneva and paid him for the tea at 10/6 per lb."

    (Parson Woodforde's Diary)

    a) *Why did so much smuggling take place in the 18th century?*

    b) *Name some of the places where smuggling was common.*

    c) *What was the economic policy which helped to cause so much smuggling?*

    d) *What was the name given to the officers who attempted to prevent smuggling?*

    e) *Discuss with your teacher how smuggling is carried on today, what is smuggled, and the methods used to catch smugglers.*

4. *What part was played in the free trade movement by Adam Smith, William Pitt the Younger, and Huskisson?*

5. a) *Why was a Free Trade policy beneficial to Britain in the 19th century?*

    b) *What part was played by Peel in bringing about Free Trade?*

    (Scottish Certificate of Education, Ordinary Grade, 1965)

6. *"Even apart from his work for free trade Robert Peel was an outstanding politician." Discuss this statement.*

7. *Imagine that you are:*

    a) *a farmer,*

    b) *a member of the Anti-Corn Law League,*

    c) *Sir Robert Peel in 1846.*

    Write a speech for each person stating your attitude towards the Corn Laws.

    (West Yorkshire and Lindsey Regional Examination Board, 1971)

8. *Why did Joseph Chamberlain campaign against free trade in the period 1903–1906?*

    (West Midlands CSE Board, 1965)

9. *Why did we finally return to protective tariffs in 1932?*

10. *Discuss with your teacher the European Common Market and all that it involves.*

15 Industry in the 19th Century

Although the Industrial Revolution began in the 18th century it was in the 19th century that Britain really became an outstanding industrial nation. Nothing showed this more clearly than the Great Exhibition of 1851 which was held in the Crystal Palace, a magnificent glass and iron building almost 610 metres long and over 120 metres wide, which was especially built for the occasion. There were 19,000 exhibits and the whole scene was so magnificent that Queen Victoria wrote in her diary: "We remained two hours and a half and I came back quite beaten, and my head bewildered, from the myriads of beautiful and wonderful things, which now quite dazzle one's eyes." British manufacturers had reason to be proud of their exhibits for nothing held the visitors' attention so much as our machinery. It was these machines and the extremely high standard of our engineering which really proved that we were " the workshop of the world".

However, we had set a pattern which other countries could begin to copy. In 1867, less than twenty years later, an International Exhibition was held in Paris. As the British observers looked at some of the exhibits from other countries they were amazed at what they saw. Although British products were still of the highest standard foreign competitors were rapidly catching up and in industries such as the chemical industry they were overtaking us.

It was, of course, inevitable that other countries should become industrialised, but despite foreign competition Britain remained for most of the 19th century the world's leading industrial power. The really disturbing feature was that in some of the new industries, particularly the car and electrical industries, other countries were far ahead of us.

Coal Mining

The nineteenth century saw a great increase in the demand for coal. Vast quantities were required for steam engines, railway locomotives, and steamships, for iron and steel industries, gas works, and for domestic use. There was an enormous increase in output. In 1800 it was 10 million tonnes, in 1860 74 million tonnes, and in 1913, when British coal output reached its highest figure, 287 million tonnes.

Throughout the century pits were sunk increasingly deeper. In 1793 one Whitehaven pit was sunk to 298m, but this was exceptional. By 1850 seams were being worked 610m underground, and the Apedale pit in North Staffordshire had reached 645m. By 1890 Ashton Moss near Manchester was sunk to almost 884m.

A number of factors played a part here. After 1815, Davy's lamp meant that deeper pits could be worked, and powerful steam engines were used for winding and draining. However, the deeper the pits were, the greater was the risk of explosions. Between 1845 and 1850 there were a series of terrible accidents in South Wales, Lancashire, and Yorkshire, and many hundreds of miners were killed or badly injured. In an attempt to prevent these disasters, experiments were made with improved methods of ventilation. In 1837 William Fourness of Leeds invented the exhaust fan and other engineers improved it.

80 *Two young girls tipping a tram of coal on to the screens at Rose Bridge Colliery, Wigan.*

81 *A group of miners at Frog Lane Colliery, Bristol.*

Eventually the modern method of ventilation was evolved by which air was forced down one shaft and drawn up another, thus disturbing any pockets of gas. To increase the miners' safety, wire cables were used after 1840 and men were raised and lowered in controlled cages.

By 1914 most pits used mechanical equipment for haulage and ventilation, but although coal cutting machinery had been introduced, over 90 per cent of all coal was still obtained by pick and shovel.

Chemicals

It was essential for the chemical industry to make considerable technical progress during the 19th century as textiles, bleaching, dyeing, soap and glass manufacture were dependent to some extent on chemicals.

Alkali was needed in soap, glass and textile manufacture, and when Leblanc, a Frenchman, discovered how to obtain alkali by treating salt with sulphuric acid in 1791, his process was commonly adopted. By 1825 Charles Tennant employed over 1,000 men making soda in

Glasgow. Tennant also manufactured bleaching powder by a combination of chlorine and lime and this obviated the laborious process of treating the textiles with buttermilk and leaving them in the fields to bleach by sunlight. At times this took months in a damp climate like Lancashire's.

The demand for salt as a chemical led to a great expansion of the chemical industries around salt works, particularly in Cheshire where there were great beds of natural salt. Another very important chemical development was the manufacture of synthetic dyes. Dyes had been made from vegetable products. For example, blue came from the indigo plant, red from madder roots, and yellow from weld. Then in 1856 William Perkin discovered how to make a purple dye from coal tar. From then onwards the chemical dye industries grew but most of the discoveries came from the continent and Germany in particular was ahead in this field.

Another important development in the 19th century was the manufacture of phosphorus matches. At first the workers in this industry suffered from the poisonous vapours of phosphorus which caused them to lose control of their jaw muscles and sometimes to become bald. It was not until after 1845 that a safe way of making matches was discovered.

We saw in Chapter 13 how science came to the aid of agriculture. At the same time doctors were also finding increasing uses for chemicals. Iodine was in such demand as an antiseptic that a flourishing industry grew up to extract iodine from seaweed. The medical profession also demanded chemicals like ether, chloroform and nitrous oxide for anaesthetics.

Electrical Industry

The electrical industry had its beginnings in the experiments of men like Benjamin Franklin who, in the 18th century, flew kites in thunderstorms and obtained sparks at the end of a cord. In the early 19th century Volta, Ohm, and Ampère carried out valuable research and gave their names forever to electricity. A great step forward was made in 1831 when Michael Faraday built an effective electric motor. After that progress was more rapid. In 1837 Charles Wheatstone patented the electric telegraph. The first submarine cable under the English Channel was laid in 1851, and in 1876 a Canadian, Graham Bell, invented the telephone. In the 1870's the incandescent electric light

82 *A steam hammer used for shingling (the process of wrought-iron manufacture) at Wigan in 1895.*

was invented by the American Thomas Edison and the Englishman Joseph Swan. Electric lighting was followed by electric power. The first electric tram ran in Berlin in 1881 and soon after an electric train was in operation in Northern Ireland. A further development in the electrical field came in 1901 with Marconi's invention of wireless telegraphy.

Many of these early inventors had been British but even so Britain lagged behind Germany and America in the consumption of electricity, and partly because of this the electrical manufacturing industry developed slowly. The output of the British electrical industry in 1913 was worth about £30 million, Germany's was £65 million, and America's £74 million.

Engineering

The 19th century saw great progress in mechanical engineering and in the manufacture of precision machine tools. One of the first of the great mechanical engineers was Joseph Bramah who lived from 1748 to 1814. Bramah was an extremely talented inventor who devised amongst other things the pull-down suction tap used in public houses, a device for printing serial numbers on bank notes, and an improved water closet. This water closet could have played an important part in public health in the early 19th century, but, as we saw in Chapter 10, town sewerage facilities were completely inadequate. One of Bramah's greatest inventions was a patent lock. He invented this in 1784 and although a challenge prize of £200 was offered it was not until 1851 that it was eventually picked. Even then it took 51 hours spread over 10 days which meant that it was really thief proof!

The success of Bramah's lock was largely due to one of his employees, Henry Maudslay, who made the tools by which the lock's complicated parts were produced. Maudslay became Bramah's foreman but in 1797, dissatisfied with his wages of £1·50 a week, he set up on his own. The accurate machine tools which Maudslay manufactured were extremely valuable to industry and in particular he improved and popularised the slide rest. With this a metal cutting machine could be held much more firmly than by hand. Maudslay also invented a screw cutting machine which enabled screws of a specific size to be made.

The fact that many of the leading engineers of the 19th century received their early training with him meant that Maudslay had a further influence on machine making. Included amongst these was James Nasmyth who invented the steam hammer (Plate 82, opposite) and who also devised a machine for planing metal. Joseph Whitworth who opened his tool-making factory at Manchester in 1833 was another of Maudslay's pupils. He improved metal planing and drilling machinery and produced a measuring machine which was accurate up to one hundredth of a millimetre. Probably most important of all was his work on the standardisation of gauges for screws and screw threads. Whilst there was no standard for screws and all machine parts varied in size, there was no possibility for mass production of identical

83

machines such as we know today. This development came out at a
fortunate time, when the cotton and textile industries and the railways
were expanding rapidly, and the demand for machines consequently
increasing daily.

Plate 83 shows a picture of one of Whitworth's factories in 1866. On
it you will see lathes and drills and you can also see how his machinery
was mechanically operated by a steam engine outside the workshop.
There is also a travelling crane.

Through the work of engineering inventors like Bramah, Maudslay,
Whitworth and Nasmyth, Britain led the way in the machine age of
the early 19th century.

Textiles

The 19th century saw the localisation of the cotton industry in
Lancashire and of most of the woollen industry in the West Riding
of Yorkshire. By 1840 cotton spinning and weaving was done almost
entirely in factories, but the handloom system was to continue in the
woollen industry for some years. Numerous improvements were made
on the 18th century inventions but the 19th century did not see any
technical advances comparable with the earlier Industrial Revolution.

However, the output of both the cotton and woollen industries increased enormously. By 1900 we were importing almost 906 million kilos of cotton and $226\frac{1}{2}$ million kilos of wool. Although the textile industries were of great importance their exports had fallen behind those of machinery, and more important still was the fact that in India textile factories were in operation using British machinery. In the 20th century both India and Japan were undercutting the prices of our cotton products and capturing much of our overseas trade.

Iron and Steel

The iron industry continued to progress rapidly during the 19th century. In 1828 James Neilson of Glasgow invented the hot air blast. This was a fairly simple device. The blast pipe passed through an oven which heated the air in the pipe. The use of hot air in the blast furnace reduced the quantity of fuel needed to produce a tonne of cast iron from 8 tonnes to less than $2\frac{1}{2}$ tonnes.

Then in 1840 James Nasmyth invented the steam hammer. This hammer was of great importance in forging iron, for not only could it strike with tremendous force, but it could also be brought down so gently as to rest on an egg without cracking the shell. Nasmyth's steam hammer was invaluable for large forgings; without it the paddle shaft of Brunel's *Great Eastern* could never have been forged.

The outstanding feature of the 19th century, however, was the progress made in the manufacture of cheap steel. In 1856 Henry Bessemer invented a converter process. Bessemer was a remarkable inventor who had already devised processes for the manufacture of plate glass, the pressing of cane sugar, and a cheap method of making embossed velvet. Strangely enough before he invented his converter he had had very little experience of the iron industry for he wrote in his autobiography:

"My knowledge of iron metallurgy was very limited and consisted only of such facts as an engineer must necessarily observe in the foundry or smith's shop; but this was in one sense an advantage for me, for I had nothing to unlearn."

As Plate 84 shows, by Bessemer's method molten iron was poured into the converter and then air was blasted upwards through the tuyères. The blast of air brought oxygen into contact with the molten metal and produced a great flame at the top of the converter. In less than half an hour all the carbon was burnt out of the iron and

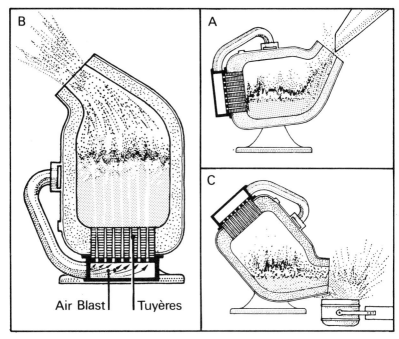

84 *Bessemer's converter.*

The converter was first charged, that is molten iron was poured into it from a ladle. The converter was then raised upright and a blast of air forced through the tuyères or pipes at the bottom of the converter. This blast had to have enough force to prevent the molten iron running down through the tuyères. As the air came into contact with the molten iron it oxidised all the impurities and carbon in it. These were burnt out and a sheet of flame erupted at the mouth B. The converter was then tilted over and the molten metal poured out.

pure malleable metal was left. To convert this into steel the correct amount of carbon was then added.

Bessemer himself wrote of what happened when the converter was first tried out.

"The silicon had been quietly consumed; and the oxygen, next uniting with the carbon, sent up an ever-increasing stream of sparks and a voluminous white flame. Then followed a succession of mild explosions, throwing molten slags and splashes of metal high in the air, the apparatus becoming a veritable volcano in a state of active eruption. No one could approach the converter to turn off the blast, and some low, flat roofs close at hand were in danger of being set on fire by the shower of red-hot matter falling on them. All this was a revelation to me, as I had in no way anticipated such violent results.

However, in ten minutes more the eruption had ceased, the flame died down, and the process was complete."

Bessemer's converter reduced the cost of making steel from £70 to £10 a tonne and Bessemer himself made a fortune out of his own iron and steel plant at Sheffield.

In 1866, William Siemens, a German who had settled in England, invented the open hearth process. The open hearth process was slower than Bessemer's method, but it produced better quality steel and by 1913 had largely displaced the converter. Siemens had been right when he claimed: "I can produce a ton of cast steel for less money than Bessemer and of superior quality."

Although these two processes were successful they both suffered from the disadvantage that neither could use pig iron which contained phosphorus. In Britain the only non-phosphoric ores came from Cumberland, and all other pig iron had to be imported from Spain or Sweden. This problem was solved in 1878 by two cousins, Sidney Gilchrist-Thomas, a London police clerk, and Percy Gilchrist, an ironworks chemist. Sidney Gilchrist-Thomas had never worked in a steelworks but he had studied metallurgy at evening classes and built his own laboratory. The two cousins discovered that if the converter was lined inside with a material called dolomite this would remove the phosphorus from the ore. They demonstrated their results at Middlesbrough in 1879 and within months they were world famous.

Their discovery meant that all British iron ores could now be used for steel making, but the process was even more important for Germany and the United States, who had vast reserves of phosphoric iron ores.

In 1840 the output of steel had been only $1\frac{1}{4}$ million tonnes a year and by 1890 it reached almost 9 million. The effects of cheap and plentiful supplies of steel were felt in many other industries. Railway lines and ship hulls, machines, bridges, and guns were all made of steel, and with the use of steel reinforcing concrete, modern skyscrapers could be built.

Motor Manufacturing

Motor manufacturing was one of the most important of modern industries to begin before the end of the 19th century. Two German engineers, Gottlieb Daimler and Karl Benz, were mainly responsible for the development of the internal combustion engine in 1885. Plate 86 shows Benz's power-driven tricycle. As can be seen the engine was

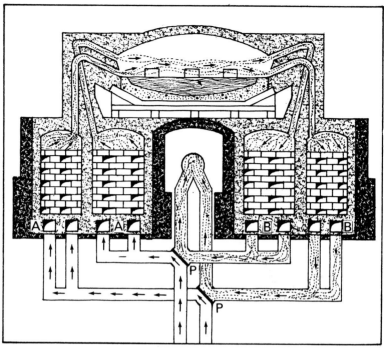

85 *Siemens's open hearth process.*
The open hearth furnace consisted of a shallow trough with a roof over it, and openings at each end. Cold air entered at P and passed through the brick regenerators A A. As the air oxidised the molten iron hot waste gases were formed which heated the regenerators B B. The valve at P was then reversed and the air flowed in the opposite direction. This time the air was preheated in the regenerators so that it was very hot when it came into contact with the molten iron. This saved fuel as well as giving even greater heat. The escaping gases now heated the regenerators A A. The valve was used once again to reverse the air flow.

at the back. It had only one cylinder and as was common with the early vehicles it was steered by a tiller. Although Benz used battery and sparking plug ignition, Daimler ignited the petrol vapour in the carburettor with a platinum tube kept heated by a type of Bunsen burner. These early cars carried water tanks and a pump forced water round the cylinder to cool the engine. The cooling systems were rarely efficient and overheating was common. By 1888 both Benz and Daimler had produced two-cylinder cars. Benz's car in that year had a two-speed gear with a maximum speed of 13km/h in first gear, and 24km/h in second.

France soon began to make motor cars. It was a Frenchman, Emile Levassor, who put the engine at the front and covered it with a bonnet.

86 *Benz's Tricycle, 1888.*

At the same time he introduced the modern differential gear system. In the 1890's two other French engineers, Renault and Peugeot, started what are now world famous firms.

American engineers showed great interest in cars and in 1896 one car won a race at what was then the amazing speed of 41½km/h. In the same year Henry Ford built his first car and in 1901 R. E. Olds was already producing 5,000 Oldsmobiles a year. The American car industry soon adopted mass production methods and with his famous Model T, the "Tin Lizzie", Ford made all his parts interchangeable. This made it much cheaper both to produce and repair cars.

In Britain the development of motor cars was delayed by the "Red Flag" Act (whereby a man had to walk ahead of every car with a red flag). This had been passed in 1865 to control steam cars, and restricted speeds to 6½km/h in the country and to 3km/h in towns. When it was finally repealed in 1896 the new British magazine, the *Autocar,* produced its entire issue in red ink, and a procession of cars was held from London to Brighton. The fact that nearly all the thirty-three vehicles were foreign indicated how backward the British car industry was. However, our car industry could now begin to grow and in 1896 the first English Daimler Company was formed. Famous names like Lanchester, Wolseley, Rover, and Morris and Vauxhall appeared, and in 1907 C. S. Rolls and Henry Royce produced the *Silver Ghost,* a luxury car of the highest class. In the same year an

187

English car, the Talbot, reached a top speed of 161km/h at the Brooklands race track.

The comfort of motor cars improved greatly with the invention of the pneumatic tyre. Dunlop had invented this in 1888 for use on bicycles, and in 1895 Michelin had built the first car tyre. At this time many of the roads were in poor condition for they had been largely neglected with the passing of the stage-coach age. Solid rubber tyres had made journeys uncomfortable, but now punctures became a real hazard, particularly as spare wheels were not carried until after 1900. One of the worst features of the roads was dust, and motorists were compelled to wear goggles. There were some attempts to overcome this dust by watering the road surface each day, but it was not until 1913 that tar spraying became common.

By 1900 the steering wheel had largely replaced the tiller, the accelerator was foot- and not hand-operated, gear changes were more advanced, and electric ignition was in common use. Even so, long journeys were still an adventure and the driver needed to be a mechanic, for breakdowns were all too frequent.

Motor Vehicles on British Roads

	Cars	Goods Vehicles (Not buses)
1904	8,000	4,000
1905	16,000	9,000
1914	132,000	82,000
1925	580,000	224,000
1935	1,477,000	435,000
1938	1,944,000	495,000

Total figure for 1965, including buses and coaches, was 12,939,800.

Between 1900 and 1914 cars improved considerably. Engines became more reliable and windscreens and hoods were the accepted thing. There is no doubt that British engineers were making some of the finest cars in the world but our total output lagged far behind the Americans'. By 1914 when they were manufacturing almost 500,000 vehicles a year our total production was only 25,000. We were also slow to adopt mass production methods and consequently our cars were far more expensive to buy. American cars cost less than £200 each when the average price of a British car was £325. Their high cost was bound to limit sales and restrict the output of the industry. As we shall see, however, British manufacturers like William Morris were soon to realise the advantage of the assembly line method of production.

Follow up Work

1. *In which major industries were Germany and the United States of America overtaking us towards the end of the 19th century?*
2. *What part was played by Bramah, Maudslay, Nasmyth and Whitworth in the growth of the engineering industry?*

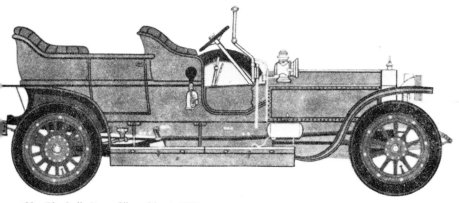

88   *The Rolls Royce* Silver Ghost, *1907.*

3. *What was the importance of Bessemer, Siemens, and Gilchrist-Thomas in the development of the steel industry during the 19th century? Show by labelled sketches how Bessemer's converter and Siemens's open hearth process worked.*
4. *Using the following guide explain how in the 19th century England became "the workshop of the world": the new industrial areas, the invention of machine tools, the development of railways, the mass production of steel.*
   (East Midlands Regional Examinations Board, 1970)
5. *Write a full account in your own words of the development of the motor car industry before 1914. Illustrate it if you wish.*

16 Trade Unions 1850-1914

The New Model Unions

The years after 1850 saw the rise of a very different type of trade union. These were to be called the "New Model Unions". Unlike Robert Owen, the leaders were not interested in transforming society but merely in protecting the interests of their own members. The first of these unions was the Amalgamated Society of Engineers founded in January 1851 (now the AUEW).

The ASE and the other new model unions which were to follow had certain features in common. First of all they were only intended for skilled men. Secondly they demanded a high subscription of five pence a week. Skilled engineers were much more highly paid than unskilled men. Although wages varied in different parts of the country, some idea of this difference can be gained from the fact that in London in 1850 engineers received as much as £1·75 a week when labourers were paid £1·00. Thirdly the new model unions offered their members security against sickness, unemployment, and old age. This was very important at a time when there were no Government schemes to help the workers. Fourthly the new model unions did not believe in strikes if they could be avoided and thought that differences with employers should be settled by discussion.

William Allan, the secretary of the ASE, had said that they wished to settle disputes "without resorting to strikes or any other hostile proceedings". The employers felt otherwise. To them all unions were dangerous and they determined to crush the engineers. At this time many engineers were unemployed and the ASE suggested ending overtime in order to provide more work. This is commonly agreed to today but in 1851 the employers had not yet accepted the right of unions to make such demands. They refused to listen and when the workers insisted on their demands they were locked out of the factories.

The lock-out lasted for over three months and the newly created union could not stand the strain. Starvation drove the workers back and the employers now forced them to sign "the Document" renouncing membership of the ASE.

The Government and the employers thought that unionism had been destroyed once more, but this time they were wrong. The skilled engineers were men of courage and intelligence. "The Document" was ignored because they maintained that it had been unfairly forced upon them and membership of the Union rose rapidly. Its growing strength was an inspiration to other skilled men. Craft unions like the Carpenters, the Bricklayers, the Plasterers, the Boilermakers and the Ironfounders began to organise themselves on the same lines as the ASE. The new model unions were a success.

Their secretaries all had offices in London and this enabled them to meet each other to discuss union matters generally. This group of leading unionists, later called the Junta, played an important part in formulating trade union policy at this time.

The First Trade Union Congress

In addition to the new model unions other trade unions were rapidly growing in strength in the 1860's. Amongst these were the Weavers' and Cotton Spinners' Association, the Ironworkers' Association, and after a great struggle against bitter opposition the National Miners' Union was formed. Many members of these unions were not skilled men; their leaders frequently disagreed with the Junta's policy of a peaceful approach, but finally in 1868 most of the unions in the country came together and the first Trade Union Congress was held.

Trade Unions and the Law

This unity amongst trade unionists was badly needed for there was much opposition to them, both from many members of the public and from Parliament. In 1866 and 1867 the Sheffield outrages occurred. There different cutlers' unions used violence against non-members. Gunpowder was thrown down the chimney of one worker's house and his wife was badly injured. The vicious attacks grew worse until an employer was murdered as he left his house. The middle class began to wonder if this was what all unions would do and the trade unions lost many influential supporters.

A Royal Commission was set up to consider the whole matter of trade unions but while it was still sitting the case of *Hornby* v. *Close* reached the courts. The Treasurer of the Bradford Boilermakers' Society had embezzled part of the Union's funds. He was charged but the judge stated that trade union funds were not protected by law and that no prosecution could be brought. This was extremely serious for it meant that any union official could appropriate funds and the union could do nothing about it.

Shortly after this the Royal Commission reported. This Report was anxiously awaited, and when published was found to be very favourable towards trade unions. According to the Report most unions were respectable and responsible bodies, economically necessary to both workers and employers. The union leaders welcomed the main body of the Report but one statement was less pleasing; the Report condemned peaceful picketing. In other words it was wrong to try to prevent non-strikers from entering a factory even though force was not used.

Two acts resulted from the Report. The first was the Trade Union Act of 1871 which provided that a union's funds were protected by law. The second was the Criminal Law Amendment Act of 1871 which made picketing, or intimidation during a strike, criminal offences. This second Act was open to many interpretations and hostile judges could say that even a threat to strike was intimidation. The trade union leaders realised immediately that this Act could be disastrous to them. They approached Mr. Gladstone, the leader of the Liberal Party which had passed the Act, but he refused to listen to their appeals. Here he made a great error for in 1867 the working men in the towns had been given the vote. At the next election many of them withdrew their support from the Liberals, and the Conservatives, under Benjamin Disraeli, were elected. In return for this support the Conservatives passed the Conspiracy and Protection of Property Act 1875 by which peaceful picketing was legalised.

The years 1850 to 1880 were of great importance in the development of trade unions. Many strong unions had emerged and the TUC claimed over one million members. In addition, two union leaders, Alexander Macdonald and Thomas Burt, had been elected to Parliament. The position of the working class was changing rapidly.

Follow up Work

*1. In the diagram below, the circle represents a shilling which was the
weekly contribution of a member of the Carpenters' Union. The right-
hand column indicates the various benefits which he could obtain from
the Union. Study this carefully, and then answer the questions which
follow.*

The Carpenters' Union

1860

Unemployment benefit
up to 10/- a week

Replacement
of tools lost

Sick benefit
up to 12/- a week

Accident benefit
up to £100

Pension up to 8/- a week

Emigration benefit £6

Funeral benefit £12

a) What do you think were the general functions of this union?
*b) Which action, which we generally associate with trade unions, is
not included?*
*c) In view of the weekly subscription, what section of the workers do
you think would become members of this type of union?*
d) Which was the first union of this type to be formed?
*e) How did the activities of these unions assist the progress of trade
unionism?*

(Welsh Joint Education Committee CSE, 1965)

*2. Explain fully which legal decisions affected the growth of trade unions
up to 1875.*

Trade Unions 1875–1914

Most of the unions which grew up before 1870 had been for skilled or semi-skilled workers. The new model unions with their high subscriptions and cautious approach held very little appeal for the masses of unskilled workers. The years up to 1914 were to see the organisation of these labourers into unions of their own.

Joseph Arch and the Agricultural Labourers' Union

One of the really great men in the story of trade unionism was Joseph Arch, who in 1872 formed an Agricultural Labourers' Union. Arch was a Warwickshire farm labourer of exceptional ability and deep feeling for the sufferings of his fellows. He knew how difficult it would be to organise farm workers who were spread over enormous areas, but as he later wrote, "only organised labour could stand up against employers' tyranny". Arch went from farm to farm slowly spreading his ideas amongst labourers who sometimes worked twelve hours a day for less than 50 pence a week. In February 1872 he was invited to speak to a group of men at the village of Wellesbourne. The meeting was held in the evening, and in the centre of the village a vast crowd of men waited. In Arch's words, "I saw the earnest upturned faces of those poor brothers of mine, faces gaunt with hunger and pinched with want, all looking towards me."

The Union was formed that night and shortly after a strike was called in Warwickshire for a wage of 80 pence a week and a working day from 6 a.m. to 5 p.m. Other workers and members of the middle class wholeheartedly supported Arch, and his Union rapidly grew to 100,000 members. In many areas wage increases were obtained, but to farmers, landowners, and country parsons this Union was something that had to be stamped out. In face of this powerful opposition Arch's Union only lasted until 1875. By then an agricultural depression had set in and there was no chance of increased wages. As for Arch himself, when the farm labourers were given the vote in 1884 he became their first MP. They had not forgotten him.

The London Match Girls

It was in the late 1880's that the movement towards unions for the unskilled really gathered force. The first union was probably the strangest of all. In the East End of London, Bryant and May employed hundreds of girls making matches under the most appalling conditions at a wage of between 40 and 45 pence a week. Led by a journalist named Mrs. Besant they came out on strike. It seemed a hopeless gesture for the strike leaders were promptly sacked, but when their working conditions were made known public opinion was roused. Girls told of how they were paid 1p for making a gross of matchboxes, they showed hands and faces discoloured by chemicals, and one pathetic girl of fifteen was seen to be almost bald through the poisonous fumes of the crowded workshops. Within two weeks the girls' demands were met and they all returned to work as members of the Matchgirls' Union.

The Dockers' "Tanner."

Shortly afterwards the London gasworkers formed a union and obtained a wage increase. Then in 1889 the London dockers struck for a minimum wage of 6d. ($2\frac{1}{2}$p) an hour—the dockers' tanner. The conditions under which they worked were amongst the worst in the country. Some days they worked, but only too often they were so hungry that after one hour's work they had to sign off to buy food with the 2p they had earned. Three men, John Burns, Ben Tillett, and Tom Mann, brought this disorganised mass of labourers out on strike; their demands were $2\frac{1}{2}$p an hour and improvements in the system of casual work. As John Burns, with his black beard and white straw hat, led processions of dockers through London, the general public's imagination was stirred by the demand for the dockers' tanner. Money poured in from all over the country, but even so after two weeks it seemed that the strikers must be defeated. Just as capitulation was near there came an unexpected gift of £30,000. The Australian dockers had collected the money and joined in the fight. Now the Roman Catholic Cardinal Manning came in as mediator and two weeks later the strike ended. The dockers had got their tanner.

The docker's victory was a stimulus to other unions. Unskilled railwaymen formed a union, the agricultural workers were organised again, the miners', seaman's and textile workers' unions developed rapidly. Even black-coated workers began to form unions. Teachers, clerks and shop assistants all began their unions at this time. In 1888 there had been about 750,000 union members; by 1892 the number was more than 1,500,000.

Laws affecting Trade Unions

The early years of the 20th century saw two very important legal decisions which affected trade unions. The first was the Taff Vale Judgment of 1901. The Taff Vale Railway Company had lost money as the result of a strike. They sued the Amalgamated Society of Railway Servants and were awarded £23,000 damages. This put all trade unions in a dangerous position for even if strikes succeeded they could now be sued and probably ruined. In 1906 twenty-nine Labour MPs were returned to Parliament. These MPs took the case up and in 1906 the Liberal Government passed the Trade Disputes Act which reversed the Taff Vale decision. This Act provided that trade unions should not be liable for losses caused by a strike.

In 1909 came the Osborne Case. Many trade unionists paid a compulsory political levy which was taken from their union subscriptions and sent to the Labour Party. These levies provided a large part of Labour Party funds. Osborne, who was a member of the Amalgamated Society of Railway Servants, was a Liberal, and objected to any of his subscription being given to the Labour Party. He took the case to court and the House of Lords confirmed his objections. No part of trade union funds were to be handed over to any political party. However, in 1913 the Trade Union Act was passed which legalised the political levy provided that any individual had the right to "contract out", that is, to refuse to pay the levy.

The Years of Unrest

The years from 1900 to 1914 were prosperous for the country as a whole but as prices rose faster than wages the workers tended to be worse off. There was a great increase in trade union membership and many bitter strikes. The experience of Liverpool shows the mood of the workers just before the First World War. In August 1911 a carters' strike began in Liverpool. It spread to other workers and soon there was almost a general strike in the city. Dockers, railway porters, road sweepers, and tramway workers all came out. This ugly incident was reported by a journalist who had been sent to the city.

"A number of men denounced as 'scabs', or blacklegs, by the strikers were found to run the trams but were stoned on their journeys. On a Sunday morning I saw many trams brought to a standstill and then set on fire. In one tramcar were passengers, including women and children, who became panic-stricken as stones came hurtling through the glass. One woman with a baby in her arms came on to the step, hesitating to jump out. The car was travelling at a furious speed. The driver had lost his nerve, as well he might, under that fusillade of stones. The woman on the step was paralysed with fear and suddenly dropped her baby. It fell into the roadway, and not a man on the side walk moved to pick it up. I tried to break through the crowd in front of me to do so but a woman dashed forward and lifted up the babe which was badly stunned. It was not a pleasant episode for a Sunday afternoon." (From *The Pageant of the Years*, Sir Philip Gibbs).

Then the railwaymen over most of the country came out on strike and at the end of August, before the dispute was settled, internal transport, except in London, had almost completely stopped. 1912 saw serious trouble in the coal mines when almost one million miners went on strike. The ill-feeling between employers and men continued right up to the outbreak of war in 1914. In fact in the first six months of that year there were over 900 strikes, and there seemed to be no solution to the problem of industrial unrest which had prevailed throughout the early years of the 20th century.

Follow up Work

1. *The years after 1870 saw the growth of trade unions for the unskilled. What part did Joseph Arch, Mrs. Besant, John Burns, Ben Tillett and Tom Mann play in it?*

2. *Why were the Taff Vale judgment and the Osborne case so important in the history of trade unionism?*

3. *What evidence is there of industrial unrest in the years immediately preceding the First World War?*

17 Parliament

Reform of the House of Commons

In Britain today we live in what is known as a democracy. This means that the government of the country is determined by the wishes of the majority of the people as shown by the way they vote at a general election. Every man and woman over the age of eighteen, who is not a convict, a lunatic, or a peer, has the right to vote. This freedom of voting is something we should prize very highly for it is probably the most important of all our liberties.

Democracy is something quite new in our history for in the 18th and early 19th centuries Parliament was completely undemocratic. The House of Lords was almost entirely controlled by the great land-owners, and even in the House of Commons all members had to own property. An MP for a borough had to own land worth at least £300 a year, and a county MP land worth £600 a year.

The right to vote was not the same in the towns as in the counties. In the counties the electors had to possess land worth not less than 40 shillings (£2) per annum, which meant that voters were quite numerous. This made county elections more democratic but as bribery and corruption were the normal means of winning an election, contests were very expensive and consequently rarely held. For example, in 1807 the three candidates contesting the two Yorkshire seats spent almost £500,000. In Northamptonshire there were only three actual elections in the whole of the 18th century, as the same member was usually returned unopposed.

In the boroughs or towns, the right to vote varied. In some, all the freemen voted, in others burgage holders (that is people who paid rent to the lord of the manor for their property); in other boroughs there were the scot and lot voters, (those who paid certain taxes); and in others the voters were given the odd name of potwallopers. These were all the inhabitants who could "keep their pots boiling". In practice this meant those who earned enough money to live on without help from the parish rates and this was the nearest approach to democracy at that time, except for Preston where most of the male inhabitants were enfranchised.

Many of the boroughs were still controlled by great landowners. There were boroughs, like Gatton in Surrey where all the houses were owned by one man, whose vote returned two MPs. These were called pocket boroughs because they belonged absolutely to one man, or to put it another way, were "in his pocket". These boroughs were openly bought and sold. In 1795 *The Star* contained this advertisement:

To be sold the borough of Newport in which freeholders have the right to voting for MPs.

Then there were the rotten boroughs where the voters had dwindled to a mere handful who could quite easily be bribed. Even in larger boroughs there were often so few voters that bribery was made easy and then the candidates vied with each other in offering free election feasts of beef and beer, while on occasions noble ladies like the famous Duchess of Devonshire bought votes by kissing the electors.

Elections lasted for days and the candidates stood on what were called the hustings, watching the electors openly register their votes, for there was no secret ballot. To the townspeople these elections were something to which they could look forward. They were far noisier and rowdier than anything experienced today and it was not uncommon for the army to have to control outbreaks of hooliganism. Afterwards if an unpopular candidate had been elected he would frequently have mud thrown at his coach and the windows broken by stones.

Even worse than the corruption was the fact that the electoral system had not taken into account the changes brought about by the Industrial Revolution. The new industrial towns of the North were growing rapidly but most were not represented in Parliament, whilst some ancient boroughs, which were almost deserted, still kept their MPs. Old Sarum in Wiltshire had two MPs and yet it was little more than a desolate hill. Dunwich in Suffolk had almost disappeared beneath the North Sea. Cornwall had 42 MPs including one for Bossiney where there was only one voter. Yet at the same time growing towns like Birmingham, Manchester, and Leeds had no members at Westminster.

At the beginning of the 19th century there were two political parties; the Tories, who were generally rich landowners and supporters of the Church of England, and the Whigs, who were mostly landed magnates, but also interested in trade, and were more tolerant of religious non-conformists. Although in many ways there were no great differences between the two parties, the Whigs were in favour of a programme of gradual reform, including some reform of Parliament. They knew that Parliamentary reform would help their party, for most of the pocket and rotten boroughs were controlled by Tories, and that many middle class manufacturers who were excluded from voting were prepared to support them if given the chance.

In the early 19th century both the middle class and the working class demanded the right to vote. To the middle class businessmen it seemed wholly wrong that although they played an important part in the country's industries many of them should still be unenfranchised. The workers merely saw in political reform a chance to improve their own social conditions.

In the trade depression that followed the end of the Napoleonic Wars there was acute poverty and unemployment in many parts of the country. The demands of the workers for parliamentary reform grew, and riots broke out both in London and in the Northern industrial towns. The Government took savage, repressive measures to crush this political unrest. In 1816 the citizen's right of Habeas Corpus, that is, no imprisonment without trial, was withdrawn. The Gagging Acts of 1817 made it illegal to hold public meetings without permission from the magistrates. In the same year the pathetic "March of the Blanketeers" took place. The starving Manchester handloom weavers, carrying a blanket and what food they could afford, marched to London to present a petition for reform. The Blanketeers were broken up and turned back before they reached Derby. Only one extraordinary brave man actually reached London, but his petition was in vain. Then in 1819 came the tragedy of the Massacre of Peterloo.

From Manchester and the towns around about 50,000 people had gathered. Many regarded the meeting as something of a holiday occasion and brought their wives and families with them. The main speaker was Henry "Orator" Hunt, a man whom the authorities had been watching for some time. As Hunt began to speak not a soldier was visible and the opening of his speech showed how peaceful the mood of the meeting was.

"My friends and fellow countrymen, I must entreat your indulgence for a short time, and I beg you will endeavour to preserve the most perfect silence. I hope you will exercise the all-powerful right of the people in an orderly manner, and if you will perceive any man that wants to raise a disturbance, let him be instantly put down and kept secure."

89 *Hogarth's engraving:* The Election. *Plate 3, "The Polling Scene."*

As he was speaking the armed yeomanry could be seen gathering and then the magistrates ordered them to arrest Hunt. It was this that led to the tragedy that followed. Some of the yeomanry were half-drunk, and their horses got into difficulties in the crowd. They began to strike out with their sabres. Panic broke out and as the crowd struggled to get clear 11 were killed and 400 injured. The viciousness of this incident is shown very clearly by this account in *The Times*.

"A man within five yards of us in another direction had his nose completely taken off by the blow of a sabre. Seeing all this hideous work going on we felt an understandable alarm. We appealed to a constable for assistance. He replied, 'Oh, oh, you then are one of their writers, you must go before the magistrates.' Then we saw a woman on the ground, insensible and with two large gouts of blood on her

90 and 91 *Left, St Peter's Fields, Manchester, called "Peterloo" ironically, after Waterloo. The "medal" in the poster below is a further grim reminder of the Napoleonic campaigns.*

A PETERLOO MEDAL.

chest ... The constables were treating Hunt in a manner in which they were neither justified by law nor humanity, striking him with their staves on the head."

The only action the Government took over the Peterloo Massacre was to introduce even more stringent measures. In 1819 the Six Acts were passed which restricted meetings, curbed the press, and gave magistrates the right of search and arrest on the slightest pretext.

During the 1820's the country was more prosperous and the Government could afford to be less repressive towards the workers. For example, in 1825 the Combination Acts were repealed and trade unions were allowed. However, the political demands of the middle class were growing and as part of their campaign to get the vote, they formed an alliance with the working classes.

The Tories under the Duke of Wellington were bitterly opposed to reform, as was the King, George IV. In 1830 George IV died and his brother William IV succeeded him. Shortly afterwards the Whigs, with Lord Grey as Prime Minister, came into power. The country was now led by a party which supported reform and a King who would not try to oppose any forceful demands.

The Whigs were to meet great difficulties. In March 1831 their first Reform Bill failed to pass through the Commons. They introduced a second. Passed by the House of Commons, it was sent in October 1831 to the House of Lords. The Lords were still predominantly Tory and there were many who supported Lord Wharncliffe when he said, "I would rather forfeit ten thousand times the amount of property I possess, I would rather resign my rank and descend to the station of a common English gentleman, than vote for this Reform Bill as now constituted."

The Bill was defeated in the Lords and as news of this rejection spread over the country, the people were furious. At Derby the gaol was broken open and the prisoners released. Nottingham Castle was set on fire, the tapestries from the walls were torn down and sold to the mob at 15p a metre. In Bristol rioting workers controlled the town for a few days and before order was restored £300,000 worth of damage had been caused, including the destruction of large stocks of Fry's cocoa. Members of the middle class threatened to refuse to pay taxes and to withdraw all their money from the Bank of England. During the last months of 1831 Britain was on the verge of revolution and in this dangerous atmosphere William IV agreed to create sufficient Whig peers to ensure that the Bill was passed. In the face of this threat the Tories in the Lords withdrew their opposition, led by the Duke of Wellington who displayed his usual common sense in ordering an about turn. On June 4th, 1832, the first Parliamentary Reform Act became law.

These were the main provisions of the Act.

1. 56 boroughs lost their MPs and 30 small boroughs were deprived of one of their two members.

2. 42 towns were given MPs. These included the large industrial towns like Birmingham, Sheffield, Manchester, and Leeds.

3. In the counties the vote was given to £10 copyholders, £50 short leaseholders, and £10 long leaseholders, as well as to the 40-shilling freeholders (£2) who had it before.

92 *The Bristol riots, 1831.*

4. In the boroughs the vote was given to anyone owning or occupying property worth £10 a year or more.

The 1832 Reform Act was very important but only the middle class really gained from it. The working classes were bitterly disappointed and as we saw in Chapter 7 many turned to Chartism.

During the years that followed the attitude of both Whigs and Tories changed. As social and political reform progressed the parties altered fundamentally, and gradually the Conservative and Liberal Parties emerged.

By 1866 both parties were determined to extend the franchise and in 1867 the Second Reform Act was passed by the Conservatives. This Act gave the vote to working men in the towns but not as yet to farm labourers in the country. The movement towards democracy now grew more rapidly. The Ballot Act 1872 had made voting secret and put an end to bribery and corruption. Then in 1884 came the Third Reform Act giving the vote to the farm workers. The vast majority of men in Britain were enfranchised, but women still had many years to wait.

The Suffragettes

Although there had been occasional suggestions that women should be given the vote, it was not until the 1890's that the women's suffrage movement really began to gather strength. At the forefront of this movement were three remarkable women, Mrs. Emmeline Pankhurst and her daughters Christabel and Sylvia.

Public opinion, including Queen Victoria herself, was against women having equal rights with men. A woman's place was in the home and it was unthinkable that she could have the same intelligence and capacities as a man. At the suffragettes' many public meetings noisy hecklers yelled insults and threw rotten eggs and even live mice at them. Despite this they continued their campaign courageously and the number of suffragettes rose rapidly. Soon Mrs. Pankhurst was able to say:

"At length the opening day of Parliament arrived. On February 19th, 1906, occurred the first suffrage procession in London. I think there were between three and four hundred women in that procession, poor working women from the East End, for the most part. My eyes were misty with tears as I saw them, standing in line, holding the simple banners which my daughter Sylvia had decorated, waiting for the word of command." (From *My own Story*, Emmeline Pankhurst.)

The suffragettes' tactics varied—sometimes they only shouted their demands at political meetings, or held orderly processions through the streets of London. But on occasion they became more militant and tried to force their way into the House of Commons or chained themselves to the railings outside Parliament, 10 Downing Street or Buckingham Palace, in an attempt to make the leading politicians listen to them. After 1906 hundreds of suffragettes were arrested and imprisoned, usually for short spells. In prison they defied the authorities by going on hunger strikes and an effectively horrifying suffragette poster of the time showed a suffragette being forcibly fed through the nose.

Parliament now introduced a new law. The starving women were released and re-arrested as soon as they were well. This became known as the "Cat and Mouse" Act because the Government resembled a cat playing with a mouse.

In 1912, embittered by the Government's failure to grant them the vote, the suffragettes turned to more violent action. On March 1st the people of London were amazed to see peaceful-looking women suddenly take stones and hammers from their bags and begin to hurl them through shop windows. Next morning's *Daily Mail* reported the scene vividly.

"From every part of the crowded and brilliantly lighted streets came the crash of splintered glass. People started as windows shattered at their sides; suddenly there was another crash in front of them; on the

other side of the street; behind—everywhere. Scared shop assistants came running out on the pavements; traffic stopped; policemen sprang this way and that; five minutes later the streets were a procession of excited groups, each surrounding a woman wrecker being led into custody to the nearest police station. Meanwhile the shopping quarter of London had plunged itself into a sudden twilight. Shutters were hurriedly fitted, the rattle of iron curtains being drawn came from every side. Guards of commissionaires and shop-men were quickly mounted, and any unaccompanied lady in sight, especially, if she carried a hand bag, became an object of menacing suspicion."

This opened an era of vandalism. Valuable pictures were slashed, railway stations burned, and bombs thrown. The suffragette movement had become deliberately hostile to the law. Probably the most tragic story was that of the young suffragette Emily Davidson who flung herself under the King's horse at the Derby. Neither her death nor the attacks on property benefited the suffragettes, for many moderate supporters left the movement. Mrs. Pankhurst herself was sent to prison for three years and many of her followers were arrested.

The troubles continued until, in August 1914, war was declared on Germany. It was the war which really ended the suffragette movement. The suffragettes realised that for the moment defeating Germany was more important than getting the vote and in addition a completely new idea was gained of the part women could play. As more and more men went into the services women were needed and conscripted to make munitions, drive vehicles, work as railway porters and operate signal boxes. It was obvious that the old beliefs about women were out-of-date. In 1918 the vote was given to women over 30, and then in 1928 a further Reform Act enfranchised all women over the age of 21.

The House of Lords

It is important to realise that before any parliamentary bill becomes law in Britain it must be passed by both Houses of Parliament; the House of Commons and the House of Lords. The House of Lords is therefore still of great importance, for not only can it introduce bills of its own but it can also amend and reject bills introduced and passed in the House of Commons.

At the beginning of the 20th century the House of Lords was far more powerful than now. Peers, except for law lords and Bishops, were hereditary, that is, their titles were passed down from father to son.

Although there were over 700 members, only a few ever attended debates and most of these were men of ability who had often something worthwhile to say. The real danger of the House of Lords lay in the fact that the majority of its members were Conservative. They were in a position to prevent any social reforms which the Liberals wished to pass.

As we saw in Chapter 10 the Liberal government of 1906 introduced a number of bills which were intended to improve social conditions. Acts like the Old Age Pensions Act of 1908 and the National Insurance Act of 1911 were the beginnings of our welfare state, but all social schemes cost money. It was obvious to Lloyd George, the fiery Welshman, who was then the Chancellor of the Exchequer, that taxes would have to be increased to pay for the old age pensions. In 1909 he introduced his "People's Budget". Income tax was raised from 1/– to 1/2 (5p to 6p) in the £ and high death duties were to be paid on estates worth between £5,000 and £1 million. In addition a super tax was introduced on incomes over £3,000 per annum, and a land value duty was to be paid by all landowners. Immediately there was an uproar from the Conservative Party. They could not accept Lloyd George's argument that he was "taxing the pleasures of the few in order to spare the sorrow of the myriad". To the rich Conservatives it seemed that they were being robbed of their rights. The House of Lords rejected the Budget and a political uproar broke out.

As he canvassed the people in support of his Budget, Lloyd George lashed the House of Lords with biting comments like, "a fully equipped duke costs as much to keep up as two Dreadnoughts (battleships) and they are just as great a terror and they last longer".

A general election was held in January, 1910, and the Liberals were returned to power. The Conservatives accepted the Budget but the Liberal Party was determined to prevent any further restrictions by the Lords. The Parliament Act 1911 limited the delaying power of the Lords to two years and laid it down that they could neither reject nor amend a finance bill of any kind. The Lords could have rejected this Act when it was debated by them but had they done so they knew that their opponents would have created sufficient Liberal peers to get it passed. For this reason many Conservative lords refrained from voting.

Since then further important changes have taken place in the constitution of the House of Lords. By the Parliament Act of 1949 the delaying period was reduced to one year. In 1958 an Act was passed making it possible to create far more life peers, and women became entitled to sit in the Lords.

Today the House of Lords has some 950 members, who are not paid, but can claim general expenses of up to £8·50 a day as well as travel expenses for attendance. But those who do are for the most part people of ability, who have often been created peers as a reward for their outstanding work for the community, and because their experience and knowledge will be of value to Parliament.

The Labour Party

As we have seen the old Tory and Whig parties gradually changed and the 19th century saw the emergence of the Conservatives and Liberals, both of whom favoured social reforms and some abandonment of *laissez-faire*, that is, a policy whereby the state interferes as little as possible. However, the closing years of the century saw the beginning of another political party which was to have profound effects in the future. This was the Labour Party.

Although the Reform Acts of 1867 and 1884 had given the vote to large numbers of working men it was not until 1892 that the first three independent Labour MPs were elected. They were Keir Hardie, a Scottish miner elected for West Ham, John Burns, one of the leaders of the 1889 dockers' strike, for Battersea, and Havelock Wilson for Middlesbrough. Of these three Keir Hardie was to be the most important in the growth of socialism.

James Keir Hardie came from a poor family and was brought up in a Lanarkshire mining area. He began work at 7 and by the time he was 10 he was working in the mines. A man of great courage and high principles he devoted his life to working class politics. When first elected to Parliament he shocked the House of Commons by arriving wearing a cloth cap and following a procession led by a brass band. In 1893 Keir Hardie helped to found the Independent Labour Party but its future was uncertain and in the 1895 election all its candidates were defeated.

It was not until 1900 that the Labour Party as we know it really began. A conference containing representatives of the trade unions and various socialist societies met and formed the Labour Representation Committee. In 1906 this group took the name Labour Party. At first the progress of this new party was slow. By 1900 it had only 2 MPs including Keir Hardie for Merthyr Tydfil. This number had risen to 29 in 1906 and 45 in 1910. By the outbreak of the First World War the Labour Party was firmly founded. It had its own MPs, its own organisation based on money largely received from the trade unions, and its own newspaper, the *Daily Herald.*

In 1918 the Labour Party issued an official programme advocating the nationalisation of coal, electricity and the railways, and the formulation of a deliberate plan to ensure full employment. At the 1922 election the Labour Party won 142 seats and was already more powerful than the Liberals. It was helped by the fact that quarrels among the Liberal Party leaders had split their Party in two. The Labour Party won an election for the first time in 1924 but as it had not an absolute majority, it depended on the support of the Liberals. Labour remained in power for less than a year. It tried to introduce some reforms but as yet it was still a party without a properly thought-out policy. At the next election it was defeated by the Conservatives.

The Conservatives remained in power for five years and then in 1929 the Labour Party was re-elected once more. Unfortunately, although it was the largest single party, it would have been defeated on any major issue if the Liberals had voted with the Tories. This in itself was a problem for the leader, Ramsay MacDonald, but far worse was the great depression of 1929. We shall read about this in Chapter 19. Here it is sufficient to note that the Labour Party could find no solution to the slump.

In 1931 Ramsay MacDonald and a number of other leaders met the Conservatives and Liberals and agreed to form a "National" cabinet containing 4 Labour, 4 Conservatives and 2 Liberals. There is no doubt that the problems facing MacDonald were immense, but to many Labour supporters this seemed like a betrayal of all their socialist ideals. In the next election the Labour Party was soundly defeated and was to remain in opposition until after the Second World War.

In 1945 the Labour Party was re-elected with an overwhelming majority. It was now able to put into practice some of the measures it had long advocated. These included improved national health services and national assistance, and the nationalisation of the Bank of England, mines, railways, road transport, gas and electricity.

Follow up Work

1. *"In 1800 Britain was almost completely undemocratic." Write an account proving the truth of this statement.*

2. *Write an account of a parliamentary election in a borough at the beginning of the 19th century.*

3. *"The Bill which has just passed into law is not the end but the means of reform." Pamphleteer, 1839.*
   a) *To which Bill does this refer?*
   b) *What Parliamentary reforms were introduced by this Bill?*
   c) *Which subsequent reform acts proved the truth of this statement? Who was given the vote by these Acts?*

4. a) *What were the arguments for and against giving women the same political rights as men?*
   b) *What actions were taken by suffragettes in their campaign for equal rights and with what justification?*
   c) *When, and in what circumstances, were equal rights achieved?*
      (Scottish Certificate of Education, Ordinary Grade, 1965)

5. *What reforms have taken place in the constitution of the House of Lords during this century?*
   Give your views on the proposed new composition of the House of Lords. What can be said for and against the hereditary system?

6. *"Four spectres haunt the poor: old age, accident, sickness and unemployment. We are going to drive hunger from the hearth. We mean to banish the workhouse from the horizon of every workman in the land."*
   Words of the Chancellor of the Exchequer 1911.
   a) *Who was the Chancellor and to what party did he belong?*
   b) *How did this party attempt to remove the "four spectres"?*
   c) *What other social reforms did this party introduce between 1906 and 1914?*
      (Metropolitan Regional Examinations Board, 1971)

7. a) *Who was Keir Hardie?*
   b) *When did the Labour Party really come into existence?*
   c) *Why were the first two Labour governments relatively unsuccessful?*
   d) *Explain some of the Labour Party's policies.*
   e) *When was it able to put some of these policies into effect?*
   f) *What happened to the* Daily Herald?

18 Communications

The Postal System

In the 19th century a revolution in communications paralleled that in industry. In the early years of the century the sending of messages was generally slow and often difficult. For example, news of Nelson's victory and death at Trafalgar in 1805 was dispatched on October 22nd but did not reach London until November 6th. The Duke of Wellington sent word of the defeat of Napoleon at Waterloo on October 19th, 1815, but even this message took three days to reach London and did not reach Manchester until eighteen hours after that, although the mail coach accomplished the journey in record time. At this time most mail and messages were delivered by horse riders or mail coaches although attempts had been made to quicken communications by semaphore signalling which was fairly successful, but only in clear weather, while the German Julius Reuter, founder of the famous Reuter's News Agency, had had the imagination to use pigeons to carry his news items.

Before the invention of the electric telegraph it was understandable that communications from abroad should be delayed, but even within Britain to send a letter was both a costly and a lengthy business. When coaches were replaced by railways after 1830, letters could be sent quicker but the disorganised state of the postal service was still an obstacle to progress.

The reform of the postal services was the work of one outstanding man, Rowland Hill. Hill's father was a Kidderminster schoolmaster of exceptional ability who had founded a school which offered an education far superior to most others at that time. Hill himself had taught at the school but ill-health made him leave teaching and work on a scheme for colonising South Australia.

In 1837 Hill, who, like Bessemer in his field had nothing to "unlearn", published a pamphlet called *Post Office Reform, Its Importance and Practicability*.

Before Hill's proposals were implemented the cost of postage varied

according to distance. There were no stamps and the letter or packet was paid for by the receiver. The system was chaotic and the cost of sending letters was almost prohibitive to poor people. Hill now advocated a low and uniform rate of postage to be pre-paid by stamps. The cost was to depend on the weight of the letter, not on the distance it was carried. He maintained that a cheaper postal service would be more profitable because far more letters would be sent. Despite considerable opposition his ideas were accepted. In 1840 the "penny post" was introduced. At first pre-paid envelopes were used but before long the adhesive stamp came into being. The first of these stamps was the famous Penny Black. "The penny post" was an immediate success and by 1860 almost 600 million letters were sent compared with 77 million in 1838.

94 *The Penny Black.*

The Electric Telegraph

Although the improved postal service was of great importance it was the invention of the electric telegraph that opened the way to a rapid system of communication. Many attempts at sending messages by telegraph had been tried but it was two British scientists, William Cooke and Charles Wheatstone, who were largely responsible for using it successfully. Railway companies soon realised how useful the electric telegraph could be to them and in 1844 the Great Western Railway had a 30½km telegraph line built from Paddington to Slough. A few months later a dramatic incident occurred which made the general public really aware of the importance of this new means of communication. On January 1st, 1845, the operator at Paddington was astonished at receiving this telegraph.

"A murder has just been committed at Salthill and the suspected murderer was seen to take a first class ticket for London by the train which left Slough at 7.42 a.m. He is in the garb of a Quaker with a brown overcoat which reaches nearly down to his feet. He is in the last compartment of the second first class carriage."

The police were contacted immediately and the suspected murderer, a man named John Tawell, was arrested as he left the train. The police now had a new weapon at their disposal.

The development of the telegraph was aided considerably by the invention of the Morse code in 1838 by an American, Samuel Morse, who had himself been experimenting with a telegraph system. The code consisted of a series of dots and dashes replacing letters. It enabled messages to be sent at great speed and is still used today by wireless operators all over the world. Throughout the 1840's telegraph lines spread over Britain and in 1843 Morse suggested the idea of a cable across the Atlantic. This scheme was not taken up, but in 1851 the first submarine cable to France was laid. This scheme was of such value to businessmen that the probability of crossing the Atlantic was given serious thought. In 1857 attempts were made to lay a telegraph cable from Britain to America but the cable broke after less than 483km had been laid. A year later a cable was successfully laid from Ireland to Newfoundland and *The Times* jubilantly announced "Since the discovery by Columbus, nothing has been done which has so enlarged the sphere of human activity." Unfortunately this cable only lasted twenty days before it snapped. It was not until 1866 that Brunel's *Great Eastern,* after a number of attempts, successfully laid a cable across the Atlantic. By the 1870's almost every capital city in the world was connected by telegraph. Messages which had once taken months to send were now being transmitted in minutes.

Meanwhile an American, David Hughes, had invented the first teleprinting machine. Letters, which were typed on a keyboard by the operator, printed themselves at the receiving end. Obviously this made the reception of messages very much easier and less subject to error.

The Telephone

The next major step forward in communications was the invention of the telephone. A German, Reis, demonstrated the first telephone in 1861 and it was with this as his model that a Scottish-born Canadian, Alexander Graham Bell, built the first successful telephone. Bell discovered that if an iron diaphragm was put very close to an electric magnet, sound waves could be transmitted along a wire. For months he and his assistant Watson tried to pass audible messages along a wire. In March 1876, when they had almost given up hope, Watson was amazed to hear quite clearly, "Mr. Watson, come here, I want you." The first telephone message had been received.

Next year when Bell's invention was demonstrated in England the magazine *Punch* reported: "On putting the telephone to my ear, I felt as if a regiment had fired a volley at a hundred yards into it." In 1879 *The Times* reported with amazement: "By its means the human voice can be conveyed in full force from any one point to any other five miles off, and with some loss of power to a very much more considerable distance."

95 *An early "Bell" telephone.*

216

96 *Left, Bell inaugurates the New York—Chicago line, 1878. Right, HM the Queen inaugurates the first STD system.*

In Britain the Telephone Co. Ltd. was formed in 1878 using Bell's patents. The receivers were good but the transmitters had to be considerably improved. This was done by placing carbon granules in the speakers. Two carbon electrodes were used. One was fixed, the other attached to the centre of a flexible diaphragm. Speech vibrated the diaphragm, moved the front electrode and altered the resistance of the carbon granules. In this way sounds could be transmitted clearly over long distances. The first telephone calls always had to be connected by an operator and it was some years before the system we use today, of dialling on automatic exchanges, became possible. In Britain the telephone network was not left in private hands for long; in 1911 it was taken over by the General Post Office.

The Wireless

Probably the greatest technical advance in electrical communication in the 19th century came with the invention of the wireless. A German, Hertz, and an Englishman, Lord Rutherford, both had some success with their experiments in wireless telegraphy, but it was an Italian, Guglielmo Marconi, who really made wireless a practical idea.

As a young man Marconi had spent years experimenting with the wireless transmission of signals. With his brother he had succeeded in sending Morse signals across the hills near his home at Bologna, but the Italian government had shown little interest in his discovery. Disappointed by the indifference of his countrymen he came to Britain

217

and took out a patent for his invention. Here he was more fortunate for the Chief Engineer of the Post Office encouraged him and even provided a laboratory where he could continue his experiments. Soon he was transmitting messages 13km across Salisbury Plain, and by 1897, using a $30\frac{1}{2}$m aerial mast, he sent signals across the Bristol Channel.

The value of wireless telegraphy was quickly realised and in 1898 an Irish newspaper asked Marconi to report the progress of the Kingston Regatta to their office in Dublin. Marconi followed the race in a boat and his messages were received distinctly on land. The importance of the wireless to newspapers had been proved decisively.

Marconi had shown that wireless signals could be sent over 30km to 40km but now he wanted to find out what the limit was to such transmissions. The vital question was whether wireless waves went in a straight line or whether they followed the earth's curvature. If the former, then there could never be any question of transmitting over thousands of kilometres. Marconi decided to carry out an experiment which he hoped would solve this problem. He built a powerful transmitter high above the cliffs near Mullion in Cornwall. Then he sailed to St. John's, Newfoundland, where, with a kite lifting it up, he raised a 122m aerial. On 12th December, 1901, with an arctic storm blowing outside their shelter, he and his friends waited anxiously for the signal from England. At noon the transmitting station was to begin sending the signal, the Morse letter S. Nothing was heard except the jumble of atmospherics and then, at 12.30 p.m., the faint sound of three dots came through the headphones. Marconi listened in triumph as again and again it was repeated. He had proved that wireless signals could be sent across the Atlantic.

Now shipping companies began to instal wireless equipment and "Marconi" men, as they were called, sailed on many large boats. The value of wireless was soon shown. In 1909 two ships collided in dense fog and it was only the wireless operator's urgent SOS that saved the lives of 1,700 passengers and crew. Soon afterwards the infamous murderer Dr. Crippen tried to escape by liner. His description, circulated by wireless, was recognised by the captain and he was arrested in Canada. In 1912 as the *Titanic* was sinking, her heroic wireless operator, Phillips, sent out his calls for help. He was drowned still tapping at his Morse key, but by his bravery 700 people were saved.

At the same time as shipping companies and newspaper offices were installing wireless, experiments were being carried out to transmit not only signals but also speech and music. Before the end of the First World War it was possible to transmit speech and music by wireless. By 1920 Marconi's company at Chelmsford were successfully broadcasting musical entertainment.

In 1922 the BBC was founded with broadcasting stations in London, Birmingham and Manchester. Technically reception was still poor for listeners had to wear headphones and constantly adjust the "cat's whiskers", as the receiving wires set in crystal detectors were called. Gradually the equipment improved and by the 1930's wireless sets were a feature of most homes.

The Camera

The idea of using a lens ·to project an image in a dark room had been known for years. The difficulty was how to capture and retain this projected image. Modern photography owes its beginning to two Frenchmen, Nicéphore Niepce and Louis Daguerre, from whose researches the daguerrotype process was evolved in 1839.

Niepce, who died before his ideas were perfected, had used silver chloride as his light-sensitive substance. He covered a pewter plate with a kind of bitumen and exposed his photograph for almost eight hours. He then dissolved the bitumen with vegetable oil and any bitumen which had been hardened by light remained and gave an outline of a picture. Niepce's process was slow and the results unimpressive. But Louis Daguerre was to learn from Niepce's experiments and to produce his own daguerrotypes which were a great improvement.

Niepce's development of the camera also helped Daguerre. It was a rectangular box with a space of 15cm between the plate and the lens, which could be adjusted to focus the picture. Daguerre now began to use silver iodide on a silver-plated copper plate. It needed less than half an hour's exposure and the plate could be developed with mercury vapour. These daguerrotypes, as they were called, were immediately popular. People flocked to buy his photographic equipment which with camera, plates, and chemicals weighed almost 50 kilogrammes!

At the same time as Daguerre was working in France, an Englishman, William Fox Talbot, invented the negative-positive process and used paper coated with silver iodide, the same light-sensitive material as Daguerre used. Fox Talbot's Calotype process, as it was called, never became really popular even though it meant that many pictures could be developed from the negative whereas only one daguerrotype could be produced. Despite this it was the Englishman's negative-positive idea that was to have most influence in the future.

Although photography was progressing rapidly by the middle of the nineteenth century it was still a highly complicated process. The fact that up to ten minutes' exposure was still needed meant that the person being photographed had to sit absolutely still during this time. To help them there were head rests and neck clamps at the back of the chairs. The fear of moving led to the rather strained expression we often see on the faces of people in mid-19th century photographs. Although it

97 *The instant reality of the camera brought actual scenes of distant wars to the home front.*

must have been a most unpleasant experience the Victorians regarded it almost as a duty to be photographed and individual portraits or family groups decorated the walls of most middle-class homes. In spite of such limitations there were pioneers like Roger Fenton through whose photographs the Crimean War of 1854 is brought to life for us, or the even greater Matthew Brady who recorded the full horror of the American Civil War.

In addition to the difficulty of taking the photograph the plate had to be developed at once. This meant that anyone using a camera away from a studio had to carry a specially darkened tent as a portable dark room (Roger Fenton had a special horse-drawn dark room). This was largely overcome when photographic plates were produced in 1871 which did not require immediate developing. A camera and a number of glass plates which had already been sensitised were the only necessary equipment. Photography was still a difficult process but one which an amateur could take up.

A great step forward was taken in 1888 when George Eastman, an American, produced the first Kodak camera. This was technically far simpler than anything which had preceded it, but even more important was the fact that it used a long roll of celluloid film instead of plates. This meant that up to 100 pictures could be taken without reloading the camera.

The Cinema

At the same time as these developments were taking place, an Englishman, William Friese-Green, invented moving pictures using celluloid films. It was two French brothers named Lumière who then went on to make and show films. The first moving picture show in Britain was given at the Polytechnic, London, in February 1896. The admission charge was 5 pence and the show lasted thirty minutes. Each film took about three minutes to show and a man stood at the front giving explanations. Many music hall managers saw the possibilities of this new form of entertainment and began to introduce occasional films into their shows. Fairground owners showed films in tents and many of them opened town cinemas. These films only lasted for a few minutes and the movements were so uneven that they were sometimes called the "shakies". It usually cost $\frac{1}{2}$p to 1p to watch, and as one person who saw these early films remembers, "We paid our 2d., and this included a bag of sweets." One of the most successful of the pre-1914 films was *Rescued by Rover,* in which the producer's dog took the leading part. The film lasted for twenty minutes and cost less than eight pounds to produce. The standard of films was slow to improve, and in fact, until Charlie Chaplin appeared in 1915 cinema-going was not very popular.

After the War techniques advanced rapidly. The actors' movements became less jerky, and the pictures were more clearly defined. All over the country cinemas sprang up and people flocked to see the early silent films. They laughed at the slap-stick farces and worshipped the romantic heroes. The impact of the screen was so great that when one star, Rudolph Valentino, died, girls committed suicide and millions queued to see his body as it lay embalmed in a glass coffin.

98a *Valentino in* Son of the Sheik, *1926.*

b *Jolson in the first Talkie,* The Jazz Singer, *1927.*

c *Chaplin in one of his later films,* City Lights, *1931.*

In 1927 the *Jazz Singer* was produced and with this first talking picture the era of silent films was over. The 1930's saw cinemas spreading to every town in Britain. It became customary for people to go to the pictures at least once and sometimes twice a week. In 1935 weekly cinema attendances were almost 20 million, and by 1945 they had risen to 30 million. Films offered a new leisure interest and the educational effects of the cinema were to be immense.

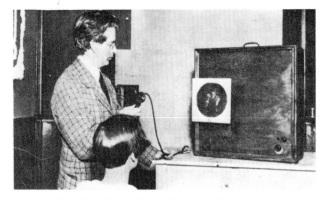

99 *Baird watching his "televisor" screen, 1926. The image of his assistant holding two dolls' heads can be seen on it.*

Television

Finally in this account of the development of communications there is the birth of television. The leading pioneer in television was a Scots engineer, John Logie Baird. His work in this field was outstanding, for not only were the technical difficulties extremely complex but because he had no financial backing he was compelled to use a mass of second-hand electrical parts. It is strange today to think that the first television consisted of disused wireless parts, pieces of cardboard, and an old biscuit tin, all held together by glue and tacks. In October 1925, Baird succeeded in transmitting a picture of a face from one room to another. Within months Baird had improved the picture so much that a company was formed to exploit his invention.

100 *Baird in his transmitting studio, holding the two dolls' heads.*

The BBC, however, were slow to take up television and it was not until 1936 that the first regular programmes were transmitted from Alexandra Palace in London. By then V. K. Zworykin, a Russian who had become a naturalised American, had also developed a television system. It was decided to try Baird's and Zworykin's systems on alternate weeks. The American's proved superior and was the one finally chosen. Although Baird was the pioneer of television the method used today has no connection with his actual invention.

Since 1945 television has spread rapidly and today it is an essential part of most homes.

Follow up Work

1. *Write an account showing the importance of Rowland Hill in the development of the postal service.*

2. *"The work of Wheatstone, Morse, Bell, and Marconi revolutionised the sending of messages in the 19th century." Write a connected account proving the truth of this statement.*

3. *What part was played in the development of the camera by: Niepce, Daguerre, Fox Talbot, and Eastman.*

4. *Write a brief account of the history of the cinema.*

5. *What part was played by John Logie Baird in the development of television?*

19 Industry 1919-1970's

In this book we have seen how the great industrial areas of the North and the Midlands grew up. We have traced their prosperity in the middle of the 19th century when Britain was the "workshop of the world". Later we saw how, towards the end of the last century, there were clear signs that we had lost our industrial supremacy. Now, in the period between the two world wars, a very different picture emerged. During these years many of our leading industries declined rapidly and unemployment and poverty were common in the North. Yet despite this our total industrial production increased by over 30% for new industries were growing up in the Midlands and the South.

The Depressed Areas

Although, as we shall see, there were many important industrial developments between 1919 and 1939, the severe unemployment problem tended to dominate these years. The graph (p. 227) shows just how serious the problem was. After 1921 the level of unemployment never fell below one million. During the winter of 1921–1922 it rose rapidly and reached almost 2 million. Then it fell and remained below $1\frac{1}{2}$ million until 1929.

Despite this recovery some of the older industries were very depressed throughout the 1920's. In South Lancashire, South Wales, Tyneside, the industrial belt of Scotland, and West Cumberland, thousands of men were out of work. The old exporting industries in these areas were the worst affected, for during the 1920's our exports never equalled those of 1913. The recovery was mainly felt in the light industries, and although there were exceptions such as the chemical plants built in Lancashire, Cheshire, and Durham, most of the expanding industries were south of Birmingham. Manufacturers of cars, cycles, radios, electrical appliances, rayon, and household products prospered and towns like Coventry, Oxford, and the industrial suburbs of outer London grew rapidly.

Thus even during the 1920's unemployment had become a feature of many districts. Then in 1929 came the American Wall Street crash and an unprecedented depression swept the world. America had seemed extremely prosperous. Her industry had boomed and the banks had lent money liberally. It was in 1928 that a slump started in agriculture and as farmers curtailed their purchases industry began to feel the strain. There was a sudden panic on the Wall Street stock market. In one week the total value of shares fell by 16 billion dollars. Banks had to close their doors, factories were shut down, and in a matter of months the number of unemployed spiralled.

As Americans cut their imports the depression spread to Europe. In Britain the unemployment figures rose alarmingly. By 1930 there were already $2\frac{1}{2}$ million out of work. Conditions worsened and by 1933 the figure had reached 3 million.

In an attempt to prevent cheap foreign imports competing with her products Britain abandoned free trade and with the Import Duties Act 1932 returned to tariffs. This could hardly be expected to help the exporting industries and in Wales, parts of the Midlands, and much of the North, men were out of work for years. Many of these mining and industrial towns became almost derelict. An air of grim poverty hung over towns like Dundee, Maryport, Merthyr Tydfil, and Wigan. Shabbily dressed men stood hopelessly at street corners or lined the pavements outside the Labour Exchanges. Some went on doing so for years. In Durham and in the South Wales valleys men were on the dole for five and even seven years. In desperation the men of Jarrow marched to the House of Commons.

The tragedy of the situation was reflected in an American popular song of the 1930's. Its tune was haunting, its words pathetic:

> *Once I built a railway, made it run,*
> *Made it race against time.*
> *Once I built a railway, now it's done,*
> *Buddy, can you spare a dime?*

The Government made no real attempt to provide work, nor until 1934 did they encourage prospering firms to open factories in the depressed areas. Its main answer to the problem was to offer some form of relief money to the unemployed. In 1931 even this dole was cut by 10% and a means test introduced. By this means test if any member of the family was earning money the father's dole was reduced. It led in many cases to the break-up of families for men hated the thought of being dependent upon their children's earnings.

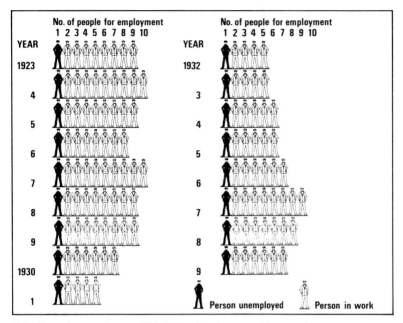

101 *Unemployment figures, 1923–1939, of workers over 16 years of age.*

The dole kept men alive but long periods of unemployment had terrible results. Men became bitter as they forgot their skills, young people who had never had a job grew up aimless and indifferent to work. This was something which parents feared as much as their own poverty. As one Rhondda Valley miner said:

"I am glad that I haven't a son. It must be a heart-breaking business to watch your boy grow into manhood and then see him deteriorate because there is no work for him to do. And yet there are scores of young men in the valley who have never worked since the age of sixteen. You see at sixteen they become insurable and the employers sack them rather than face the extra expense."

(From *Time to Spare*, ed. F. Green)

The women suffered worst of all, for unemployment did at least give the men leisure. Their wives had to economise on everything and only too often Monday morning saw them at the pawnshop.

"On the whole my husband has worked about one year out of twelve and a half. He fell out of work about four months after I was married so I've hardly known what a week's wage was . . . I've just put the eighth patch into a shirt of his. I take the sleeves out of one and put them in another, anything to keep going.

When we've finished with the clothes they go into making a mat...

Many a time I put a bit of black polish on a white thread to put a patch in, because I haven't any black thread... Many a time my husband has had to make cups for the children out of empty tins." (From *Time to Spare*)

Far more practical help came from voluntary sources than from the Government. Religious groups like the Salvation Army and the Quakers started clubs and residential educational centres. Some Southern towns tried to help by adopting towns in the depressed areas and sending gifts. For example, Surrey adopted Jarrow. In some districts the unemployed were encouraged to have allotments and to follow instructional courses. These were commendable efforts but they only touched the problem. New industries and public works were needed, and here the Government failed miserably.

The Prosperous South

This was the grim side of Britain in the 1930's. There was, however, a very different picture. The great depression had affected the new industries in the Midlands and the South but by 1933 they were recovering rapidly. Their unemployment figures were down to an average of 5%. There is no doubt that the general standard of living was rising and it was these areas which benefited most of all. Radio sets, cars, and better houses added to people's enjoyment of life. Seaside holidays became an accepted thing, electrical gadgets relieved the drudgery of housework, and the great chain stores offered smart and attractive clothes at prices people could afford.

Britain was undoubtedly more prosperous but this prosperity was unevenly distributed. An unemployed ship builder on Tyneside might sacrifice a little of his dole money at a cinema where he could escape into another world, but in Oxford and Dagenham a car worker's family could enjoy many of the benefits of a richer life.

Finally, if you look once more at the graph (p. 227) you will see that unemployment was beginning to rise again in 1937. This time the threatened slump was averted by the need to re-arm against Hitler's Germany. It was, however, a clear indication that our economy was far from healthy if serious unemployment could only be staved off by war. This was the general situation in Britain between the wars; the

228

fortunes of the main industries now need to be considered in more detail.

Coal

In 1913 Britain had mined a record total of 287 million tonnes of coal but this figure was never reached again. During the 1920's the output was falling and in the great depression it had sunk to 209 million tonnes. There was a slight improvement after 1934 but by 1938 it was still only 227 million tonnes. One of the most important reasons for this decline in output was a serious fall in the amount exported. Countries like France, which had previously bought from us, now mined their own while other European countries were buying German and Polish coal. The coastal coalfields in South Wales, Durham and Northumberland, and the Scottish fields were badly hit. The South Wales steam coal trade was also severely affected by boats substituting oil for coal. In the 1930's more than half the merchant ships used diesel fuel (compare the figures for steamships and motor vessels in the table on p. 122). At home there was an increased consumption of gas and electricity, and although these fuels depended on coal in the first place, scientific advances had reduced the amount of coal needed. At the same time improved techniques in the iron and steel industries had lessened the quantity of coal used in the blast furnaces.

The fact that many mines were small, and that in others the seams were difficult to work, tended to delay mechanisation. However, by 1936 almost 60% of our coal was machine cut. This meant that although coalfields such as those in South Yorkshire and Nottinghamshire now prospered because the seams were thick, many of the older pits were unable to compete. The introduction of machinery also reduced the number of miners needed and by 1938 there were only two-thirds as many pit workers as in 1923. In 1921 the mining and quarrying industries could count some 1,204,000 workers; in 1931 1,083,000, while by 1951 there had been a dramatic drop to 675,000.

During the 1960's there was a deliberate policy of running down the coal industry. Lord Robens, then Chairman of the N.C.B., planned these closures both sensibly and diplomatically. Most redundant miners were transferred to economic mining areas or absorbed by other industries. In the pits that remained open new methods were applied and the output per miner increased. The labour force was reduced from 711,000 in 1952 to 419,000 in 1967, and in 1972 had fallen to 268,000. It was then that the sudden oil crisis and the soaring cost of oil made the Government aware of the importance of coal as a source of energy. It is now recognised that coal has a vital part to play in the economy.

Cotton

Between 1919 and 1939 the output of cotton goods fell continuously and by 1938 was only half that produced before the First World War. No other industry had depended so much on exports as had the cotton industry, and the loss of overseas markets was the main reason for the severe unemployment in South Lancashire. The Japanese were selling cotton cloth at a price far below ours for they had the advantages of cheap labour and the most modern machines. Then India, once one of our largest markets, began to manufacture cotton cloth. Most of our trade with the Near and Far East was gone for ever, and towns like Oldham and Blackburn, where cheap cloth had been made, were very badly hit. However, in the manufacture of expensive cotton cloth Lancashire could still compete with the Japanese.

Since 1945 many millions of pounds have been spent on modernising the cotton textile industry. Yet, despite these efforts, the contraction of the industry has continued. Between 1951 and 1965 imports of raw cotton fell from 451,000 to 205,000 tonnes, and both the spinning and weaving industries have suffered considerable reduction in size. The actual output of cotton cloth fell from 2,202 to 1,015 million yards. All over Lancashire mills were closing and the labour force in 1967 was only 108,500, 15% less than in 1966. To emphasise the fact that the cotton industry had really lost its greatness the imports of cloth in 1967 were greater than the amount produced in Britain.

Shipbuilding

After the First World War, when ship owners began to replace vessels which had been sunk, the world's shipyards boomed. Their output was so great that by 1921, only three years after the war, there were already more merchant ships in the world than in 1914. Then in the 1920's and, particularly during the great depression, international trade declined. Ships were laid up all over the world and orders for new ones cancelled.

Throughout the 1920's idle shipyards were a common sight and in the 1930's conditions grew worse. By 1934 over 60% of all shipyard workers were unemployed. It was obvious that there were far too many shipbuilding companies. An attempt was made to combine some of these companies and to reduce competition by closing inefficient yards. One consequence was the closing of Palmer's Shipyard at Jarrow. As a result of this Jarrow became known as the "town that was murdered", for over 70% of its men were unemployed in 1935.

The Government gave very little effective help except to grant loans to complete the *Queen Mary* and begin work on the *Queen Elizabeth*. The building of these ships did at least bring some work to Clydeside. Even by 1939 the shipbuilding industry was still depressed. The fact remained that there were too many shipyards in the world.

After the Second World War shipyards were kept busy replacing wartime losses. By 1956, however, the old problem of too many shipyards in the world was causing many firms to close. The North East of England was particularly badly hit; two yards closing down at Sunderland, one at Hartlepool, and one at Blyth.

British shipbuilding was in a poor position to face foreign competition. A combination of out-dated equipment, inefficient management, and restrictive trade union practices had caused Britain's shipyards to fall well behind those of Japan and Germany. In 1966 the Geddes Report was published stressing the need to concentrate production on fewer and more efficient units. Despite the bankruptcy of the Upper Clyde shipbuilders in 1971, there was a marked improvement in the efficiency of many yards. However, the industry is suffering an international slump and British yards are affected.

Iron and Steel

So far we have studied those industries which were particularly depressed between the Wars. Although the iron and steel industry cannot come under this category its fortunes did fluctuate considerably. The industry was badly hit by the 1929 slump, but after 1932 steel production in particular rose considerably. This was mainly because of the demand from the rapidly growing motor vehicle industry and from engineering firms. Then in 1938 the need to re-arm also stimulated iron and steel.

There was a general fall in the number of workers employed in the industry, for manufacturing techniques were displacing labour. New areas were becoming increasingly important. The Gilchrist-Thomas process enabled the phosphoric ore of the Midlands to be worked, and this had the advantage of being easily quarried. Scunthorpe and Corby, which grew up on this iron ore field, became prosperous steel towns during the 1930's. In addition new plants were built at Middlesbrough and Margam, conveniently close to the coast where ore imported from Spain and Sweden was landed. A steel works was also erected at Ebbw Vale, but this was one of the few deliberate political moves to ease unemployment.

It has been recognised for some time that if the British steel industry is to compete with Germany and Japan considerable sums of money will have to be invested in the most modern methods of production. At the same time the work force will have to be cut and certain plants will be closed. The steel industry is an example of an industry which has to rationalise and modernise to survive, but in which trade union and local fears of redundancy have to be overcome.

Since 1945 a large part of the steel industry has been nationalised and is now controlled by the British Steel Corporation. The industry is mainly concentrated on five regions. The largest production area is Wales, followed by Yorkshire and Humberside, the North East, Scotland and the West Midlands. The United Kingdom is, after West Germany, the second largest steel producer in the European Economic Community.

Electrical Industry

We have seen that although British inventors led the way in the early development of electricity Britain fell behind in actual output. The years between the Wars saw a great expansion in the production and consumption of electricity. At first the existence of a number of small producing companies had restricted development but, with the setting up of the Central Electricity Board and the National Grid, power could be distributed all over the country. The number of users of electricity increased enormously and industries making bulbs, fires, and electrical appliances flourished, as did those manufacturing generators and dynamos. In 1925 1,000 million units of electricity were consumed, and by 1937 this figure had risen to 6,500,000 units. There is no doubt that the benefits brought by electricity raised the general standard of living considerably. We have only to think of electrically operated domestic labour-saving devices to realise this.

Building Industry

This industry was very badly hit by the 1929 depression and in 1931 almost 30% of all building workers were out of work, although the total labour force had increased from 738,000 in 1921 to 970,000 by 1931 (by 1951 it had risen to 1,268,000). Then after 1933 the industry, particularly in the Midlands and the South, really began to boom. Mortgage interest rates were low and many people began to buy their own houses with loans from Building Societies. By 1936 almost 300,000 houses were being built each year. This was the time when the estates of semi-detached houses, which appear on the outskirts of most big cities, were built. Few of them were beautiful but they meant that more and more people could enjoy the comforts of modern housing.

It was also during these years that over one million council houses were built. Most of these were subsidised by the State which meant that the rents charged could be reduced. Many of these council estates were built to replace the hideous slums which had grown up during the 19th century.

Chemical Industry

The chemical industry had begun to grow rapidly during the 19th century and by the 1930's it was one of the most important industries, producing such products as rayon, bakelite, and plastics. In addition it contributed to economic and social progress with its continued experiments with disinfectants, fertilisers, and a wide variety of drugs and medicines. In 1926 Imperial Chemical Industries, one of the largest firms in the world, was formed.

I.C.I. have continued to exercise major control over the chemical industry, although they do not have a monopoly. It is generally an efficient industry and great strides have been made in all branches. Recently, however, certain criticisms have been levelled against it, particularly in the way Britain has fallen behind European countries in the production of plastics.

The Motor Industry

Of all the growing industries none were as important as motor manufacturing and the numerous subsidiary industries which grew up with it. We saw in Chapter 15 that the motor car industry was

102 *Austin 7, 1922, "Britain's Model T Ford".*

established before 1914 even though its progress was slow. After the War it developed much more quickly and by the 1930's had become a major industry.

In 1915 William Morris had adopted American mass production methods and, except for luxury cars, the assembly line became the recognised way of manufacturing cars. It meant that they could be built much more cheaply and manufacturers soon realised that there was a vast market for small cars. The Austin 7, Ford 8, and Morris Cowley were bought by thousands of people who had once thought cars an undreamed-of luxury. By 1926 there were 676,000 private cars in Britain.

The motor car industry grew up mainly in the Midlands and the South and this was an important factor in the prosperity of Birmingham, Coventry, Oxford, and outer London. Also the growth of the car industry led to the development of a number of subsidiary trades. Tyre, battery, and engineering firms prospered and with the increased demand for car bodies so did the steel manufacturers.

Between the Wars cars were taxed according to horse-power which made it increasingly dear to own a large car. For this reason British manufacturers were encouraged to build small or medium sized cars. Unfortunately this practice tended to affect our overseas sales for some countries preferred the more powerful American cars. Even so car exports doubled between 1930 and 1939 and the industry at that time was definitely ahead of our European competitors.

Even before 1939 many small car firms had merged to form larger units and by 1970 the industry was virtually dominated by four groups, British Leyland (Austin, Morris, Triumph, Jaguar, Rover, MG), Ford, General Motors (Vauxhalls) and Chrysler. All except British Leyland are American owned.

In the years after the war British manufacturers felt they could be proud of their efficiency for the output of vehicles increased by 88% between 1955 and 1964. During the same period, however, European and Japanese output increased by 195% and there is no doubt that they have captured some of our foreign markets as well as competing in the home market. In 1971 Japan was producing twice as many cars as Britain. In 1972 25% of cars sold in Britain were foreign, by late 1975 the proportion had risen to 40%.

The motor industry has become of such national economic importance that the Government has persuaded manufacturers to build new plants in depressed areas where new industry was needed to combat unemployment. Chrysler have a factory at Linwood in Scotland, General Motors at Ellesmere Port, British Leyland at Llanelli and Speke (Liverpool) and Fords at Halewood (Merseyside). Nothing shows this economic importance more clearly than the Government's decision in 1975 to rescue the mighty British Leyland, which was behind its competitors both in efficiency and productivity, from the risk of bankruptcy. On the recommendation of its industrial adviser, Sir Don Ryder, the Government decided to invest £900 millions in the company between 1975 and 1978.

Many people have criticised this decision for there is certainly no guarantee that the investment will be warranted. Not only is the British motor industry facing serious competition, particularly from Japan, but there is a real danger that the world car industry is now too large. The whole industry, not including the United States, has the capacity to build twenty million cars a year against an expected demand of fourteen million. Even if there is an increased demand from less developed countries such as India, there are countries like Brazil, Spain and South Korea now anxious to build their own cars.

The Energy Problem

There is no doubt that one of the major problems facing Britain and other industrial countries is what is called the "energy crisis." For years this danger was disguised by the cheapness and abundance of oil but inevitably the oil-producing nations came to realise the immense power they had in their hands. Since 1973 two huge price increases and a cutback in Arab oil supplies have transformed the energy market. Not only has the very high price of oil been a major cause of world inflation but the threat by Arab countries to withhold supplies has highlighted the unhealthy dependence of many industrial countries on imported oil, and led to a reappraisal of energy supplies.

Coal

The end of the cheap oil era has reversed Government thinking completely with regard to the coal industry. The 1960's policy of allowing the industry to decline has been reversed and no one doubts the great importance of Britain's vast reserves of coal. The National Coal Board accepts that the demand for domestic coal will continue to fall but anticipates an increase in demand from the power stations from 75 million tonnes in 1974 to 90 million tonnes in 1985. It is also believed that the demand from the steel industry for coking coal will remain steady at about 23 million tonnes.

To produce this increased coal more money is to be invested in pits which are economic and there is to be considerable exploration in areas like Selby in Yorkshire and the East Midlands where great reserves of easily mined coal are believed to exist. In addition there is to be an increased recruitment of men.

Natural Gas

Since the 1960's the gas fields below the North Sea have been providing Britain with immense new sources of heat and power for domestic and industrial use; by 1974 natural gas was contributing about 11% of the United Kingdom's energy demands. Within the next decade some of the fields now producing will decline, but the huge Frigg field far out in the North Sea, and the gas known to be present alongside the Brent oilfield east of Shetland will ensure adequate supplies for many years to come. It is, in fact, believed that natural gas will play an increasingly important part in Britain's energy requirements, contributing probably as much as 16% of the total demand.

North Sea Oil

The Montrose field was the first commercial oilfield to be found in the British sector of the North Sea in 1969, followed by the Forties field in

1970. Numerous other fields have been opened up and, considering the difficulties under which they work, particularly in winter, the oilmen have made considerable progress. Pictures of vast oil platforms being towed out to sea have become a familiar news item and there is no doubt that oil has changed the way of life in Eastern Scotland and the Shetland Isles where over 40,000 people are employed by the industry.

The first oil from the British sector was brought ashore by tanker from the Argyll field on June 18th, 1975. Three other oilfields started production towards the end of 1975 and it is expected that production will be more than equal to Britain's oil demand by the 1980's although some heavier crude oils will still be imported for technical reasons.

The future importance of North Sea oil to Britain's economy cannot be overestimated. Although it should be possible for Britain to actually become an exporter of oil it has been stressed that oil is a valuable raw material that should be conserved as much as possible. However, it has cost the oil companies vast sums to develop these North Sea fields and as the well head equipment will have a relatively short life in such conditions it seems likely that the companies may opt for a policy of maximum production immediately.

The Government, realising the importance of the vast reserves of oil in the North Sea, has established a British National Oil Corporation with headquarters in Glasgow.

Nuclear Power

Despite intensive research and development over the last twenty years the present contribution of nuclear power to Britain's energy requirement is limited to a fairly small output of electricity. Britain was the first country to adopt nuclear power on any scale when her first commercial station was commissioned in 1962. In the years that followed too many reactors were built without adequate research and there have been many technical difficulties. This has led to overcaution and a reluctance to buy advanced American reactors. The result is that electricity produced by nuclear power stations is very expensive and at the moment few engineers are confident of nuclear power playing an important part in the immediate future.

237

Follow up Work

1. On a map mark in the areas which were depressed between 1919 and 1939. Indicate clearly the industries which these areas relied on.

2. How did the Government attempt to help the unemployed? What other measures do you think should have been taken?

3. Write an account showing the probable social consequences of prolonged unemployment.

4. "He was nearly fourteen when the great upheaval came. His father, who had worked all his life in the pit just below their cottage in the North country village, moved his job, and the family with him, to work in a car factory in the Midlands. The whole family moved into a new house in a very new town, and everything was strange—the modern house, new neighbours, an enormous supermarket at the end of the road, and a new school. Even the strange accents of his new companions confused him. His elder brother became a mechanic, and his sister went into the local factory ..."

   Read the above extract carefully and then answer the following questions:

   a) What does the extract reveal of the general changes in the pattern of British industry in the 20th century?

   b) Why did this particular family decide to move? Write a paragraph about the new industries in which they found employment.

   c) Write an account of the changes in the life of this family brought about by the "new house", the "new town", the "supermarket", and the "new school".

   (West Midlands CSE Board, 1966)

5. Name two twentieth-century inventions you consider important (Aeroplanes may not be chosen). State what you know about their invention and the results of their use.

   (Metropolitan Regional Examinations Board CSE, 1966)

6. Why was there so much unemployment in Britain in the period 1920–37? In your answer you might consider such things as:
   the effects of World War I,
   competition from abroad,
   the decline of certain industries,
   free trade.
   Include other factors if you can.

   (Associated Lancashire Schools Examining Board, 1971)

20 Between the Wars and After

Trade Unions 1918–1945

During the War trade unions had increased their membership considerably and by 1919 they had almost 8 million members. Full employment during the war years had removed the fear from trade union members of being blacklisted by employers and in addition the unions had been successful in raising wages. Therefore when the War ended the workers were well organised.

By 1919 industrial unrest had spread once more over the country. There were a number of strikes, the most successful being the railwaymen's. The railwaymen had been embittered by a series of wage negotiations which had led to reductions in pay from £2·65 to £2 per week for many of them. When the National Union of Railwaymen called its members out, the Government, which still controlled the railways after the War, made plans to break the strike, but underestimated the strength of its opposition. The Union fought back and on its side were many other unions, the Co-operative Societies, and the *Daily Herald*. Within a week the NUR had won. Terms were agreed providing a minimum weekly wage of £2·55 for all railwaymen.

The end of the War also saw the amalgamation of unions into much bigger and more powerful bodies. These included the Amalgamated Engineering Union, the National Union of General and Municipal Workers, the National Union of Textile Workers, and the Transport and General Workers' Union.

These vast unions seemed powerful groups on their own, but one agreement which the employers viewed with suspicion was the Triple Alliance of miners, railwaymen, and transport workers. In 1921 the strength of this alliance was tested for the first time. Wage negotiations broke down between the mine owners and the men, and the miners came out on strike. Immediately the Government proclaimed a state of emergency, for it seemed as if a general strike was inevitable. The expected clash never came, for when called upon to act the Triple Alliance collapsed miserably. On April 15th, to be known thereafter as "Black Friday", the railwaymen and transport workers deserted the miners who were left to fight alone. They struggled on for a few weeks but were compelled to go back defeated.

The discontent of workers generally, showed itself in a series of strikes throughout 1921 and 1922. However, the wartime boom was over and with almost two million men unemployed the power of the unions was considerably weakened. There were far fewer strikes after 1922 but in 1926 the industrial discontent came to the surface.

The General Strike

The trouble began with the miners. The coal industry had been declining since 1918. Loss of export orders had caused a considerable fall in output and there was no doubt that many mines were un-economic. To try to combat this, new agreements were proposed which would have meant longer hours but less pay for the miners. The Miners Union refused to accept any agreement by which the owners seemed to be making no concessions. A. J. Cooke, their leader, coined the phrase, "not a penny off the pay, not a minute on the day". Both the miners and owners refused to yield and on May 1st, 1926, the miners struck. This time they had the sympathy of almost the whole trade union movement, and at midnight on May 3rd, the Trade Union Congress called a general strike.

With the exception of journalists, sailors, firemen, and electrical engineers, every union supported the strike. The response was over-whelming as all over the country workers stayed out. Hardly any trains or buses ran, newspapers ceased, factories stood idle. Occasion-ally lorries moved through the streets carrying yellow and black placards with the words "Permit from the TUC" written on them. There was a strange, uneasy atmosphere as the Government and the TUC prepared to fight.

The local trade union branches worked heroically to help their members. Arrangements were made to provide pickets, to ease cases of serious distress, and to send teams of motor cycle despatch riders from town to town. In London, at the headquarters of the TUC, there was less order and far less optimism. No real plans had been made for a general strike and there seemed little unity of policy amongst the trade union leaders.

The Government was far better prepared. Winston Churchill was

103 *A street scene during the General Strike.*

made editor of the *British Gazette,* a news-sheet which the Government published as a propaganda weapon against the strikers. Phrases like, "the General Strike is a challenge to Parliament and is the road to anarchy and ruin", were bound to influence members of the middle class. The BBC refused to take sides, but tended to be biased towards the Government and would not allow the Archbishop of Canterbury to broadcast an appeal for a settlement. The Government could rely on the support of a large section of the middle class. Strange sights were seen all over the country as businessmen drove trains and undergraduates took charge of buses. To the students the strike was something of a lark. They even amused themselves writing slogans on their buses like, "The driver of this bus is a student of Guy's Hospital, the conductor is a student at Guy's. Anyone who interferes with either is liable to be a patient at Guy's."

The police were strengthened with special constables, and lorries protected by troops were a common sight in the streets. There were outbreaks of violence but considering the seriousness of the situation these outbreaks were not particularly threatening. Buses were overturned in Glasgow and there were fights with the police in South Wales and Yorkshire. Yet at the same time the police played a football match with the strikers at Plymouth!

241

The strike lasted for nine days and most of the workers were firmly opposed to ending it. It was the TUC leaders who broke down before the Government's attack. On May 12th, to the dismay and astonishment of many workers, the strike was called off. When the men returned to work they were often victimised. Sometimes their jobs were refused them, their wages were reduced, or they were compelled to leave the unions. As for the miners, embittered by this desertion, hating their employers as few other workers did, they continued the strike for another six months. Then sheer starvation forced them back and they were compelled to accept lower wages and longer hours.

The Government had defeated the TUC and to strengthen their own position they passed the Trade Dispute and Trade Union Act in 1927. By this Act general strikes were declared illegal, and civil service unions were forbidden TUC membership. The Act also provided that all members who wished to contribute to their union's political fund must personally contract in. This reversed the Trade Union Act of 1913 and was intended as a blow to the Labour Party. The 1927 Act was not repealed until 1946.

The failure of the general strike cost the unions over £4 million in strike pay and caused almost 1 million members to leave the unions. It was not until 1937 when industry was fairly prosperous again that the membership rose to almost 6 million

Industrial Relations Since 1945

After 1945 the unions were in a strong position. With full employment and a friendly Labour Government in power the unions were able to bargain more effectively, and by 1950 they had 9 million members. At first there was a deliberate policy of wage restraint as the country tried to strengthen its economic position after the war. Since 1949, however, this policy has been abandoned and each year has seen the unions submitting claims for wage increases. For this reason various attempts were made in the 1960's to arrive at some form of prices and incomes policy, all of which ended in failure. The Government's view is now that large increases in wages are a major cause of the rising inflation which has been seriously damaging the economy. In 1975, the Government, with the agreement of the TUC, imposed a maximum wage increase of £6 per week for all workers. An even stricter limit on wage increases was imposed in 1976, again with the agreement of the TUC.

In some respects the unions have shown a willingness to work with the employers. Time and motion schemes have been accepted and so has the upgrading of unskilled workers. The employers in turn have shown greater consideration towards the workers and numerous benefit schemes have been introduced.

However, there is no doubt that many unions cling to old forms and practices which cannot but help to harm the economy. Restrictive practices have certainly been a major factor in holding back the modernisation of British industry. The Luddites met the threat of machinery by smashing it. Their 20th-century descendants often use their power to retain obsolete manning standards on newly invented equipment. It has been estimated that the motor industry is as much as 40% overmanned. It takes three times as many men to produce a tonne of steel in Britain as in the United States. The Royal Commission on the Press in 1961–2 revealed that national newspapers had to employ one-third as many men again as they needed. Even in Smithfield market at one time they had various categories of porters to carry meat in different parts of the market.

Many traditional craft skills have been made obsolete by new techniques and materials, for example plaster boards have largely taken the place of the skilled plasterer. Yet many skilled craft unions still demand unnecessary apprentice schemes. Much worse has been inter-craft rivalry which has led to considerable waste of resources. For example, in 1965–6 there was a five-week strike in a Bristol shipyard over which workers should pencil guide lines for a new type of steel-cutting machine.

It is possible to trace many of the unions' attitudes to workers' fear of unemployment and historically this is understandable. But there is no doubt that many workers could have had higher standards of living if restrictive practices had been swept away; as it is overtime has had to be worked to compensate for low basic wage rates. It has not always been accepted by unions that the introduction of labour-saving techniques can in the long run bring greater leisure and higher living standards.

Another great weakness in British industry is the working time lost through strikes, particularly unofficial ones not called by the union. The Conservative Government passed the Industrial Relations Act in 1971 in an attempt to exercise greater control over unions. The Act met with much opposition and as it was clearly not going to succeed it was repealed by the Labour Party when they came into office.

It is possible to point to many instances where unions and employers have co-operated to the benefit of both but labour relations is a field where great progress needs to be made.

Follow up Work

1. *"Tuesday, May 4th, started with the workers answering the call. What a wonderful response. What loyalty. What solidarity. From Land's End to John o'Groats the workers answered the call to arms to defend us, the brave miners in our fight for a living wage...*

   It was a wonderful achievement, a wonderful accomplishment that proved conclusively that the Labour Movement is capable of providing the means of carrying on the country. Who can forget the effect of motor vehicles with posters saying, 'By permit of the TUC'." (The Nine Days, *A. J. Cooke*)

   a) *What was the main cause of the miners' strike?*
   b) *Which unions did not join the general strike?*
   c) *Which supplies do you think the TUC allowed through?*
   d) *What was the weakness of the TUC during the general strike?*
   e) *What preparations had the Government made to defeat the unions?*
   f) *Is it true that the strike was wholly peaceful?*
   g) *For how long did the strike last?*
   h) *In what ways were many workers victimised after the strike?*
   i) *How did the Government attempt to weaken the unions after the strike?*
   j) *How did the strike affect the union membership?*

2. *Discuss with your teacher and then write brief accounts about:*
   a) *Inflationary spiral*   b) *Prices and Incomes Policy*
   c) *Devaluation.*

Agriculture 1919–1970's

During the First World War one of the greatest perils had been the packs of German U-boats which blockaded our sea routes. Merchant ships carrying food suffered appalling losses as thousands of boats were sunk. So serious were these losses that at one time it seemed as if we might be starved into ending the War.

To combat the submarine menace it was essential that we grew as much food as possible. All over the country parks and school playing fields were dug up and lawns turned into vegetable plots. These patriotic measures helped but it was to the farmers that the Government turned to provide as much food as possible. As the imports of foreign grain were cut, land which had been neglected or laid to pasture after the 1880's slump was ploughed up again and wheat became a common crop in Eastern England once more.

For the farmers these were prosperous years and even the Government seemed confident of the future of agriculture. They fixed minimum wages for farm workers and guaranteed to protect farmers against serious price falls. By 1921, however, the boom was over. Cheap imported food was once more flooding Britain. Agricultural prices fell rapidly and the Government, finding itself faced with a huge bill under its guarantee, hurriedly withdrew its protection to both farmers and labourers. Wheat farmers reverted to pasture once more and many farm workers' wages fell from over £2 a week to £1·25. To some countrymen it seemed as if there was no escaping these slumps. Thousands of farm workers began to leave the land. Some because of lack of work or reasonable wages, others because the towns, particularly in the South, were far more attractive than the villages. For at this time although electricity was reaching some villages, more than one half of all country parishes had no piped water, and often village cottages were little better than hovels. To an outsider a village may look picturesque but there is little pleasure in living in a dilapidated cottage with no running water and where the toilet is an earth closet in an outside shed.

During these depressed years many farmers faced bankruptcy and the struggle that some of them had is shown very clearly if rather light-heartedly in this account which was given on the radio.

"Our worst experience of the depression was when we were faced with two months and no money coming in whatsover. We were employing five men and they needed their wages on the Friday night, and to us those men were our friends as well as our workers. My husband had in those days two beautiful Cleveland bay horses; they were the first to go, and we lived on the proceeds of them and paid our wages for the first month. Then came the second month, and the men queueing up on the Friday night. My husband said to me: 'I can't pay the wages. What are we to do?' And I suddenly remembered that we had up in the attic quite a lot of silver which had been given to us as wedding presents, and a few priceless possessions. We filled the back of our old Wolseley car and my husband and I went into our nearest market town and, believe me, it was the hardest day's work I've done to sell that silver to raise the wages, but we did it and afterwards we went across to the nearest pub and had a good meal and a drink, which we badly needed, and then home to pay our men and carry on until the milk cheques worked round." (*Scrapbook for the 1920's*, Muller.)

Government Assistance

Some attempts were made by the Government to help farmers but it was in the 1930's that the Government's attitude to agriculture really changed. Since the repeal of the Corn Laws in 1846 farmers had received very little Government assistance. After 1931 there was a determined attempt to help the farmer even though this meant that the price of food would have to rise.

In 1931 and 1933 Agricultural Marketing Acts were passed which enabled marketing boards to be set up. The object of these marketing boards was to buy, process, and sell the product, and in this way to decide how much was to be produced and the price to be charged. If two-thirds of the main producers approved, the schemes were to be compulsory. Eventually there were marketing boards for hops, potatoes, milk, bacon, and pork. This scheme eliminated competition and ensured the farmers a regular source of income although, of course, it restricted some farmers' earnings. Further help was given by paying subsidies to farmers to enable them to lower their prices and to compete against foreign imports. The paying of a subsidy meant in fact that the farmer was receiving a grant from the Government. Subsidies were paid to farmers growing wheat, barley, oats, and sugar beet, and to livestock and bacon producers. Finally the imports of foreign food were deliberately restricted by tariffs and by quotas. We adopted a policy of Commonwealth and Imperial Preference which adversely affected such European countries as Denmark.

Partly as a result of these measures the farmers became sufficiently confident to invest in many technical advances. Mechanisation proceeded rapidly. Tractors largely replaced horses, electric milking machines were introduced, and on large farms combine harvesters could be seen cutting, threshing, and bagging wheat as they moved along. Great improvements took place in the standard of animal foodstuffs, and the output of meat, milk, and eggs increased considerably. At the same time the food canning industry was growing which led to a great increase in the acreage of fruit and vegetables under cultivation. Although there were still instances of backward farming many British farmers were taking advantage of the new techniques and the output per man increased by over 40%.

Gradually in the 1930's living conditions in the villages improved. Council houses began to replace rural slums, and bus services broke down the isolation of many communities. Women's Institutes which had come into being during the War spread rapidly, and the wireless offered wider horizons to the remotest hamlet.

During the Second World War British farmers were again called upon to produce as much food as possible. To encourage wheat growing a subsidy was paid for ploughing up land which had been unploughed for seven years. With the exception of cattle which were needed for both milk and meat, far less livestock was kept, but in terms of calories and proteins home production of food was increased by 70%, and we were able to cut food imports by half.

The end of this War did not see a slump in agriculture. In 1945 it was essential that we kept our imports as low as possible in order to safeguard our reserves of foreign currency. Farmers were urged to continue to produce as much as possible. In 1950 British farmers were actually producing twice as much food as they had been in 1939. This was achieved by the use of chemical fertilisers, by keeping poultry in batteries and deep litter to increase egg production, and by improved seeds and grasslands. At the same time far more machinery was used.

Throughout the 1960's successive Governments stressed the need to produce as much food as possible so that imports could be reduced, and there is little doubt that the policies adopted were reasonably successful.

Almost every branch of farming now has machine aids and there has been a considerable economy in labour. Taken as a whole British agriculture is amongst the most advanced and efficient in the world.

Follow up Work

1. Why were so many workers deserting the land in the early 1920's?

2. Describe the history of British agriculture during this period, mentioning the effects of the two Wars, and how the industry has been helped by the Government.

(East Midlands Regional Examinations Board, CSE, 1966)

Transport 1919–1970's

Today when we consider railways we automatically think of the term British Railways. In 1914, however, the railways were not under a unified control but were operated by over 120 different companies. If you look on railway bridges near your home you can often see old notices telling you the name of the company which owned the railway in your district. These companies may have been efficient, many of them served small areas well, but it was obvious that as railway transport was absolutely vital during the War, they would have to be controlled by the Government. This was really the end of the small companies for the war years showed how much more efficient the large groups were. After the War the railways were not nationalised, but by the Railway Act 1921 the whole network was divided between four huge groups; the Great Western—the Southern—the London, Midland and Scottish, and the London and North Eastern. These companies were to be subject to considerable state control.

The four great companies had many problems to face. Much of their rolling stock had deteriorated and their lines and stations needed modernising. Vast sums of money needed to be invested if the railways were to be brought up-to-date. Yet the railways were no longer an attractive investment for the fact remained that many of them were unprofitable. An even greater problem was the rapid development of road transport. Buses, lorries, and cars were increasing every year and were taking more and more business from the railways. People who lived on the outskirts of the towns preferred to use buses, and lorries could deliver many goods both quicker and cheaper.

104 *The LNER* Silver Jubilee, *1936.*

In the face of this competition the railway companies did begin to improve their services. The number of express trains travelling at over 96km/h increased considerably. In 1936 the LNER *Silver Jubilee* reached a top speed of 181km/h and the *Coronation Scot* averaged 115km/h from London to Edinburgh. The Southern Railway made considerable technical progress by electrifying some lines. In many parts of the country unprofitable lines were closed and economies made on staff. Unfortunately this often led to· dirty carriages and unpunctual trains, particularly on branch lines.

Despite their efforts the railways continued to decline. When the Second World War ended in 1945 they were nationalised. Since then thousands of millions of pounds have been spent on them. Vast electrifi-

105 *Use this plate together with the maps in Chapter 6. Try to find some up-to-date labour figures for the years from 1931 to the present.*

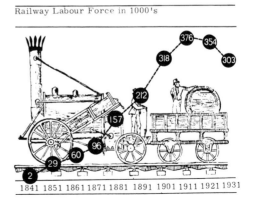

Railway Labour Force in 1000's

1841 1851 1861 1871 1881 1891 1901 1911 1921 1931

249

cation schemes have been carried out, goods departments have been automated, stations brought up to date. At the same time the Beeching Plan has led to lines being closed down for there were still far too many unprofitable sections. It seems unlikely that railways will ever become profitable again but there is no doubt that they are of great value to the community. The Inter-City services give fast, reliable journeys between the main centres of population, and by 1976 trains were running at more than 125 m.p.h. (201km/h). Railways relieve the pressure on the roads even further by serving as important freight carriers particularly for bulky goods such as iron ore, coal, cement, chemicals and petroleum.

Motor Transport

Long before the First World War motor transport had ceased to be a novelty. Cars and lorries were to be seen in small numbers over most of the country and in the towns people were becoming accustomed to travelling by bus. In fact motor buses were to be seen in London soon after 1900 but the first really reliable vehicles were the "B" type in 1910. These replaced horse-drawn buses which were finally withdrawn in 1911.

After 1918 buses became increasingly popular and there appeared what were known as "pirate" buses. These were owned by numerous small companies and only ran at peak hours. Their object was to steal as much trade as possible with the result that there were many dangerous races between rival bus drivers. As one observer said, "It was possible to stand waiting for a bus and to see two drivers racing madly towards me. The fare was only a penny and I was the only passenger, but this did not seem to matter." This practice had become so dangerous that in 1924 the Government was forced to control the number of buses allowed. Despite the increasingly popular motor buses, electric trams and trolley buses survived in many towns and the last London tram only stopped running in 1951. Glasgow's famous "caurs" remained until 1962.

Between 1919 and 1939 the number of motor vehicles in Britain rose from over 450,000 to more than 3,000,000. This was to bring with it countless problems. The responsibility for roads lay with the local authorities and many roads were improved. In Scotland new roads were built, in England the Mersey Tunnel was opened in 1928, two road bridges were built on the Great North Road over the Tyne and Tweed, and outside London the North Circular and the Kingston

106 *General Omnibus Company "B" type bus, official speed, 19km/h.*

by-pass were opened. Unfortunately these improvements were too few and by 1939 much of our road system was still antiquated.

One very important step was the Road Traffic Act 1930. Before this Act the speed limit had been 20 m.p.h. (32km/h). This ridiculous limit was frequently disregarded. The 1930 Act abolished it and also introduced third-party insurance. Then in 1935 a definite speed limit of 30 m.p.h. (48km/h) in built-up areas was introduced.

Since 1945 conditions on our roads have grown worse. The number of motor vehicles has increased yearly and today we are living in a motor car age. Great steps have been taken towards improving the roads. Vast stretches of dual carriageways have been constructed and even more important are the motorways which now connect many of our main cities.

Holiday periods still lead to considerable hold-ups but the greatest problem is probably in the town centres, most of which were never planned to deal with the enormous amount of traffic which enters them. Attempts are being made to ease traffic congestions but it is undoubtedly a problem which will continue to grow and to which there can be no permanent solution in the foreseeable future.

Air Transport

The history of the aeroplane really began on December 17th, 1903, when, at Kitty Hawk, North Carolina, two American brothers, Wilbur and Orville Wright, flew a powered aircraft for the first time. On the fourth flight of the day the aircraft flew 260 metres and stayed in the air for 59 seconds. The Wrights had proved that controlled flight was possible. The two brothers continued their experiments and by 1908 they were flying for over two hours at a height of 91 metres. By then they were technically well ahead of any other aviators but in the years which followed up to the First World War, great progress was made by flyers in America and Europe.

In 1909 Louis Blériot flew the English Channel in 37 minutes at a height never exceeding 30 metres. In Britain the *Daily Mail* offered tempting prizes to ambitious airmen and increasingly longer distances were flown by such pioneers as "Colonel" Cody, T. Sopwith, and Claude Grahame-White. By 1911 the first air mail service was in operation. The wartime potential of aircraft was soon realised and in 1912 the Royal Flying Corps, the forerunner of the RAF was founded.

Although aircraft only played a small part in the 1914–1918 War, these years acted as an incentive to aircraft designers. When the War began the average speed of aircraft was only 128km/h, but by 1918 they were flying at speeds of 240km/h and reaching heights of some 9,144 metres.

When the War ended an era of long distance flights began. In 1919 two Englishmen, Alcock and Brown, made the first non-stop trans-Atlantic flight from Newfoundland to Ireland. That same year two Australian brothers, Ross and Keith Smith, flew from England to Australia in 28 days. Alan Cobham made adventurous flights over India and Africa. Charles Kingsford-Smith crossed the Pacific in his *Southern Cross* in 1926. In 1927 an American, Charles Lindbergh, flew solo from New York to Paris, an incredible journey lasting over thirty hours. And in 1930 an intrepid woman, Amy Johnson, made a solo flight from England to Australia.

The first commercial aircraft company, the Aircraft Transport and Travel Co. was formed in 1919. At first it was a daily service between London and Paris and only two or three passengers a day were carried at £20 a trip. Other companies were formed to fly to Amsterdam and Brussels but they soon found that they could not compete against the French firms which were receiving Government assistance. To help

107 *A 1930 Imperial Airways De Havilland Hercules 66, seating up to 14 passengers. Cruising speed about 152km/h.*

these British firms our own Government began to subsidise fares and by 1921 the flight from London to Paris cost £6·30.

In 1924 the Government recommended that all air routes should be controlled by one company and this led to the formation of Imperial Airways. To enable it to expand and seek new routes the company was granted a subsidy of £1 million. By 1932 Imperial Airways had planes flying to India, the Far East, and Australia. Aircraft carrying

108 *A BOAC Comet 4, 1958, seating 70, with a cruising speed of 800km/h.*

109 *The BAC–Aerospatiale Concorde under construction. It has seating for 110–28 passengers and a cruising speed of around 2,200 km/h. This photograph shows clearly its vast size and beautiful design.*

up to 20 passengers now reached Australia in 12 days, when the journey by sea took from 4 to 6 weeks.

In 1935 another company, British Airways, began to compete with

Imperial Airways, particularly on European air routes. The companies attempted to undercut each other's prices and it was obvious that both were losing by this competition. Consequently the Government decided to nationalise the companies and in 1939 the British Overseas Airways Corporation was formed.

At the outbreak of the Second World War airlines were operating over most of the world and aircraft had made considerable technical advances. Sea planes were then in common use on long-distance routes. More and more people flew to the continent for their holidays and almost 250,000 passengers flew over Britain in 1936. Even so air transport was really still in its infancy.

The 1939–1945 War helped to lead to revolutionary advances in aircraft design. Wartime bombers and fighters were heavier and faster than anything known before and in 1943 Sir Frank Whittle's jet engine had been put into effective use. When the War ended the aircraft industry benefited from the improved techniques. By the 1950's BOAC was using the famous jet airliner, the *Comet*, and BEA an advanced propeller turbine plane, the *Viscount*. In 1958 the American Boeing 707 was carrying 100 passengers from New York to London in less than 7 hours.

The aircraft industry has also undergone great structural changes. As with cars the number of manufacturers has grown less and less, for giant aircraft costing millions of pounds can only be built by vast firms. Today, in fact, a huge firm like British Aerospace, which is a combination of many famous firms, is finding difficulty in competing against the even bigger American companies.

Concorde, which cost over £900,000,000 to develop, was made possible by Britain and France combining their technical and financial resources. It is doubtful whether either country would have agreed to the project had they realised what the final cost would be. The aircraft is now in service but some experts question whether it will ever be profitable to run.

Follow up Work

1. *What problems faced the railways after 1918? How did they attempt to solve them?*

2. *Discuss with your teacher the changes which have taken place in railways in your locality since 1945. Write an account of these changes.*

3. *What changes in road transport took place between 1919 and 1939?*

4. *"The most striking feature of all 20th century advance in transport has been the development of the aeroplane..."*

   Write an essay which starts with this sentence. Your answer will include among other points, the work of the Wright Brothers, Blériot, Alcock and Brown, and Amy Johnson, as well as the effect of the two World Wars on development.

   (West Midlands CSE Board, 1965)

5. *This is a general question and to answer it you may need to re-read Chapters 10, 11, 12, and 18.*

   a) Compare the way you spend your leisure time with the way you might have spent it had you been alive in 1905.

   b) Compare the standard of living of a working class family in 1905 with the same type of family today.

   (Southern Regional Examinations Board, 1965)

21 Course Work

Course work has become a compulsory part of many examinations. The fact that it involves a detailed consideration of a specific subject and much individual work can make it a most rewarding study. Also it can be fascinating for it provides an opportunity to study history at first hand and not merely learn facts from a textbook. However, preparing worthwhile topics can be difficult. It will not be sufficient just to copy from books, and it is a waste of opportunity to choose a subject which offers no chance for field study.

Each student will, of course, want to choose a subject which interests him or her. In this chapter ten possible subjects have been taken and an outline given on how to prepare a study of each. The outline is meant only as a guide and can be adapted to suit individual needs. These guides can also be used for many other subjects.

There are, however, certain requirements which must be considered no matter what subject is chosen.

1. It must be a subject which can be studied in detail from books, in museums, from original documents, or by field study.

2. Rough notebooks or loose leaf files should be used at first but these must be kept in such a way that the information is not mislaid.

3. Sources of information should be noted before they are forgotten.

4. When all the information has been collected great care should be taken in setting it out. Pages should be numbered, chapters or sections clearly marked. Diagrams and photographs must be put in against the relevant text and should be clearly labelled. Where the information has been obtained by field study or from original documents, this should be stated.

5. Spend time on careful titling for you must show pride in your work.

6. If you have specimens or models these should be collected together separately, and clear reference made to them in the text.

7. Give your list of sources at the end of the study.

Railways

1. Discuss with your teacher whether your local railway is worth studying. It must have had an important influence on your district and offer interesting features. You must also be able to visit the railway and to find ample information about it in your school library, the public library, and the local museum.

2. Now decide what information you are looking for. It could be in this order.

a) Transport in your area before the railways. Make brief notes about packhorse tracks, turnpike roads, and canals. Draw a map to show where they were.

b) An account of the surveying and planning of the railway. Here your geography teacher will help you to draw geological and geographical sections to show the difficulties facing the engineers.

c) The formation of the first company. Share capital, directors, etc.

d) Any information you can find on the actual building of the railway.

e) Make notes of where the stations were built and copy any pictures you can find of these early stations.

f) Find out what traffic the railway took and the rates charged for passengers and freight at various times. Check on its importance to local industry and agriculture.

g) Find out all you can about the early engines and rolling stock. Where possible make drawings of these.

h) Note when it amalgamated with other companies. This may have occurred during the 19th century or it may have been in 1921 when the Government formed the four large companies.

i) Find out how it was affected by road competition even before 1939. It may have closed down in that period.

j) Obtain full information of what has happened to it since 1945. It may have been closed down or it may have been modernised.

Using your school library, the public reference library, and the local museum find out all you can about these points. Remember that you can often make your information clearer by using diagrams, photographs, sketch maps, and statistics.

3. Field Study

Do *not* attempt to walk along railway tracks which are still in use. This is both illegal and highly dangerous.

a) Check the track from bridges, stations, or high points overlooking the line. Take photographs and make sketch maps of any interesting features connected with the track. This may include such things as viaducts, unusual bridges, old signal boxes, level crossings, and what were obviously difficult engineering feats.

b) Visit the main stations and make notes of any points of interest. You may see remains of old style waiting rooms, sidings, goods yards, etc. The effects of any modernisation schemes should also be noted. Sketch maps and plans can be drawn and photographs taken, but if the light is poor it is doubtful whether an ordinary camera will be of any use.

4. Draw a sketch map of the railway network in your area showing tunnels, cuttings, embankments, bridges, branch lines, mineral lines, stations, level crossings, and any other points of interest.

5. Put all your information together. Do not put the library notes and field study into separate parts, but make it clear which information has been obtained by visits.

6. Check all local newspapers for they frequently give useful information and photographs.

Canals

1. Discuss with your teacher which local canal he thinks will be the most rewarding to study. You must be able actually to visit the canal and to find ample information about it.

2. Now decide what information you are looking for. It could be in this order.

a) Transport in your area before the canals.

b) An account of the planning and surveying of the canal. Here your geography teacher will help you to draw geological and geographical sections.

c) The formation of the first company.

d) Any information you can find on the actual building of the canal. Include reservoirs and feeders.

e) Find out what traffic it took and the rates charged at various times. Also check on its success.

f) Find out if the railway took it over and its subsequent history during the 19th and 20th centuries.

g) Check to see whether any recommendations have been made as to its future. Using your school library, the public reference library, and the local museum find out all you can about these points. Remember that you can often make your information clearer by using diagrams, photographs, sketch maps, and statistics.

3. *Field Study*

a) Walk along the canal and make notes of the main engineering difficulties, e.g. tunnels, locks, embankments, basins, etc. Take photographs or make sketch maps of any interesting features.

b) Take photographs or make sketch maps of the reservoirs. Make a plan of the feeder system.

c) Talk to lock keepers and make notes of any interesting information they can give you.

4. Draw a map of the canal showing contours, warehouses, basins, feeders, etc.

5. Now put all your information together. Do not put the library notes and the field study into separate parts, but make it clear in your topic which information you have obtained by visits. For example, an account of the building of the canal should be a combination of the information discovered in books plus the pictures you took and the facts you discovered on your visit. Its condition and use today should depend on photographs, discussions with lock keepers, and accounts in local papers.

A Village

If you live in a village (or even near a village) this can provide a most enjoyable topic. You will often find that a history of the village has been written at some time or other. Church guides can also be useful. If you visit the nearest town library or county archives you will usually find references to your village in local history books or in documents.

1. First of all find out when the village came into existence and what its original name meant. Then check on why it grew at that particular spot. With mining and industrial villages the reasons are generally obvious but there were a number of reasons for the siting of some agricultural villages.

2. Now find out all you can about its history.

a) Is it mentioned in the Domesday Book? To where did the village fields extend? Where was the mill? Where was the manor house?

260

Which of the roads radiating from the village were tracks then? How was it affected by the Black Death? These are only a few of the interesting facts which you may be able to answer.

b) Make notes of any subsequent growth or decline. Write full accounts of any old buildings which still exist.

c) When were the village fields enclosed? If possible draw plans to show how the land was divided up.

d) Find out all you can about any turnpike roads, canals, or railways in or near the village.

e) Try to discover how changing agricultural methods have affected the village, e.g. some areas which were once arable have turned over largely to market gardening and pasture farming.

f) Make notes on the village today. Include such things as where the people work, how they spend their leisure, connections with the town, and the use of modern agricultural techniques.

g) Make a detailed study of the church. Draw plans of it and write an account of its history. Do not neglect tombstones and memorials. Frequently the church gives a very good picture of the history of the village.

h) Draw a plan of the village. Mark in the different periods of growth clearly. Also show any important features which have disappeared, e.g. castles, mills, manor houses, etc.

3. If you live in an industrial or mining village write a full account of the history of this industry. This account must be as detailed as possible.

4. *Field Study*

Take photographs and make sketches of all the interesting features of the village. These may include:

a) Any castle, manor house, or mill, or any remains there may be.

b) Any instances of early agricultural methods. Sometimes the strip system can still be traced and often ridge and furrow ploughing methods are visible.

c) Any features of the village such as a green, market cross, smithy, ancient houses, pumps, stocks, etc.

d) Any interesting transport changes. These may vary from packhorse tracks to modern roads.

e) Photographs of any mines or industrial remains.

f) Photographs to show the history of the church.

5. Write about any interesting local customs. These can include such things as well dressings, rush gatherings, dances, etc.

6. Find out what you can from older people. They can frequently tell you of interesting changes which they remember.

7. Put all your information together. Make sure that as far as possible the field study and the book notes are combined, not written up separately.

Studies of Famous Local People

This is quite an easy topic but because there can be very little field study, it will not be as interesting to write as some of the others.

Most of the information needed can be obtained either in your school library or in the local public library. However, it is always advisable to read books by local authors for they will have included interesting details which ordinary biographers omit. It will not be sufficient merely to summarise a well-known biography. The examiner will expect you to give considerable local detail.

If the person you have chosen was an important statesman then show in your biography that you have a good knowledge of the political situation when he was alive. If you are writing about soldiers or sailors you must give details of the battles or voyages in which they were involved. If you write about an important inventor or industrialist, then a detailed account of what he made or the industry with which he was connected must be given. With a writer or musician or artist an understanding of his work must be shown.

Field study is obviously limited but you must take photographs or make sketches wherever possible. For example the house in which he lived may still remain, there will in all probability be local spots associated with him, and certainly there will be information about him in the museum. Try to show that you have traced his association with your district as closely as possible.

Roads

This topic will depend upon the existence of a wide variety of roads in your locality. For example, if you are able to write accounts of Roman roads, packhorse tracks, turnpike roads, and motorways, this can be a most interesting and rewarding study.

1. Using your school and the public library, and also the museum, try to find information on the following.

a) Evidence of Roman roads, when they were built, and what was their importance.

b) Find out what you can about any packhorse routes, where they were, and what was usually carried.

c) Make notes on the history of turnpike roads in your area. Find out where the turnpike gates were, what inns existed, which engineers built the roads, and any other interesting details.

d) On a map mark the Roman roads, the packhorse tracks, and the turnpike roads. Indicate which still exist to this day.

e) If there is a motorway nearby find out what you can about its construction.

2. *Field Study*

a) Trace the Roman road and packhorse routes on foot, and take photographs or make sketches of any interesting remains.

b) Take photographs of any remains of the turnpike roads such as toll houses, mile posts, inns, etc.

3. If you are able to, draw or find pictures of packhorse teams, stage coaches, inn scenes, etc. These can all improve your topic.

4. Use diagrams to show the changes in techniques in road construction.

5. Put all your information together. Make sure that anything you have obtained by field studies is clearly shown. Combine this with the notes you have made from books.

Local Architectural Styles

If you are interested in art and architecture this can provide a most rewarding topic. However, before you can begin you must have some knowledge of your subject. Therefore if you choose this topic ask your teacher to recommend a general book on the history of architecture. He will also tell you which sections are likely to be of most use to you in your area.

Clearly you will not have time to study every important local building. Your teacher will suggest those which show the greatest variation in architectural style.

1. From books in the public library find out what you can about the history of the buildings you have chosen.

2. a) It is advisable to visit the buildings in the order in which they were built.

b) Take a book on architecture with you. This will help you to know what to look for. (The *Observer's Book of Architecture*, published by Warne, is a very handy size).

c) Carry a rough notebook and a drawing pad. Write down all the important details of the building and draw the most interesting architectural points. These drawings may be rough provided they are clear enough to be copied later.

d) Take photographs where they will be useful.

3. When you write up your work give a detailed account of each building. Remember that you must have a large number of illustrations and that these must be well drawn.

It is important to remember that very little of this topic can be done from books.

Local Trade Unions

This topic depends upon whether in the past a certain trade union was particularly important in your own area and whether there are sufficient books and documentary evidence available in the local library.

Discuss with your teacher which local union offers a good study and then visit the municipal reference library to see what information is available. Then write to the local union secretary to see what information he can give you.

Now begin to collect your information in this order.

1. Find out when the union began, with particulars of its early strength and membership. Then check on what was happening to unions generally at the same time. For example you may be able to trace the union back beyond 1799 or it may have been part of the new model unions, etc.

2. Trace its history up to the present day showing all outstanding incidents, e.g. did it take part in politics, strikes, and local affairs. Make notes of how its membership rose or fell.

3. If the local secretary or librarian can show you any interesting documents make copies of these or of parts of them, e.g. early membership cards, strike pay slips, letters from members, etc.

4. Conclude with particulars of membership today showing how one becomes a member.

5. Arrange your information in this order and make sure that all pictures are clearly marked. At the same time indicate from where you have obtained your information.

Study of an Outstanding Historical Building

This can offer a most interesting topic. It will, however, require considerable field study and the building must be important enough to provide adequate material. Of course, this can be overcome by studying more than one building.

1. It is advisable to visit the public library and to write to whoever is in charge of the building in order to ascertain what information is available. Once you are satisfied that the facts can be obtained the topic can be approached in this way.

a) What the building is, when it was built, and by whom.

b) Obtain a detailed account of its actual construction. This should include the cost, wages paid, price of materials, where the workers came from, etc.

c) If it played any part in local or national history, or in the local economy, explain this.

d) If it is now in ruins explain when and why it fell into decay. Also try to copy old diagrams showing the gradual collapse of the masonry.

e) If it is still intact but has been enlarged or restored in any way obtain full particulars of these alterations.

When you have obtained full details of its history you can then begin a detailed study. A cursory visit will not be enough. You must be prepared to spend some time in and/or around the building.

2. *Field Study*

a) Take your note book with you and obtain a copy of the guide book if there is one.

b) Write a detailed account of each part of the building. The guide book itself will not provide all the details.

c) Wherever possible take photographs or make sketches. Remember that indoor phtotographs need flash bulbs and that for such shots it will probably be cheaper to buy postcards.

3. Put all your information together. Do not separate the facts you

265

obtained from books from your field study; the two should be combined and all illustrations put in their appropriate places.

Local Industry

Many areas have industries which are very localised. Some still exist and even where they have largely declined there may be sufficient information to provide a very good topic. Amongst such industries are shoes, glass, slate quarrying, pottery, hat making, tin mining, coal mining, shipping, lead mining, wool, cotton, silk, etc.

1. Discuss with your teacher whether there is a local industry which will provide a good topic. You must be able to find ample information about it in your school or public library, and in local museums. It will improve your topic if you are able to visit old sites or factories.

2. Now decide what information you are looking for. It could be in this order.

a) The origin of the industry in your district. Why it began there. Whether it was ever a domestic industry. The size and output of the early industry.

b) Draw a sketch map where possible to show its original situation.

c) Make notes showing how it grew. Information should be found on output, size of firms and plants, labour employed, any labour disputes, changes in technology, and the spread of the industry.

d) In certain cases the industry may have been dominated by a few firms. In this case the history of these firms can be traced and much information obtained by writing to the company if it still exists.

e) A sketch map may be useful to show the spread of the industry and the growth of canals and railways to serve the various firms.

f) Where the industry has declined find out why and what effect this decline had on the area generally.

g) If it still exists trace its history up to the present. Write a full account of the industry as it is today.

3. *Field Study*

a) Visit any old sites and make sketches or take photographs. If you are studying topics like mines or quarries be *extremely careful* for these old workings can be dangerous. Keep away from actual mine shafts.

b) Visit all local museums. Make sketches and take notes of any examples which show the progress of the industry.

c) Take photographs of the tracks, canals, or railways which served the industry.

d) If there are firms still in existence they will usually give you valuable information relating to the history of the industry and of its present methods of production.

4. Put all your information together. Do not put the library notes and the field study into separate sections. Indicate clearly the facts you have obtained by actual visits.

A Town

Writing the history of a town can be fascinating but as all towns differ it will be necessary to discuss this most carefully with your teacher. It may be possible to write a topic on your town in Roman times, or during the Middle Ages, or probably when it grew up during the Industrial Revolution. However, if information is sparse you may have to trace its history from the beginning. Consider this very carefully for your topic might become too long.

This is a guide of what to look for in your school library, the public library, and your local museum.

1. *Roman Britain*

a) Copy any plan or model of the town noting the street arrangements, the main buildings, and the wall, if there was one.

b) Make notes of what has been discovered about the town at that time. These can include such things as its population, everyday life, purpose, and importance.

c) Visit the local museum and write down what you see of any Roman remains. These usually include pottery, weapons, coins, tools.

d) Check whether your town was founded in Saxon times and make notes of its history at that time. Some of these Saxon towns were mints, others were the capitals of the shires, and many were fortified. There is not usually much written about this period in history.

2. *The Middle Ages*

a) Draw a plan of the town in the Middle Ages. Include, if they existed, the castle, the wall, and the main buildings.

b) Make notes of all you can discover about the town. Include such things as any political turmoil in which it was involved, how the people

267

110 *Old horse whim and mine shaft, Pinxton, Notts. (See Plates 9, 10)*

lived, any schools, any trade and industry, how the town got its freedom, and when it received its charter.

c) Visit the museum to see what evidence is available there.

3. The Tudors and Stuarts

a) The growth of the town during these periods. How far it was affected by the Reformation. Any political troubles in which it was involved. What part it played in the Civil War. Make notes of any new industries which grew up. Any schools which were built. Parliamentary representation. How the medieval town changed its appearance.

b) Check the museum again for evidence of these years.

4. 1714 to 1970's

a) Draw a plan of its growth during these years. In the case of industrial towns this may have been rapid. Show on your plan the areas where the industry began and how it spread. Also show the gradual expansion of the residential districts. To make the plan clear indicate any main roads, canals, railways, and important buildings.

b) These were the years when the industrial towns grew extremely rapidly. Make notes on the industries, any slum districts which appeared, public health, communications, education, political activity, and all other points of local interest.

5. *Field Study*

If you are making a broad historical study of the town choose a few representative areas to visit. These should include such things as remains of castles and walls, the guildhall, Tudor buildings, 18th century houses, industrial sites, Victorian civic buildings, and present day development. If, however, you are making a particular study of one part of the town or of one period in its history, then your field study must be detailed.

Make sure that any photographs or sketches clearly indicate what you intend.

Further Reading

General Histories

British Economic and Social History 1700–1939, C. P. Hill, Edward Arnold.

A Sketch Map Economic History of Britain, J. L. Gayler, Harrap.

A Practical Guide to Modern Economic History, R. Sellman, Edward Arnold.

Picture Source Books for Social History, ed. M. Harrison, Allen and Unwin.
18th Century, Early 19th Century, Late 19th Century.

They Saw it Happen, Blackwell.
Volume III 1689–1897
Volume IV 1898–1945

Rockliff New Project Series, A. B. Allen, Rockliff.
18th Century England 1714–1800
The 19th Century 1800–1850
Victorian England 1850–1900
20th Century Britain

Living through the Industrial Revolution, S. Davies, Routledge and Kegan Paul.

Life since 1900, C. Firth, Allen and Unwin.

Britain 1906–1951, P. Teed, Hutchinson Educational.

The Industrial Revolution

Industry and Technology, W. Chaloner and A. Musson, Vista Books.

The Wonderful Story of British Industry, P. Smith, Ward Lock.

James Watt and Steam Power, Jackdaw Series, Cape.

Methuen's Outlines:
The Growth of Mechanical Power
Forge and Foundry
Coal Mines and Miners
Spinning and Weaving

The Story of Davy, A. Ellis, Methuen.

Great Inventors, N. Wymer, OUP.

The Past and Present Series, Batsford:
Power
Factories

Agriculture

The Agrarian Revolution, Then and There Series, Longman.

The Land, J. Higgs, Vista Books.

Old Farm Tractors, P. A. Wright, A. and C. Black.

Old Farm Implements, P. A. Wright, A. and C. Black.

The Story of Agriculture, J. G. Crowther, Hamish Hamilton.

Harvests and Harvesting through the Ages, N. Lee, CUP.

The English Village, D. R. Mills, Routledge.

The Story of Farming, G. E. Fussell, Pergamon.

The Past and Present Series, Batsford:
Country Life
Farming

Transport

An Illustrated History of Transport, Anthony Ridley, Heinemann.

A History of British Transport, J. Ray, Heinemann.

Transport and Communications, N. P. Bray, Hart Davis.

Transport by Land, T. Insull, J. Murray.

The Past and Present Series, Batsford:
Transport
Ships and Shipping

Roads

Wheels on the Road, S. E. Ellacott, Methuen.

Thomas Telford, L. T. C. Rolt, Longman.

Stagecoach to John o' Groats, L. Gardiner, Hollis and Carter.

Transport, J. Simmons, Vista Books.

The Shape of the Motor Car, L. A. Everett, Hutchinson.

Motoring History, L. T. C. Rolt, Dutton/Vista.

Blind Jack of Knaresborough, G. Hogg, Phoenix.

The Rolls-Royce Men, J. Rowland, Lutterworth.

Gottlieb Daimler, A. Bird, Weidenfeld.

The Past and Present Series, Batsford: Roads.

Railways

Railway Revolution 1825–1845, Then and There Series, Longman.

From Rocket to Railcar, L. Snellgrove, Longman.

The Story of British Locomotives, R. Barnard Way, Methuen.

G. and R. Stephenson, J. Williamson, A. and C. Black.

Isambard Brunel, L. T. C. Rolt, Longman.

Railways and Life in England, S. Gregory, Ginn.

A History of Railways, J. Ray, Heinemann.

Railways in the Making, R. M. Gard and J. R. Hartley, University of Newcastle-on-Tyne.

It Happened Round Manchester, J. Clarke, ULP.

The Past and Present Series, Batsford: Railways.

Canals

Inland Waterways, P. Thornhill, Methuen.

Inland Waterways, L. T. C. Rolt, ESA.

The Story of Our Inland Waterways, R. Aickman, Pitman.

James Brindley, Pioneer of Canals, L. Meynell, Bodley Head.

Britain's Inland Waterways, R. Wickson, Methuen.

British Canals, Charles Hadfield, David and Charles.

Aircraft

The Story of Aircraft, S. E. Ellacott, Methuen.

The Wright Brothers, H. Thomas, A. and C. Black.

A Pure History of Flight, Vista Books.

Six Great Aviators, J. Pudney, Hamish Hamilton.

The History of Flight, J. Ray, Heinemann.

Transport by Air, T. Insull, J. Murray.

Labour Movements and Factory Reform

Strike or Bargain, D. J. Williams (Today is History Series), Blond Educational.

Early Trade Unions, Jackdaw Series, Cape.

Social Reformers, N. Wymer, OUP.

Shaftesbury, G. F. Best, Batsford.

Shaftesbury and the Working Class Children, Jackdaw Series, Cape.

The Slave Trade, Jackdaw Series, Cape.

The Man who freed the Slaves, A. and H. Lawson, Faber.

The Past and Present Series, Batsford:
Trade Unions
The Welfare State

Medicine and Public Health

The Man who discovered Penicillin, W. A. Bullock, Faber.

The Chloroform Man, J. Rowland, Lutterworth Press.

I Swear and Vow, E. J. Trimmer (Today is History Series), Blond Educational.

The Story of Nursing, J. M. Calder, Methuen.

Louis Pasteur, Nesta Pain, A. and C. Black.

The Town, G. Martin, Vista Books.

House and Home, M. W. Barley, Vista Books.

Six Great Doctors, J. G. Crowther, Hamish Hamilton.

The Story of Health, G. Howat, Pergamon.

The Development of Surgery, J. Gibson, Macmillan.

Pasteur and the Germ Theory, Jackdaw Series, Cape.

Parliament

Peterloo and Radical Reform, Jackdaw Series, Cape.

The Vote 1832–1928, Jackdaw Series, Cape.

The Story of Mrs. Pankhurst, J. Kamm, Methuen.

Government, R. Evans, Vista Books.

Our Parliament, S. Gordon, Hansard Society.

Women in Revolt, Jackdaw Series, Cape.

The Past and Present Series, Batsford:
Government
Elections
Political Parties

Communications

From Pillar to Post, L. Zilliacus, Heinemann.

Britain's Post Office, H. Robinson, OUP.

Television, F. Roberts, ESA.

Lives of Great Men and Women (Series III), N. Wymer, OUP.

The Press, B. Inglis (Today is History Series), Blond Educational.

Marconi, L. Reade, Faber.

Edison, H. Thomas, A. and C. Black.

Faraday, J. G. Cook, A. and C. Black.

The Past and Present Series, Batsford:
The Post
News and Newspapers

Industry in the 19th and 20th Centuries

Industry and Technology, W. Chaloner and A. Musson, Vista Books.

The Wonderful Story of British Industry, P. Smith, Ward Lock.

The Great Exhibition, Jackdaw Series, Cape.

Lord Nuffield, E. Gilbanks, Cassell.

Six Great Inventors, N. Wymer, OUP.

Six Great Engineers, J. G. Crowther, Hamish Hamilton.

Epics of Invention, J. Rowland, Bodley Head.

A Short History of Technology, Derry and Williams, Oxford.

A History of Invention, Larsen, Phoenix House.

The Past and Present Series, Batsford:
Inventions
Towns
The Environment

Course Work

Discovering Local History, D. P. Titley, Allman and Sons.

Index

277